At the crossroads where humanity
us consider the effects of what hu
selves, other animals, and to Earth. As we are increasingly faced with
the global consequences humans have created, ancient wisdom from
these traditions can serve as an inspiration and guide for compassion
and activism for animals that, in the long run, will affect everything.

—**Julie Andrzejewski**, Department of Human Relations
and Multicultural Education, St. Cloud State University

In a time such as our own, when religion is commonly used to legitimate war and terror, *Call to Compassion* importantly gestures to how
world religions might variously find common cause in their work for
peace between the species. A liberation theology for the animals such
as this has never been more necessary.

—**Richard Kahn** Core Faculty at Antioch University Los Angeles

This book will shed much-needed light on the intersecting beliefs of
animal advocates and religious groups, and will be an insightful and
indispensible tool for animal activists in helping bridge the narrow
gap between their work and the compassionate message at the core
of all faiths.

—**Nick Cooney**, author, *Change of Heart*

A classic in the making, the book offers a unique examination of animal rights in other cultures through the perspective of world religions, demonstrating compassion isn't the exclusive purview of any
one culture or species. A must read for students and activists in our
era of globalization!

—**John Asimakopoulos**, Director,
Transformative Studies Institute

Harmony with nature and respect and compassion for all life forms
were original tenets of geographically separated but spiritually con-

nected movements. Recognizing the importance of these religious movements to the development of the major ethical and philosophical ideas shaping human thought can only give one pause in imagining a present quite different from the global market and technological culture we now inhabit, based as it is on the deaths of approximately 55 billion land animals alone killed annually for food worldwide. This book fills that pause with the knowledge and wisdom we need to move forward in imagining, and acting on, a different present and future based on that original harmony.

—**Carol Gigliotti**, Emily Carr University, Media and Critical and Cultural Studies, Vancouver, B.C., Canada

Kemmerer and Nocella should be praised for compiling a pivotal book that will have profound influence on how animals are viewed in society.

—**Sarat Colling**, VIVA, Canada

Religion has an important role to play in animal rights and this book takes a major step to making the case for a theology of animal liberation. An urgent book for urgent times.

—**Peter McLaren**, UCLA, Graduate School of Education and Information Studies

Truly a pivotal book that challenges what it means to be ethical. *Call to Compassion* is a powerful book with an amazing list of outstanding contributors. Read now!

—**Richard White**, Editor, *Journal for Critical Animal Studies*

This book is influential in impacting the way people reconstruct the internal logic of their religion. The first of its kind to help change what has been viewed as right and wrong.

—**Justin Hand**, F.A.C.T.

At a time when the animal rights movement has been repeatedly smeared as extremist, or even "terrorist," this volume shows that, in fact, its core values stem from a long history of nonviolent teachings in all of the world's major religions.

—**Will Potter**, GreenIsTheNewRed.com

Finally, a book that connects animal advocacy with the profound spiritual resources of world faiths. This landmark collection of learned and impassioned essays will doubtlessly be widely read and admired.

—**Uri Gordon**, author, *Anarchy Alive!*

We live in a time in which humanity's need for spiritual healing through compassion is unparalleled. We have pushed the boundaries of our destructive capabilities with nuclear weaponry, genocide, factory farming, and vivisection. *Call to Compassion* is an immensely important and timely contribution to a world that yearns for rebirth.

—**Adam Wilson**, CEO, Downbound

An innovative collection that brings together diverse perspectives and will expand ethical debates about our treatment of other living beings.

—**John Sorenson**, Department of Sociology, Brock University, Canada

From Islam to Christianity to Daoism and more, traditions of compassion toward nonhuman animals abound in the world's faiths. Here we have thoughtful discussions of those many interpretations of that one simple yet profound theme.

—**Rik Scarce**, Associate Professor of Sociology, Skidmore College

Threading together religion and animal liberation, *Call to Compassion* is a vital read.

—**Maxwell Schnurer**, Professor of Communication, Humboldt State University

An inspiring and honest view of the treatment of animals and animals as sentient beings through the various cultures and religions, *Call to Compassion* breaks down various viewpoints and merges them into one critical message that resonates through them all: animal liberation.

—**Shannon Keith**, Director of the
award-winning film *Behind the Mask*

CALL *to* COMPASSION

Reflections on Animal Advocacy
in World Religions

EDITED BY

LISA KEMMERER *and* ANTHONY J. NOCELLA II

LANTERN BOOKS • NEW YORK
A Division of Booklight, Inc.

2011
LANTERN BOOKS
128 Second Place
Brooklyn, NY 11231
www.lanternbooks.com

LIBRARY OF CONGRESS CATALOGING-IN-PUBLICATION DATA

Call to compassion : reflections on animal advocacy from
the world's religions / edited by Lisa Kemmerer and Anthony J. Nocella, II.
p. cm.
Includes bibliographical references.
ISBN-13: 978-1-59056-182-9 (alk. paper)
ISBN-10: 1-59056-182-1 (alk. paper)
1. Animal welfare--Religious aspects. I. Kemmerer, Lisa. II. Nocella, Anthony J.
BL439.C35 2010
202'.4—dc22
2010007226

Contents

PART TWO — ABRAHAMIC TRADITIONS
Jewish, Christian, and Islamic Traditions

Contents

Foreword

STEVEN M. WISE

As a practicing animal protection lawyer, writer, and adjunct law professor teaching animal rights jurisprudence, I feel privileged to write this foreword. My legal writing often focuses on the use of Anglo-American common law—the judge-made law of English-speaking countries—to protect nonhuman animals, to the point of granting such fundamental rights as bodily liberty and bodily integrity. But I know something of religious attitudes toward nonhuman animals and the rest of creation, both present and past. These topics occupied a central place in my recent book, *An American Trilogy*, which answers the question of why one piece of land in Tar Heel, North Carolina, first supported Native Americans who were nearly wiped out, then became a slave plantation, and today is the site of the world's largest slaughterhouse, where thirty-six thousand hogs are killed each day. These were all "genesis disasters."

As do contributors, I theorize about the good and the right, and how common law can become what it ought to be. In the eternal process of "working itself pure"—Lord Mansfield's phrase—the common law reflects society's ideas about what is good and right, as well as its experience. But in certain important areas common law is, and ought to be, primarily influenced by principle. Religion has long been one important source for the principles integral to common law. Former George W. Bush presidential speechwriter, evangelical, and animal protection advocate Matthew Scully (2002, 12–13) writes that "at least here in America . . . no moral cause ever got very far that could not speak to religious conviction, drawing on the deeper sensibilities that guide public opinion in our more secular era." Rice University Sociologist Michael Lindsay believes religion to be "the single most important factor that drives American belief, attitudes, and behaviors. It is a powerful indicator of where America will end up on politics, culture, and family life. If you want to understand America, you have to understand religion in America" (Bannerjee 2009, A1, A12). Not just in America, of course.

Nonhuman animals have long been characterized as "things" under the common law. In his influential eighteenth century commentary on the laws of England, William Blackstone (1765a) identified the legal thinghood of nonhuman animals as having been mostly derived from the Book of Genesis. Indeed, Blackstone saw Genesis as the exclusive source of humanity's claim to ownership of nearly everything (Blackstone 1765b):

[I]n the beginning of the world, we are informed by holy writ, the all-bountiful Creator gave to man "dominion over all the earth, and over the fish of the sea, and over the fowl of the air, and over every living thing that moveth upon the earth." This is the only true and solid foundation of man's dominion over external things, whatever airy metaphysical notions may have been started by fanciful writers on the subject. . . .

The earth, therefore, and all things therein are the general property of all mankind, exclusive of other beings, from the immediate gift of the Creator. (Gen. 1:28)

In *An American Trilogy*, I illustrate how even today's fundamentalist Southern Baptists are rejecting the idea of "dominion as license to exploit" in favor of a "duty to faithfully steward God's creation." This book's contributors take mighty steps toward clarifying that the principle of the divine license of human beings to exploit the animate world has always been error. Here they push society toward a more accurate and nuanced understanding of the proper place of nonhuman animals in religion. By moving society, they nudge the law in the same direction. They are unlikely to succeed in abruptly replacing the present "animal as thing" conception with a modern paradigm that more accurately reflects who nonhuman animals, and human beings, are. But these authors inject a much-needed modern view of these archaic principles that helps to neutralize them. This will allow modern judges to look at laws pertaining to nonhuman animals with fresh eyes, unblinkered by outmoded principles, more open to change. More importantly, it will catalyze new thinking among those who are now too young to be judges, so that when they attain these positions, they will arrive with more open minds. Eventually, this new outlook will lead to the adoption of new legal paradigms based on more accurate understandings of the religious base for the relationship between humans and nonhuman animals, in which humans adopt less exploitative legal relationships.

Preface

The Time Has Come

STEPHEN R. L. CLARK

Thirty or forty years ago most philosophers, most theologians, most scientists, most casual commentators simply assumed that only human beings "had rights" or merited any serious moral consideration. We might acknowledge sentimental attachments to particular nonhuman creatures. We might also acknowledge that "cruelty" was wrong (that is, that it would be wrong to *enjoy* inflicting pain on animals—a bad habit to get into), but we would not likely acknowledge that causing such pain was very wrong in itself. Until recently, it was assumed that "animals" might not feel pain at all, or if they did, it was of another sort than ours—it was axiomatic—as they were thought to lack any sense of their own identity, any notions of "before and after," memory, cause, or purpose. Analytical philosophers and existentialists agreed, in effect, that there were only "things" (which included animals) and "persons" (human beings). They might notice that there were other philosophical and theological traditions that gave nonhuman animals a larger part to play, but— for that very reason—those traditions were considered foolish.

It was just *obvious* to all right-thinking people that human beings were all that we should mind about, whether because it was only human beings who could make a verbal bargain with us, or because it was only human beings, obviously, who were *human*. That Egyptians once worshipped cats, or that Indians found cows to be sacred, just showed how primitive they were. Yet even in the Western philosophical and theological traditions there were voices who spoke otherwise. But the very fact that Jeremy Bentham, for example, thought that animal pains and pleasures should be counted in his moral calculus was reason enough to think that "utilitarians" of that sort did not appreciate human nobility, or else were misled about the nature of "mere brutes."[1] People who minded about "animals" (beyond a certain limited, sentimental point) were considered freakish. Laws established in the United Kingdom at the start of the Victorian era to protect domestic and farm animals from deliberate cruelty and neglect held some influence,[2] but were reckoned, if they were mentioned at all, to be concessions to British sentiment, which should not be taken so seriously as to prevent commercial or scientific progress.

These (Western) attitudes are actually of relatively recent origin. Older, more commonsensical traditions have usually acknowledged that nonhuman animals have their own lives to live, and merely denied that we had any right or duty to interfere with them, any more than with other human nations. Nonhuman animals entered human households and economies before recorded history began, and our duties towards and about them were not very different in kind from those we owed other humans. In older traditions it was not especially wrong to kill or enslave "others"—*any* others—and species was not a moral dividing line. But it was often considered wrong to deny to anyone, human or "brute beast," a proper exercise of their God-given natures.

The growth of universal humanism, encouraging us to think that human beings of whatever race or sex or caste were equally deserving of respect, inevitably meant that creatures who were not human had a lower status. Some humanists, then and now, might see this as mere "species solidarity," founded solely on our attachment to close kin. Most humanists, whether they owed more to Stoic or to Epicurean philosophy, preferred to rationalize the human–nonhuman animal distinction and were driven to insist, as above, that "nonhumans" had no sense of their identity, no "rational capacity," no sense of justice, and even—in a strange reversal of common sense—no sense at all. Nonhumans were merely "things," and any care we might have for them was only sentiment, on a par with a child's care for dolls, or an adult's care for landmarks, historic buildings, and antique ceramics.[3] The warm-hearted could think that animals might deserve some "charity," but never justice. A few Platonists retained a better notion, believing with Anne Conway (1631–1679) that "any man who is just and good loves the brute creatures which serve him, and he takes care of them so that they have food and rest and the other things they need. He does not do this only for his own good but out of a principle of true justice" (Conway 1996, 35).

Notions that nonhuman animals are utterly unlike humans, and that species boundaries are significant in a way that racial, sexual, and cultural boundaries are not, fit very poorly in the modern biological synthesis, which takes the fact of evolution as its guiding principle. The more we understand our evolutionary past, the less we can believe that our particular species is radically "other." Our species is not even the crowning glory of evolution, but one branch among many. Once there were other hominid species, and there may be again. Similar capacities for social life, play, affection, cunning contrivance, and cruelty—unfortunately—can be identified in many nonhumans. Animal differences also excite a proper admiration and concern. It isn't that they have failed to achieve humanity, or that they are "less evolved" (such notions have no place in modern evolutionary theory). They have their own lives to live.

The scientific discovery that human beings are one species, one set of interbreeding populations among many, and that our distinctively "human" capacities do not show us to be superior, is not, of itself, enough to *make* us care about nonhumans. We might choose instead to care only for our conspecifics, merely because they are closer kin, because they "share our genes" (though in fact we share genes with every living being on Earth). One pretext for this genetic focus is a popular variant of evolutionary theory, in which we only mind about things "our genes" mind about. Out of our muddle of motives and inhibitions, only those that have a reproductive edge will last. "Human behavior—like the deepest capacities for emotional response which drive and guide it—is the circuitous technique by which human genetic material has been and will be kept intact. Morality has no other demonstrable function" (Wilson 1978, 167).

Even on this assumption, of course, it's not *obvious* that "speciesist" moralities will prevail. On the contrary, it seems more likely that we shall have more descendants if we also manage to be concerned about nonhuman animals, to befriend them when we can, and at least not ruin their lives and habitats (which we also require). Maybe we will feel more concern if we open our eyes and hearts to see nonhumans as embodying values of their own. To say that my child is only important to me because she carries some of my genes does not say how I think and feel about her, but offers a feeble explanation for why I have these feelings. If that really is all I mind about her, I would have and use other strategies to obtain my genes' survival! Maybe we can imagine some similar explanation for my concern for other creatures, who may momentarily need my care (a blackbird scrabbling in a pond to escape from drowning, a hedgehog unable to climb out from beside a cellar window), but it would be ridiculous to suggest that this concern stems from a concern for my future genetic heritage, and equally ridiculous to suggest that it's only "genetic fitness" that makes an action or an attitude correct. "*Virtuous*" is not the same as "reproductively advantageous."[4]

Most moral philosophers who have addressed these issues in the last thirty or forty years have chosen to argue only within a naturalistic or secular paradigm.[5] They have offered both utilitarian and rights-based arguments as to why we ought to treat our nonhuman companions better, though they have rarely bothered to explain how exactly we acquired a liking for universal welfare, or universal justice.

It is perhaps partly for this reason that religious believers have sometimes concluded that any concern for "animals" demonstrates a failure to realize the sacred nature of humanity, the central importance of God's plan. Though I think these believers are making a mistake, their concerns aren't foolish. Abandoning the moral and legal barrier between the human and nonhuman might improve conditions for nonhumans, but it might also permit morally intolerable use of humans.

Abandoning moral realism in favor of a merely naturalistic, evolutionary account of moral concern leads to a merely pragmatic, short-term, and nepotistic solution to the current problem. If there's no real or absolute difference between the human and the nonhuman, then we have lost one reason (not that it has been an altogether effective one) to treat *human* kindred (especially the poor) differently from how we treat domestic and "experimental" animals.[6] If we are not to fall further into corruption, we need to recall some reason against treating others—including nonhumans—in such an expedient and cruel manner, one that will be secure against temptation.

My own approach has been to seek to awaken a new way of looking at the world and the creatures who share this world with us—a new way that is also very old, part indeed of the "perennial philosophy" to be discovered in the Platonic tradition.[7] Crudely, humanism as it has ordinarily been conceived is a diversion: a diversion, no doubt, with many good effects, but nonetheless an error, insofar as it has led us to suppose that the world and its creatures matter only inasmuch as they can serve us, that we *own* them—somehow or other—though we did not make them.

The truth that our ancestors acknowledged (even as they made use of their nonhuman and human neighbors) is that nonhuman animals show us something beautiful, wonderful, sacred, something to which we owe our care and admiration. They are not to be seen only as tools or useful stuff, but as living beings in their own right, who should be given the chance to live out their "natural" lives, the lives for which, in some sense, they were "made." Different religious traditions have articulated this in many different ways, and these essays collected by Lisa Kemmerer and Anthony Nocella testify to this variety, and also to this underlying message. It is an important collection, demonstrating not only that concern for the nonhuman isn't a peripheral and easily neglected aspect of religious and ethical traditions, but also that there are many robust and creative religious and spiritual traditions whose contribution to humane endeavor has been too long neglected by merely academic theorists, unthinkingly obedient to fashionable varieties of naturalistic humanism.

My own attitudes are owed mostly to the Christian synthesis of Platonic and Hebrew thought: the Hebrew declaration that "God hates nothing that He has made,"[8] and the Platonic declaration that every creature exhibits some form of beauty, unite to demand respect for even the "least" of these. Both of these traditions, at one time distinct, may also suggest that "humanity" is in the image or form of God, but this is only, really, to say that we are called to *care* for things. Godliness is not shown in tyranny, but in service. That we so easily forget this does us little credit. As the eighteenth century Anglican cleric Humphrey Primatt (1736–1779) wrote: "When a man boasts of the dignity of his nature, and the disadvantages of his station, and then and from thence infers his right of oppression of his inferiors, he exhibits his folly as well as his malice" (Primatt 1992, 33).

Acknowledgments

This book emerged from shared concerns about animal suffering and deep commitments to social change. Lisa, a scholar of religion and philosophy, and Anthony, a scholar of peace and conflict studies, share the belief that religion has an important role to play in bringing animal liberation. Our hope in creating this book is that more people from a variety of religious traditions will come to understand that religious practice requires, at a minimum, a vegan diet. We also hope that religious people might come to see that their religious teachings overtly demand a commitment to animal advocacy.

We would like to thank our families, whose love and support make our work possible, the good people at Lantern Books (Kara, Gene, and Martin), Lillia Gajewski and Ashley Mosgrove for editing assistance, and our website creator, Nick Cooney. We would also like to thank each contributor, and their extended families, because we know the time and patience it takes to create a chapter for an anthology.

Additionally, Lisa would like to thank Anthony for his dedication to social justice issues of every kind, and also to thank each individual who practices their religion with gentle dedication, thereby helping to protect and tend nonhuman animals everywhere.

Anthony would like to thank and honor Lisa Kemmerer, a wonderful friend and co-editor; Maria, Chris, Nahshon, Jim, and the whole board from Save the Kids; Ashley Mosgrove, Judy Bentley, Janet Duncan, Sarat Colling, Kevin, Joshua Calkins, Brittani, Brittany, Jackie, Jamie, Terell, Colette, Danielle, Jay, Jeremy, Brian, Jared, Owen Hoppe, Bister, Jennifer, Liat, Matt, Andrew, Abe DeLeon, Luis Fernandez, Deric Shannon, Nick Cooney, Bill Martin, pattrice jones, Ramsey Kaanan, Charles Patterson, Stephen Clark, Steve Wise, Will Potter, Justin Hand, Tom Regan, Carol Gigliotti, Jim Mason, John Feldman, Sarah Kramer, Julie Andrzejewski, and Annie Potts; Richard White with the *Journal for Critical Animal Studies*; Richard Twine, Jason Bayless, John Alessio; Adam Wilson with Downbound; Anastasia Yarbrough, Karen Davis, Uri Gordon, Kaltefleiter, Vasile Stanescu, John Sorenson, Lauren Corman, Maxwell Schnurer, Shannon Keith, Rik Scarce, Helena Pedersen, Roger Yates, Leesa Fawcett, Amie Breeze Harper, Charlotte Laws, David Nibert, Constance Russell, Anuj Shah, Patrick Hoyt, Alma Williams, Nicola Taylor, Cary Wolfe, Amy Fitzgerald, Nicole R. Pallotta, Sherryl Vint, Mark Rowlands, Lindgren Johnson, Veda Stram, Carrie Smith, Corey Lewis, Jodey Castricano, Ward Churchill, Piers Beirne, Richard Loder, Peter Castro, and Carl Boggs; Charles Weigl Zach, Lorna, and Kate with AK Press; Sviatoslav Voloshin, Ali Zaidi; John Asimakopoulos from Transformative Studies Institute; elana levy; Andy Stepanian, and with great respect to all of SHAC 7, Daniel McGowan and Jenny; Dave (with Hugs for Puppies); Maury Harris, John Burke, John Taylor, Steve Best, Richard Kahn, Barron Boyd, Nancy Piscitell, Cliff Donn, Jeff Chin, Robert A. Rubinstein, Lisa Mignacca, Micere Githae Mugo, Bill Skipper, Richard Kendrick, Mecke Nagel, Andrew Fitz-Gibbon, Caroline Tauxe, Caroline Kaltefleiter, Herb Haines, and Peter McLaren; Ben, Kevin, and Jimmy; everyone at the Program on the Analysis and Resolution of Conflicts; 03–04 PARC Crew—Marco, Jason, Heather, Matt, Jamie, Micah, Mike, Megumi, Trish, Michelle, Amy, Sandra, Egle, Amber, Monique, Diane, Holly, Angie, and Naomi; Syracuse Bicycle (the best bike shop ever!)— Paul, Christian, Brian Dan, Bobcat Brian, Hoag, Chris, Turbo, and the rest of the crew; everyone with New York Alternatives to Violence Program inside and outside, especially at Auburn Prison; American Friends Service Committee in Syracuse—Linda, Chrissie, and Twiggy; Outdoor Empowerment; Transformative Studies Institute; Institute for Critical Animal Studies; Save the Kids, Green Theory and Praxis; Central New York Peace Studies Consortium; *Peace Studies Journal*; of course all of Nocella's wonderful and amazing students at Le Moyne College, Hillbrook, SUNY Cortland, and Syracuse University; and all of the wonderful hardworking staff at Hillbrook Youth Detention Facility.

This book is dedicated to nonhuman animals throughout history who have been tortured, sacrificed, exploited, and killed in the name of religion, or simply because religious traditions failed in their duty to challenge animal exploitation.

A portion of all proceeds from this book will be returned to animal advocacy.

Introduction

LISA KEMMERER

*Ethics are complete, profound and alive only when addressed
to all living beings. Only then are we in spiritual connection
with the world. Any philosophy not representing this, not based on
the indefinite totality of life, is bound to disappear.*

—ALBERT SCHWEITZER

*Personally, I would not give a fig for any man's religion whose
horse, cat, and dog do not feel its benefits. Life in any form
is our perpetual responsibility.*

—S. PARKES CADMAN

Across time and around the world, religions have provided human beings with a moral framework that outlines human responsibilities for other creatures, and which inevitably underscore the virtue of compassion. Simultaneously, religions have battled human tendencies such as greed, indifference, cruelty, and selfishness.

Religions are too often twisted, or simply sidelined. Although religions tend to teach generosity and nonviolence, people have grabbed and snatched, squabbled and slaughtered. Although religions tend to teach responsibility and simplicity, people have exploited and plundered for profit. Although religions tend to teach social responsibility and compassion, we have shown remarkable selfishness and shameful indifference. Religions generally call people from exploitation and greed to compassion and service, teaching us to walk lightly and live gently. Whatever we might *wish* were true, religions teach peace and kindness. Consequently, few are surprised when people of faith speak out against war, build communities in fragmented populations, or protect the defenseless against injustice. Yet comparatively few people in industrialized nations have focused on the needs of nonhumans; few among those of comparative affluence understand the spiritual importance of choosing a vegan diet.

Factory farming causes acute suffering, prolonged misery, and premature death to billions of nonhuman animals every year (see Appendix). Most of us never see the creatures that we eat, their long eyelashes or shiny beaks, marvelous colors or curious eyes. We never know a cow or a turkey as an individual with preferences, anxieties, and curiosities. Most of us only see a specific "edible" body part wrapped in plastic—and we fail to recognize that body part for what it is. Food labels rarely speak the truth. This, your "food," is part of someone else's body.

From factory and fur farms to medical laboratories and the pet industry, nonhumans are perceived as objects for our purposes, and mere means to our ends. Technology, mass production, and the sheer number of human beings now crowded onto Earth have exponentially increased the volume and intensity of nonhuman animal exploitation. Yet most of us never see truckloads of cats and dogs euthanized at the local shelter. We don't see the billions of mice and pigeons who are trapped in tiny laboratory cages, powerlessly awaiting whatever befalls them at the hands of humanity. We don't see the stale, barred quarters of tigers and chimpanzees imprisoned between circus gigs or TV programs, where they spend their thwarted lives for frivolous human ends. Although most of us never see these animals' much-diminished lives, we collectively use our dollars to support these forms of exploitation.

In our daily lives, we often act without thinking, behave without conviction, and live without intent. Our spiritual lives too often take a backseat to convention, habit, convenience, and the mindless ritual of day-to-day life. But what is the point of religion if spiritual beliefs don't touch and improve human lives? What is the relevance of sacred writings if they fail to mold our interactions with other creatures—the vast *majority* of sentient life on Earth? What is the value of religion if we are no less barbaric for belief?

How do religions guide us in our interactions with nonhumans? What is our responsibility for white turkeys and spotted hogs? Religions offer an impressive array of teachings that encourage compassion and service. Collectively, religions teach adherents not to neglect, abuse, exploit, or slaughter nonhumans, but rather to assist, tend, and respect the myriad other creatures with whom we share so much in common. Why do we so often fail to notice these dominant religious teachings, which encourage us to change our ways? Why are we largely unaware of these powerful texts and teachings?

When called to our attention, these sacred teachings, similar across centuries and continents, are likely to amaze even those who claim no religious beliefs. How much more so will they do for those who claim a particular religious tradition! The religions of the world offer a universal call to compassion, if only we would listen, if only we would make a sincere commitment to adhere to the core teaching of our religion, if only we would allow our religious convictions to change our hearts and guide our actions. In these teachings, were we to pay attention to them, we would find reason to reconsider our responsibility for a stray cat or wounded snake alongside the road, our willingness to invest in drugs tested on mice or dogs, and our choices at the supermarket.

This anthology carries readers from India and China to Malaysia and America, from sacred writings to core religious ideals, from time-honored practices to contemporary animal advocacy. We hope that this anthology will encourage readers to reexamine their religious beliefs and/or those of friends, family, and their local community. Ultimately, we hope that readers will revisit daily habits—most importantly, the consumption of products rooted in animal suffering—in the hope that we might move toward a more peaceful, spiritual world.

ESSAYS

Christopher Key Chapple begins our examination of religions and nonhumans by introducing Hindu, Jain, and Buddhist traditions. He focuses on religious symbols, texts, moral teachings, practices, and the stories from the lives of founders and exemplars. He calls attention to yogic poses, which imitate and are named after nonhumans, and which reveal an appreciation for the powers of these nonhuman animals. Chapple also profiles the lives and teachings of Mahavira and the Buddha, the founders of the Jain and Buddhist traditions; he stresses the importance of reincarnation and karma, which maintain an animal-friendly religious philosophy. Finally, Chapple introduces the Hindu Bishnoi, and describes how Bishnoi religious practice led them to protect the natural world—plants and nonhuman animals— even at the cost of their own lives.

Steven J. Rosen examines a particular Hindu branch, the Vaishnava tradition. He explains the Hindu concept of nonviolence, and the Vaishnava version of the Golden Rule (found in most religious traditions): Whatever we do to others will also be done to us. While he notes that a few Hindu sects continue to sacrifice nonhuman animals, he explains the origin of this practice, and notes that the karmic Golden Rule speaks against such ongoing violence—while encouraging veganism. He quotes Bhishma in the Hindu epic, the *Mahabharata*, speaking out against eating flesh. Rosen also explains Hindu reverence for cattle, and reminds readers that nonviolence does not require passivity—nonviolence requires that aggression be used only as a response to violence—to protect self or another who is in need of protection.

The next essay focuses on the International Society for Krishna

Consciousness (ISKCON), commonly called the Hare Krishnas. Krishna Kripa Das and Peter Alan Medley (Sarvabhauma Das) introduce ISKCON's founder, A. C. Bhaktivedanta Swami Prabhupada (1896–1977), who carried Krishna consciousness from India to the United States in 1965, bringing Indian vegetarian meals to Americans. Das and Medley note that Prabhupada did not focus on a vegetarian diet first and foremost to reduce suffering, but as a form of devotion to God. Those who love God foster a love for all creatures, which naturally affects diet. The authors explain the importance of the Hare Krishna chant, taught by Prabhupada (now familiar in many countries around the world). Das and Medley note parallels between the *Bhagavad-Gita* (a key portion of the *Mahabharata*) and teachings from other religious traditions, particularly those of Christianity. They also compare ISKCON teachings with voices from the animal liberation movement, demonstrating a shared core.

Charlotte Laws writes of her exploratory adventure into a Jain temple in Southern California. She describes the beauty of the temple, and the comparatively safe and trusting environment that she found within. She explains the rudiments of the Jain religious tradition, including strict ascetic practices, as exemplified by the founder, Mahavira. Laws then focuses on the Jain emphasis on karmic liberation, which requires a life of nonviolence—especially in the kitchen. Laws shares her conversations with Jains during her temple visit, unraveling their understanding of fundamental Jain religious practices, most notably their tendency to purchase and release captive nonhuman animals (especially those destined for slaughter), and their willingness to found and manage sanctuaries, whether for birds, mammals, or insects. In the course of her visit, Laws ponders the strict Jain practice of dietary nonviolence, which excludes not only flesh and eggs but also tubers—yet does not lead Jains to engage in animal advocacy. In her search for understanding, she presents a few brief scenarios to the temple teachers, and then asks not only what they would do, but why.

Norm Phelps, writing from inside the Buddhist tradition, defines good and evil as joy and suffering; he also notes that joy and suffering are undeniably experienced by every living being. Phelps grounds the Buddhist call to animal liberation in a fundamental, deep equality that stems from our shared existence as living beings, exemplified by the perfect "Buddha Nature" that is inherent in all creatures. He then turns to compassion and empathy, and the first and most important Buddhist precept: Do not kill. He notes that this precept, which protects all sentient creatures, is accepted by Buddhists universally, and requires that we choose a vegan diet. He also explains Buddhist attempts to justify the flesh habit, concluding that the teachings of the Buddha are clear: "Meat eating I have not permitted to anyone, I do not permit [it], I will not permit [it]" (*Lankavatara Sutra* 1999, 219).

Matthew J. Walton focuses on the Buddhist understanding of karma as linked to intention, then applies this understanding to animal liberation. In the process, he explores the basics of Buddhism, including fundamental concepts such as the unavoidability of suffering and change, craving as the source of suffering, and the importance of "nondiscriminating compassion for all beings"—compassion that does not allow separation between "self" and "other." From a Buddhist perspective, Walton notes, we can only liberate ourselves, and liberation is not physical, but spiritual. Nonetheless, he asserts that liberating nonhumans not only sets suffering beings free (physically), but also liberates animal exploiters from the negative karma that is accrued through exploitation and causing harm. Walton concludes that Buddhist animal liberationists would do well to act without malice and anger, and with right intentions—as required by Buddhism. He explains how this change of attitude will, ultimately, lead to more effective animal advocacy.

Louis Komjathy carries readers to China to explore Daoism and diet, examining Daoist teachings and practices both ancient and contemporary. Daoist precepts, like Buddhist precepts, include an injunction not to "kill or harm any being." Yet Komjathy notes that the Chinese diet has rarely been shaped by any concern for nonhumans or the environment, and has instead been determined by such notions as ritual purity, or an interest in attaining immortality. Overall, Chinese who can afford to eat meat do so, and those who cannot, eat as much meat as they are able—which has been precious little until recent times. But a conception of vegetarian Daoist deities eventually emerged, elevating the fleshless diet to one most likely to bring a devotee closer to gods and heavenly realms. Additionally, Buddhism was introduced in the eighth century, and the Chinese people "recognized vegetarianism as a clear requirement" of Buddhist teachings. Buddhist views of compassion and karma influenced Daoism, most notably the School of Complete Perfection, the school in which Komjathy has been ordained as a monk.

Richard Schwartz shifts attention to Abrahamic religions, focusing on Hebrew Bible passages that teach compassion, preservation of health, and the duties of dominion. He notes that human health is harmed when we consume animal products; he also cites Biblical passages that reveal the Hebrew Creator as compassionate toward all beings. Schwartz recalls Isaiah and Psalms, and the Peaceable Kingdom, establishing the Creator's plan for future peace. He highlights the connection between global warming and animal agriculture, and provides Biblical teachings in support of a vegan diet (though he often uses the more familiar term, "vegetarian"). Schwartz then responds to eighteen common arguments against moving toward a vegan diet, including Biblical passages that offer humans "dominion" and note that we are created "in the image of God," as well as Jewish feast days, dietary laws, agricultural reform, and a faulty conception of what constitutes a healthy human diet. In a world plagued by factory farming, global warming, world hunger, and oil wars, Schwartz unveils a Jewish imperative that the faithful turn away from animal products.

Judith Barad explores the place of nonhuman animals in the Christian tradition through celebrated Catholics: popes, theologians, and saints. She begins with the words of Pope John Paul II, and then explores St. Thomas Aquinas's "proof" that all nonhuman animals have souls. Barad then recalls stories that demonstrate St. Francis of Assisi's compassion for nonhuman animals, especially those under the cruel thumb of humanity, whether turtledoves, rabbits, or lambs. He also extended his caring to humans and wolves, settling a dispute peacefully between these often antagonistic species. Barad explains how Catholic moral exemplars, from Aquinas through St. Francis to contemporary popes, remind Christians that they are to be compassionate, and that they owe these vulnerable creatures of God their kindness, protection, and mercy.

Andrew Fitz-Gibbon investigates animal advocacy through the lens of Christian mysticism. He notes that the ascetic, world-denying tendencies of mystics would seem to work against any animal liberation teachings among mystics, but he notes that this is not the case. He discusses the central role of unity (or Oneness), and explains the difference between pantheism and panentheism. In the absence of dualism—with all contained in One—Fitz-Gibbon notes that mystics can harbor no human/nonhuman distinction. He then explores the lives of Christian mystics who have lived close to other creatures, providing them with protective care. Fitz-Gibbon reminds readers that hagiographies recalling the lives of saints were written long before there was any need for animal liberation, and that these mystics therefore can't speak directly to a contemporary movement, but that Christian mystics provide an example of "a way of life deeply sympathetic to animal advocacy."

Through Society of Friends insights and spiritual visions, Gracia Fay Bouwman Ellwood explores the central importance of the Inner Light, which is present in all human beings, and is also shared by the divine. Ellwood explains how love is connected with this Light, and with God. She quotes mystics and poets to unveil the Hidden Paradise that is "present throughout our world, despite pervasive alienation, violence, and pain"—despite the "ocean of darkness" in which we live. In the tradition of "prophetic challenge," Ellwood explains how Friends created boycotts and petitions, and worked with the Underground Railroad to further the cause of abolition. Through Society of Friends' spiritual understandings and practices, Ellwood outlines a precedent for animal liberation.

"Scapegoating" is when a dominant group blames a subordinate group (or vulnerable individual) for personal or community misfortunes, or natural disasters. Stephan R. Kaufman explores two authors, René Girard and Ernest Becker, to examine scapegoating as a social phenomenon, as central to the Christian tradition, and as informative for animal advocacy. Girard observed that humans mimic one another, while Becker noted that social conditioning teaches us what is "good." Putting these two ideas together, Kaufman argues that humans who share a sense of what is good are likely to experience shortages, leading to conflict. When conflict escalates, social cohesion is threatened. At such times, humans frequently band together against a scapegoat, whether human or nonhuman. Kaufman calls attention to the conflict that developed around Hebrew sacrificial tradition, as demonstrated by the prophets. He also comments that the New Testament presents Jesus as an innocent scapegoat, crucified by the Romans in the hope of preventing a Passover rebellion. Jesus-as-scapegoat reveals "the lies that underlie scapegoating" in a religious tradition that teaches "that God sides with those who are weak and vulnerable."

The next chapter (Lisa Kemmerer) carries us into the world of Islam, exploring sayings from the life of the Prophet, and core teachings from the Qur'an, such as the importance of love and compassion, the human obligation to tend what Allah has created, and the imperative for *zakat* (sharing, almsgiving). Muslims are to be compassionate and to share with those in need, no matter who "those" might be. This chapter also explores Islamic laws, revealing what is likely Islam's strongest and most unique contribution to animal liberation. Islamic law forbids cruelty to nonhuman animals, especially for frivolous or unnecessary ends, thereby protecting the myriad creatures from the fur industry, the entertainment industry, and almost all exploitation for science. For most of us, eating animal products is also unnecessary, and Islamic laws therefore extend to protect factory farmed animals as well, requiring that Muslims avoid the consumption of factory farmed products, whether flesh, nursing milk, or reproductive eggs, when they are able to make other choices.

Academics and activists alike view Al-Hafiz Basheer Ahmad Masri (1914–1992) as a pioneer in the field of animal welfare/rights and Islam. Masri's grandson, Nadeem Haque, leads readers through Masri's life—from a noteworthy youth in India, to a tumultuous political life in Africa, to the animal welfare movement of the mid (to late) twentieth century in England. Masri, who became an important religious leader and lecturer, strengthened Christian understandings of the Islamic world, and Muslim understandings of Islamic obligations in the area of animal welfare/rights. He worked with the World Society for the Protection of Animals and Compassion in World Farming (CIWF), and was commissioned to publish papers and books on the subject of Islam and animal welfare/rights, culminating in his most definitive work, *Animals in Islam*.

"Indigenous Peoples: Kinship and Killing" (Lisa Kemmerer) retells a variety of lively indigenous myths explaining how nonhumans and humans morph from one species to another, engage in competitions that outline their fates, and maintain a delicate balance of power. This vision of an extended community—of kin across species—leads indigenous peoples to view nonhuman animals as they view human animals, with respect and responsibility. Indigenous peoples tend to recognize that they are dependent for survival on the larger world, and that amiable relations with nature and nonhuman animals are therefore beneficial. It is therefore not surprising that many indigenous myths—indeed, myths from every religious tradition—hearken back to a peaceable community, a time when all beings lived without bloodshed, and explain how this universal harmony was destroyed. Indigenous traditions (like all religions) teach that peaceful relations are preferable, so what does this mean for hunting traditions at a time when many natives are able to make different dietary choices?

Linda G. Fisher is Ojibway and Cherokee. She describes childhood experiences with fish and snakes, commenting: "I do not understand cruelty and indifference, whether directed toward people or other creatures." Consequently, she cannot understand contemporary Native American ceremonial costumes made of leather and feathers, the ongoing glorification of "traditional" fishing and hunting, or other practices that demonstrate a lack of empathy or respect for nonhumans and "Mother Earth." She reflects on oppression—against her people and against nature—and fears that all Americans (natives and immigrants alike) now share the same path, a path of exploitation and destruction. Fisher, an artist and animal activist, is a vegan; her mother is vegetarian. Fisher is also fully Indian. She attends powwows and wears beaded jewelry passed down from distant ancestors. She even keeps a picture of Chief Seattle in her art studio, lest she forget his words: "We are all one breath."

Dianne Sylvan describes Wicca as "a religion of Earth and stars, wind and rain, of ivy growing in spirals and people dancing in spirals," a religion that allows for both the feminine and the masculine, a religion that has emerged to satisfy the needs of those who no longer feel comfortable with the religion of their childhood. Sylvan comments on contemporary tendencies—alienation from nature, exploitation of nonhuman animals, male domination, materialism, and the unending quest for profits—all inimical to Wicca. There are no established Wiccan laws, Sylvan notes, only general understandings and tendencies. She provides a few Wiccan basics: freedom for all, individuality, and "not to harm." She notes that the Wiccan vision is holistic, leading many practitioners to activism. For Sylvan, "not to harm" is central to her ongoing animal advocacy. Where strands of belief and practice are interwoven, where change "is the only eternal truth," Sylvan's vision highlights the power of the individual and supports grassroots activism.

The final chapter, written by Fireweed, reveals a Wiccan path rejecting contemporary dualisms and forms of hierarchical dominance, whether patriarchy, animal exploitation, or environmental degradation. Fireweed makes clear that she can only speak as one practitioner among many, but notes a few common links between Wiccan spiritual visions and practice and the feminist, anarchist, environmental, and social justice movements. She expresses frustration with Wiccans who fail to include nonhuman animals in their circle of compassion, who prefer to ritualize or otherwise justify and rationalize killing sentient beings for food. For example, some Wiccans and ecofeminists reference an assumed "natural" food-chain hierarchy even though they strongly reject all other hierarchies as unnatural and harmful. Some Wiccans feel—against medical evidence—that animal products are necessary to human health, or that a prayer or a moment of thanks neutralizes an exploitative diet of flesh, eggs, and dairy products. Fireweed, in contrast, notes that there are many feminists, ecofeminists, and Wiccans who rightly include other creatures in their "earth-honoring spiritual practice based on immanence, interconnectedness, and harm reduction." Fireweed reminds readers that "healing from the wounds of patriarchy requires radical shifts in perspective," and that these shifts have the power to free wounded individuals—including nonhuman individuals—from the constraints of limited vision.

Note: Many terms stemming from religious traditions around the world have a variety of English spellings due to the complications inherent in transliteration—moving words from a particular language to another written language, where it is sometimes impossible to match sounds or their ascribed notations in a particular alphabet. While some of these diverse spellings have been unified across essays, others have been left to the particular expressions preferred by authors behind the individual essays that comprise this anthology.

PART ONE

RELIGIONS OF ASIA

Hindu, Jain, Buddhist, and Daoist Traditions

1

Indic Traditions and Animals

Imitation, Reincarnation, and Compassion

CHRISTOPHER KEY CHAPPLE

INTRODUCTION

The Hindu, Jain, and Buddhist religious traditions accord high status to animals as exemplars, friends, and past relatives. This chapter explores traditional and contemporary examples of how attitudes toward nonhuman animals in these Asian traditions have supported and continue to support advocacy for the well-being of all living beings.

The vast and complex cultures of Asia find a common historical legacy in the Indian subcontinent. From the arid river regions of the west, to the lush peninsular region of the south, to the Gangetic plain up into the Himalayas, India has nurtured numerous religious traditions: Hinduism in its various local and pan-Indian forms, most notably Vaishnavism, Shaivism, and Advaita Vedanta; Buddhism; Jainism; locally flavored varieties of Islam; and Sikhism. India also holds the world's largest population of Zoroastrians as well as several million Christians. India has developed universal spiritual practices that include physical movement, ritual (*puja*), and prayer (*mantra/japa*) that have traveled across religious traditions and continents.

ANIMALS IN HINDUISM, BUDDHISM, AND JAINISM

Perhaps the most well-known practice from the Hindu tradition is Yoga, a technique for minimizing one's mental distractions for the purposes of deepening one's spirituality (Patanjali's *Yoga Sutra*, I:2–4). Among its many practices and approaches, from ethical observances to meditation, Yoga includes movements that align human physicality with the larger animal order.

Yoga postures, often animal in reference, emerged as a distinct expression of religious devotional practice over a course of many hundreds of years. Early images from the Indus Valley civilization of Mohenjadoro and Harappa (ca. 3000 B.C.E.) depict humans surrounded by animals, both fierce and domestic, in an idyllic tableau. Terra-cotta sculptures show humans imitating the countenance of animals, most notably the tiger (Kenoyer 1998, 82, 167). Historian of religion Mircea Eliade, in his classic work on shamanism, notes that animal imitation is common among shamans worldwide. He writes that "forgetting the limitations and false measurements of humanity [by imitating animals, offers] . . . a new dimension in life: spontaneity, freedom, sympathy with all the cosmic rhythms and hence bliss and immortality" (Eliade 1953, 460). The earliest image of what might be deemed a proto-Yogi shows a cross-legged figure sitting upon an animal skin, adorned with a headdress that includes horns from a buffalo or antelope. (Similarly, Native Americans donned the skins and horns of a totem animal, indicating that they had harnessed the special power associated with that particular animal.)

Following the decline of the Indus Valley around 1500 B.C.E., India moved into a creative phase characterized by wood-based cities. No stone monuments or significant terra-cotta images remain from this period, making it impossible to know with certainty the

nature and precise shape of Indian cultures, aside from literary
accounts preserved orally and, with the advent of writing inspired
by the Phoenicians in 500 B.C.E., texts that were composed much
later. For example, the Vedas, ancient sacred Hindu texts from the
Indus Valley and beyond, extol the cow in dozens of hymns, liken-
ing the beneficence of the cow to the dawn, to speech, to the rain
clouds, and to creation itself.[1]

Enduring material evidence of Indian civilization reemerges in
approximately 300 B.C.E. with excavations of numerous sculptures
from Mathura, south of Delhi, and Ashokan pillars scattered throughout the subcontinent. From this time forward we have consistent
physical testimony corroborating the importance of animals as indicated in Indian religions and Hindu epic literature.

Great religious figures of classical India, from stories such as those
of the Jina (Jain religious tradition) and the Buddha, to stories about
the pantheon of gods and goddesses, include animals in various ways
in their narrations and iconic depictions. The Jina, also known as
Mahavira (ca. 500 B.C.E.), was described as containing animal-like
qualities:

> His senses were well protected like those of a tortoise;
> He was single and alone like the horn of a rhinoceros;
> He was free like a bird;
> He was always waking like the fabulous bird Bharunda;
> Valorous like an elephant, strong like a bull;
> Difficult to attack like a lion . . .
> Like the earth he patiently bore everything;
> Like a well-kindled fire he shone in his splendor. (Jacobi 1884, 261)

Hindu texts called the Upanishads introduced the idea of reincarnation, moving yet further from a decisive separation between human
and nonhuman animal. The *Kaushitaki Upanishad* states that "[one]
is born again here according to [one's] deeds (*karma*) as a worm, or as

a moth, or as a fish, or as a bird, or as a lion, or as a wild boar, or as a snake, or as a tiger, or as a person" (Hume 1921, 303).

Many stories of the Buddha's past births are contained in a collection of narratives known as the Jataka Tales. These stories include references to more than seventy different types of animals. The Buddha himself took many animal forms in past incarnations, including different monkeys, elephants, jackals, lions, crows, deer, birds, and fish (Chapple 1997, 135). The Buddha, when he lived as a wealthy prince, had a close relationship with many animals, most notably his white stallion Kanthaka (Warren 1896, 62–67).

In Hinduism, animals are past incarnations and beloved companions, and are also elevated to deity status, such as the Eagle Garuda, the Monkey Hanuman, and the Elephant-headed Ganesh. Each anthropomorphic deity has a well-known companion animal, including Ganesh's rat, Durga's lion, Saraswati's peacock, Lakshmi's elephant, and Shiva's bull. Animals also figure prominently in Jain symbols. The iconography of each great Jain teacher, or Tirthankara, seems nearly identical. To distinguish between the twenty-four different Jainas seated in meditation, one needs to consult the insignia at the base of each sculpture. Rsabha's companion is the bull; Ajita is marked by an elephant; Sambhava, a horse; Abhinanda, an ape; and Sumati, a partridge. The two historical Tirthankaras, Parsvanatha (ca. 800 B.C.E.) and Mahavira (ca. 500 B.C.E.), are signified by a snake and a lion, respectively (Chapple 2006, 245).

While the symbolism of animals *as* animals clearly holds great importance in these traditions, it's also clear that humans sought ways in which to capture the variety of powers embodied by animals. In the medieval period, Hindus composed detailed Yoga manuals to provide instruction on how to mimic the stance and mood of specific animals. Many postures (*asana*) carry the names of animals. The *Hatha Yoga Pradipika* (HYP), written by Svatmarama in the fifteenth century, lists several poses named after animals: the Cow Head's Pose (*Gomukha asana*; HYP 20), the Tortoise Pose (*Kurma asana*; HYP 24), the Rooster

Pose (*Kukkuta asana*; HYP 25), the Peacock Pose (*Mayur asana*; HYP 32), and the Lion's Pose (*Simha asana*; HYP 52–54) (Svatmarama 1997). Additionally, later Yoga manuals, such as the *Gheranda Samhita*, include several additional poses with animal names, including the Serpent Pose (*Naga asana*), the Rabbit Pose (*Shasha asana*), the Cobra Pose (*Bhujanga asana*), the Locust Pose (*Shalabha asana*), the Crow Pose (*Kaka asana*), the Eagle Pose (*Gauruda asana*), the Frog Pose (*Manduka asana*), and the Scorpion Pose (*Vrischika asana*), to name a few (Gheranda 1979). When imitating animals through the practice of Yoga, one takes on the qualities associated with each animal, from the regal bearing of a lion to the great balance and insight of an eagle.

One outstanding characteristic of Jaina attitudes toward animals can be found in their detailed categorizations of species. According to the theology of Jainism, 8.4 million different species exist, each part of the cycle of birth, death, and rebirth. Based on the karma that one accrues during each particular birth, one will be reborn accordingly. Moral agency is therefore not the exclusive provenance of the human, but extends to all beings, from the souls that dwell in rocks (for up to twenty-two thousand years) to the fleeting birth that one might experience as a bacterium.

The Jaina taxonomy places animals in a graduated order starting with those beings who possess only touch, the foundational sense capacity that defines the presence of life. These include microorganisms, plants, and earth, water, fire, and air bodies. The next highest order introduces the sense of taste; worms, leeches, oysters, and snails occupy this domain. Third-order life-forms add the sense of smell and include many insects. Fourth-level beings, in addition to being able to touch, taste, and smell, can also see; these include butterflies, flies, and bees. The fifth level, which includes hearing, holds birds, reptiles, mammals, and humans (Tatia 1994, 45–46).

Nonhuman animal births are generally fraught with difficulty, but animals learn lessons that eventually result in rebirth as human beings. One of the most famous of reincarnation narratives was written by Haribhadra (over twelve hundred years ago), and entails a drama between a husband and wife over issues of infidelity, murder, and revenge. In a sequence of follies, the husband, Yasodhara, and his mother had both been killed by Yasodhara's wife. The two reincarnate respectively as a peacock and a dog, as a mongoose and a snake, as a fish and a crocodile, as goats, as a buffalo (the mother only), as chickens, and eventually as twin human beings, who grow up to enter the monastic life, and convince an entire kingdom to give up animal sacrifice (Hardy 1990).

In some stories animals themselves perform great acts of merit, prompting Padmanabh S. Jaini (2000) to write:

> Like humans, animals are able to assume the religious vows. . . . This similarity with humans may partly explain the penchant of Indians— and particularly Jainas—to consider all life as inviolable. While this is not the same as exalting animals as holy beings, as some Hindus have done, it has prompted many Indians to renounce all violence toward living beings, and recognize the sacredness of all forms of life. (Jaini 264)

Buddhism, particularly in the Jataka Tales, also suggests that animals hold moral agency, learn from their mistakes, and suffer or benefit from the consequences of their actions. In one particularly robust tale, the Buddha dwelt deep in the forest as a tree spirit. A ferocious lion and tiger also lived in this forest, and were so effective and rapacious in their killing that they left behind copious offal to fester and decay. Out of fear, no humans dared enter the forest, even to fell a tree. One of the future Buddha's fellow tree spirits was deeply offended by the stench oozing from the predators' excessive victims. One day, the tree spirit assumed a dreadful form and scared off the tiger and the lion. The people of a nearby village noticed that the feared predators were no longer leaving tracks into the forest, and began harvesting trees. Soon the entire forest was gone, the land was brought under cultivation, and all the tree spirits lost their homes, moving on to new births (story 121 in Cowell 1895–1907, I:267–69). This fable, like many of the rebirth stories, teaches us to let tigers and lions be tigers and lions, warns of human greed, and highlights the sorrow (and inevitability) of change.

On the Indian subcontinent humans maintain a remarkable intimacy with animals. Cows, water buffalo, goats, camels, and elephants ply roadways with humans, providing labor that in the developed world is supplied by machinery. To honor such working animals, celebrations are held each year—such as Pongal, when animals are given a special day of rest and decorated with brightly colored dots and other patterns.

While no place in the world can claim a more pervasive and diverse vegetarian cuisine, animals are not always treated kindly in India. People within the country fear roving bands of marauding elephants and predatory tigers. Monkeys have become a major nuisance in urban areas, requiring special "monkey whisperers" to manage and remove these busy primates. Sometimes nonhuman animals are perceived to present a threat that elicits harsh treatment.

Animal sacrifice, which was practiced extensively during the Vedic period, still persists in small pockets, particularly in Nepal and eastern India. Historically sanctioned, particularly in the ancient ritual known as the horse sacrifice, such practices make magical correlations between the body parts of nonhuman animals, the human body, and the cosmos. The *Brhadaranyaka Upanishad* proclaims of the sacrificed horse that "the sun is his eye; the wind, his breath; universal fire, his open mouth; the sky, his back; the atmosphere, his belly; . . . days and nights, his feet; rivers, his entrails; plants and trees, his hair" (Hume 1921, 73). The text goes on to state that the forces of the universe dwell within the human frame, and that gaining intimacy with the senses and with the body can help one grow to deeply understand and empathize with all things. Years ago, horse sacrifice was replaced with the sacrifice of smaller animals, particularly goats, and in most places in India such sacrifices are strictly forbidden. However, the popular press of India provides descriptions of ritual killings by the Nepalese royal family and by movie stars, as a means of giving thanks (Nelson 2006, 180).

Buddhists from the outset have decried and condemned the practice of animal sacrifice and, along with the Jainas, helped convince many Hindu rulers to abandon this practice. In fact, many Buddhists in China, Korea, and Japan participate in an alternative ceremony of releasing captive animals. However, like stranded bunnies and newly hatched chicks who are abandoned after Easter, many "released" animals are often recaptured to be sold again to those with pious intentions, for release (Williams 1997, 149–62).

India maintains an extensive network of organizations advocating for animal welfare. The most famous of these is the Hindu *goshala*, shelters that exist across India for unwell and elderly cattle (Nelson 2006; Rosen 2004). Though perhaps less well known, the Jaina *pinjrapoles*, which number in the thousands, give shelter, food, and medical care to countless birds and animals. While visiting one of their bird shelters, I witnessed the care and attention given to each wounded or sick pigeon and sparrow.[2] Such work isn't limited to India and has traveled with immigrants to other lands. In a conversation with the director of the Jain Society of Greater Detroit, Manish Mehta, I learned that the society has developed a service project to benefit both humans and birds. Youth from the Jain Center in Farmington Hills, Michigan, build, install, and maintain bird feeders outside the windows of convalescent and nursing homes, providing tender bonds between young and old, human and nonhuman.

Perhaps the most famous animal advocacy movement in India outside the Jaina and Buddhist communities can be found in the work and life of the Bishnoi. The founder, Jambhesvara, also known as Jambhoji, was born in Pipasar, a rural region of Rajasthan, in 1451 (died in 1536). According to some accounts, his father was a Rajput prince and his mother was a Muslim—both Hindu and Muslim communities lay claim to his story. Though they self-identify as Hindu, the Bishnoi maintain practices associated with Islam; they bury their dead and keep no temple images of deities. Before partition, the shrine table devoted to Jambhesvara's memory was covered with a green cloth, indicating a connection with Islam. (Since partition, the color of the cloth has been saffron [Jain 2008].)

Having served as a cowherd for more than twenty years before receiving a religious vision, Jambhesvara established the Bishnoi community in 1485 for the protection of humans, animals, and plants. He composed twenty-nine rules to be followed by all members of this community, which include the following:

18. Be compassionate towards all living beings;
22. Provide common shelter for goats and sheep to avoid their being slaughtered in abattoirs;
23. Do not castrate bulls;
28. Do not eat meat or nonvegetarian dishes.[3]

Another of his works, the *Jambha Sāra*, lays out six rules of nonviolence. First is the *jhampari pāl* prohibiting animal sacrifice; second is the *jeevani vidhi* requiring the filtering of water and milk. Third is the requirement to return water-creatures to the water; fourth is to make sure that firewood and cow dung used for fuel do not hold creatures or insects that might be accidentally burned. Fifth is the *badhiyā*, to avoid harming bullocks—not to sell them to butchers—and to send them to animal shelters. Sixth is the protection of deer in forests, who are classed with cows, goats and other nonviolent beasts (Jain 2008, 109).

According to traditional lore, the Bishnoi commitment to the protection of plants and animals has cost them hundreds of their own lives since the fifteenth century, including a group of 363 Bishnoi who, under the leadership of Amrita Devi, resisted deforestation in 1730. Because of this tragedy, the ruler of Jodhpur, Maharaj Abhay

Singh, apologized and issued decrees that prevented such slaughter in the future:

(A) All cutting of green trees and hunting of animals within the revenue boundaries of Bishnoi villages was strictly prohibited.

(B) If by mistake any individual violated this order, he would be prosecuted by the state and severely penalized.

(C) Even the members of ruling families were not permitted to shoot animals in or near the Bishnoi villages.[4]

Amrita Devi inspired the renowned 1970s Chipko tree-protection movement, and to this day the animals within the Bishnoi area, which includes most of Rajasthan and parts of Gujarat and Haryana, are afforded extraordinary protections. In 1998, Hindi film actor Salman Khan was sentenced to five years in prison for killing a blackbuck in Bishnoi territory.

In modern times, Bishnoi have established the Community for Wildlife and Rural Development Society and the All India Jeev Raksha Bishnoi Sabha, a wildlife protection organization. The Amrita Devi Award was established to reward someone for their contribution in the field of wildlife protection, for having shown exemplary courage or exemplary work to protect wildlife. In 2000, the award was given to the family of Gangaram Bishnoi, who lost his life while protecting a Chinkara deer. In 2004, the award was bestowed on the family of Chhailuram Singh Rajput, a Bishnoi who lost his life saving a blackbuck. The Bishnoi maintain an active website, which includes an award-winning film about their movement, *Willing to Sacrifice*.

CONCLUSION

From earliest recorded Indian history, animals have been an integral part of Indian culture. The core philosophies of India hold animals in great regard, not only for the gifts these creatures offer humanity, but also in their own right, as exemplified in yoga and the perdurability of more recent resistance movements, such as the Hindu Bishnoi. From India's philosophies that emphasize the interconnectedness of life, lively stories of past animal births, and from India's long history of women and men who have been willing to make sacrifices to protect trees and animals, the world can learn a great deal about building an ethic of animal advocacy.

2

Vaishnava Hinduism

Ahimsa and Vegetarianism

STEVEN J. ROSEN

INTRODUCTION

Although not all Hindus are vegetarians, the Hindu world, in general, has a healthy reverence for all of God's creation, often extending to a nonmeat diet. Why do some Hindus adamantly stand behind the importance of vegetarianism while others go so far as to endorse animal sacrifice?

The question is multifaceted, but its resolution begins with the following simple truth: contrary to popular belief, Hinduism isn't a monolithic religious tradition. Rather, *Hinduism* is an umbrella term for a number of diverse religions, such as Vaishnavism, Shaivism, and Shaktism—all with different scriptures, practices, and conceptions of God. While some Hindus sanction meat eating, others do not. This chapter explores Vaishnava Hinduism, the numerically largest segment of the Hindu population,[1] to see what role vegetarianism and *ahimsa* play.

NONVIOLENCE

Vaishnavism, with a following of hundreds of millions of people, is for the most part vegetarian.[2] Vaishnavas have always advocated the equitable treatment of humankind's four-footed, feathered, and scaly kin. All are considered brothers and sisters under God's divine fatherhood.

Ancient India's scriptural legacy, Vedic literature, is firm in its support of both monotheism and animal rights—though many verses alluding to these two subjects have been lost over time.[3] Still, according to the Vaishnava sages who passed down these texts—and according to India's vast storehouse of supplemental Vedic literature (such as the epics and the Puranas)—God is the ultimate Father, as in the Judeo-Christian tradition, and all living entities are His children. Consequently, a strong tradition of *ahimsa* arose in the Vaishnava tradition, teaching harmlessness and love for all creatures, who are spiritually bonded in relationship to God. Indeed, the *Mahabharata*, chief among Vaishnava epics (and arguably the most important scripture in India), teaches *ahimsa paro dharmo*: "Nonviolence is the highest duty" (*Mahabharata* 1.11.12 and 3.198.69).

This nonviolence, it should be noted, is expressed in the most general terms. It is meant to be all-inclusive. The *Mahabharata* extols *sarva-bhuta-hita*, which means "kindness to all creatures," as opposed to the more limited vision of *loka-hita*, or "kindness to one's own species."[4] The former includes the latter, and so Vaishnava scripture teaches practitioners to be kind to all.

VAISHNAVISM'S GOLDEN RULE

Just as the Bible teaches the Golden Rule—"Do unto others as you would have others do unto you"—the *Mahabharata*, which in its earliest form predates the Bible, teaches a similar truth in almost the exact same wording.[5] But Vaishnavas extend this teaching to its logical limits, showing kindness to all species of life—and this, of course, means vegetarianism. You're not doing to others what you would have others do to you if you're eating them. It's hard to be kind to animals when you're eating them!

The Hindu teaching of "do unto others" is reflected in the origins of the Sanskrit word for meat, *mamsa*, which means "me-he," or by implication, "The fate of this animal will also be *my* fate." This etymological derivation of the word can be traced to the *Manu-samhita* (5.55): "He will eat me in the next world, whose meat (*mamsa*) I eat in this world. This is why meat is called *mam-sa*, or 'me-he.'"[6] The Golden Rule is clearly at work here. If what I "do unto you" is to eat you, then you have every right, in some future life, to "do the same unto me." In other words, the karmic reaction for eating a living being is evident in the language itself: "I will be eaten in the same way that I eat others."

Thus, devout Hindus oppose killing. They know that every action holds an unavoidable reaction (karma), and that the idea of reincarnation—of taking birth commensurate with our deeds—is as close to karma as the butcher is to meat. That which we do to others will be done to us. This is the universal law of cause and effect, echoing, once again, the Golden Rule. In other words, killing begets killing, and since we reap what we sow over many lives, violence and killing eventually return to those who are violent, to those who kill—if not in this life, then in the next.

Of course, this action–reaction schema had little meaning for Vaishnavas, who didn't eat meat. Rather, these verses address the practices of early Vedic cults, Shaktas and others, who engaged in animal sacrifice. Traditionally, worshippers of Kali, for example, as part of an elaborate ritual, were obliged to chant the Sanskrit word for meat just before slitting a creature's throat. By chanting the "*mamsa* mantra," the priest's heart was supposed to be softened, and he was pardoned from the sin of killing.

There are other linguistic connections between meat eating and the severe karmic reactions awaiting those who kill animals for food.

For example, the Sanskrit noun *pashu-ghna* ("he who kills the body") can apply to both a "meat eater" and to "one who commits suicide," thus reinforcing the notion that consuming flesh is tantamount to destroying one's own body. Indeed, the word can even refer to murder, to one who takes human life; thus, there's a correlation between killing nonhuman animals and killing human animals. Narada Muni (a renowned sage, glorified in Vedic literature) indicates something similar in his instructions to King Prachinabarhi, a ruler from the Vedic era who was enamored of opulent animal sacrifices:

> O ruler of the citizens, my dear King, please see in the sky those animals that you have sacrificed, without compassion and without mercy, in the sacrificial arena. All these animals are awaiting your death so that they can avenge the injuries you have inflicted upon them. After you die, they will angrily pierce your body with iron horns and then eat your flesh. (*Srimad Bhagavatam* 4.25.7–8)

Such ideas about karma with regard to killing are consistent with the traditional understanding of the word *mamsa*. In fact, all Vedic texts in support of animal sacrifice endorse the karmic idea that the perpetrator's future life hangs in the balance (*Jaimaniya Brahmana* 1.42–44; *Kaushitaki Brahmana* 11.3; *Shatapatha Brahmana* 11.6.1).

That said, animal sacrifices and the necessary mantras to perform such sacrifices, are ideally things of the past. They are actually considered "prohibited in the age of Kali (*kali-varjyas*)," the age that Hindus believe we now live in (Nelson 2006, 184). By the thirteenth century, great Vaishnava reformers (such as Madhvacharya) recommended "animal effigies," images of animals made of flour, for example, to satisfy ancient scriptural mandates for sacrifice, and to appease traditionalists who might still be attached to outmoded animal sacrifices (Nelson 2006). One common contemporary sacrifice for Kali is now *sankirtan-yajna*, or the congregational chanting of God's holy names. It is this, say the sages, that awakens God-realization in the current epoch of world history, just as animal sacrifices once did in days of old (*Bhagavata Purana* 12.3.51; *Padma Purana, Uttara-khanda* 72.25; *Vishnu Purana* 6.2.17).

Indeed, one may wonder why animal sacrifices were ever deemed necessary. Though scriptures are never quite clear on this point, the *Skandha Purana* offers an interesting history of how such sacrifices began. While these rituals were, in fact, ordained by the saints and sages of the Vedic era, they were never encouraged, but were instead frowned upon. As the story goes, a Brahmin once cursed the world with a devastating famine. The common people, unable to bear it, slaughtered animals to satisfy their hunger—to stay alive. But the sages did not kill animals for food, even at the cost of their own lives. The sages would rather die, the *Skandha Purana* tells us, than feast on the remains of dead animals. Still, to accommodate the masses, the sages allowed meat eating not merely to stay alive, but only as part of a religious sacrifice. Highly qualified priests would sacrifice very specific animals to the Supreme, and the common people would eat the remains. This became an established part of Vedic religion, *even though the spiritually advanced (sages) did not partake of fleshy spoils.* Gradually the calamity subsided, but animal sacrifices were already in place, and the ritualists continued this bloody practice (*Skandha Purana* 2.9.9).[7]

AHIMSA AND THE VAISHNAVA TRADITION

Ahimsa is often said to mean "nonviolence," but refers more specifically to "nonaggression," and this requirement is a high priority in the practice of Vaishnavism. It is important to understand the distinction between nonviolence and nonaggression. Violence is sometimes necessary, for example, if a loved one is attacked, or if one's own life is threatened. In such cases, violence may be in order. But it's never appropriate to initiate violence. *Ahimsa* is to be practiced not only on the physical level, but also on mental and emotional levels, requiring practitioners to avoid abusiveness of any kind, whether overtly, or in more subtle ways.

Qualities such as gentleness, humility, compassion, and other related characteristics are necessary components of *ahimsa*, without which one is not practicing true spiritual life; Vaishnavas put a premium on such behavior. Over time, they came to see gentle cows as symbolic of all finer qualities, and as representing the animal kingdom as a whole. For this reason, Vaishnavas venerate cows as an emblem of *ahimsa*. The Vaishnava position is clear: as the cow is dear to Lord Krishna, the divine cowherd, so should she be dear to us all.

Cows are appreciated for their practical value as well, noting the five magical products that come from their bodies: urine, cow dung, milk, ghee, and yogurt. Amazingly, these items—especially urine and dung—have been found effective (and cost efficient) as fertilizer, compost, medicines, pest repellents, cleansing products, and biogas fuel. The cow is also considered sacred as a natural mother for human society; as one's biological mother feeds her young on milk, so the cow can nurture humans with her milk. Caring for mother cow is thus seen as an important component of *ahimsa*.

Vaishnavas seek to develop compassion and kindness because such characteristics are virtuous in their own right. Hindus are not simply interested in avoiding karmic backlash in some future birth, but in honoring God. To understand the pervasive practice of nonviolence in Hinduism, one must understand how Hindus view the life force itself. Why is life sacred? For India's ancient thinkers, life is part of God, an emanation of the divine that must be respected and honored. Love for God cannot be attained if one does not develop love for God's children, for the sparks of divinity that flow from His (or Her) essence. Accordingly, Hindus have a natural reverence for life, which is part and parcel of their reverence for God.

VEGETARIANISM: A SCRIPTURAL BASIS

Vegetarianism has always been widespread in India, as evidenced by traditional religious literature. For example, the *Manu-samhita*

(5.49, quoted earlier) states: "Having well considered the origin of flesh foods and the cruelty of fettering and slaying corporeal beings, let man entirely abstain from eating flesh." The same work tells us that "killing living beings is an impediment to heaven" and that "one should therefore abstain from meat" (5.48). The text thus abjures the use of flesh foods in no uncertain terms. Though the *Manu-samhita* includes a provision for meat gathered from Vedic sacrifices, it shuns all other uses of nonvegetarian fare (5.42–44).

In the *Mahabharata*, the respected grandsire, Bhishma, has much to say about the harshness of eating animals. While instructing Yudhisthira, eldest of the Pandava princes, he says that the meat of animals is like the flesh of one's own son; eating meat is repugnant, he says, and it should be avoided. Bhishma goes on at some length:

Meat is not born of grass, wood or rock.
Meat arises from killing a living being.
Thus, in the enjoyment of meat there is fault.
The beloved, sincere, truthful gods
have in hand (for nourishment)
oblations, sacrificial offerings, and nectar.
(By contrast,) consider the tortuous,
unrighteous ways of flesh-eating demons.
O King, in not eating meat
one goes without fear in moonlight
or in the dreadful, dangerous darkness
or in the twilight approach of night
or at the crossroads or in the assemblies of people.
If there were no meat-eaters,
there would be no killers.
A meat-eating man is a killer indeed,
causing death for the purpose of food.
If meat were considered not to be food,
there would be no violence.

Violence is done to animals
for the sake of the meat-eater only.
Because the life of violent ones
is shortened as well (due to their deeds),
the one who wishes long life for himself
should refuse meat, O splendid one.
Those fierce ones who do violence to life
are not able to go for protection (when they need it).
They are to be feared by beings as beasts of prey. (26–32)[8]

The *Mahabharata* further explains that meat eating is a dark mode of existence, causing ignorance and disease, making clear that a healthy vegetarian diet is *sattvic*, "in the mode of goodness," able to increase purity of consciousness and longevity. Thus, there are many Indian scriptural texts endorsing the vegetarian way of life.

In the *Tirukural*, composed two thousand years ago by the South Indian Tamil saint, Tiruvalluvar, it is written that "all suffering recoils on the wrongdoer himself. Thus, those desiring not to suffer should refrain from causing pain to others" (Chakravarthi 1953, 154). The *Tirukural*, literally "Holy Couplets," is a text revered among Hindus worldwide, often quoted for its wisdom, specifically in regard to ethics and animal rights. For Satguru Shivaya Subramuniyaswami (1927–2001, founder of *Hinduism Today*, which reaches millions of people in many different nations), this was among his favorite scriptures, and he often used it to explain Hindu vegetarianism in general:

Hindus teach vegetarianism as a way to live with a minimum of hurt to other beings, for to consume meat, fish, fowl or eggs is to participate indirectly in acts of cruelty and violence against the animal kingdom. The abhorrence of injury and killing of any kind leads quite naturally to a vegetarian diet, *sakahara* [which is the Sanskrit word for vegetarianism]. The meat-eater's desire for meat drives another to kill and provide that meat. The act of the butcher begins with the desire of the consumer. Meat eating contributes to a mentality of violence, for with the chemically complex meat ingested, one absorbs the slaughtered creature's fear, pain and terror. These qualities are nourished within the meat-eater, perpetuating the cycle of cruelty and confusion. When the individual's consciousness lifts and expands, he will abhor violence and not be able to even digest the meat, fish, fowl and eggs he was formerly consuming. India's greatest saints have confirmed that one cannot eat meat and live a peaceful, harmonious life. Man's appetite for meat inflicts devastating harm on Earth itself, stripping its precious forests to make way for pastures. The *Tirukural* candidly states, "How can he practice true compassion who eats the flesh of an animal to fatten his own flesh? Greater than a thousand *ghee* offerings consumed in sacrificial fires is not to sacrifice and consume any living creature." (Subramuniyaswami 1993, 201)

CONCLUSION: SPIRITUAL VEGETARIANISM

According to traditional Hindu texts, all of life should be a sacrifice to God: "All that you do, all that you eat, all that you offer and give away, as well as all austerities that you may perform," Lord Krishna says, "should be done as an offering unto Me" (*Bhagavad-Gita* 9.27). The *Bhagavad-Gita* specifies: "If one offers Me with love and devotion a leaf, a flower, a fruit, or water, I will accept it" (9.26). The remnants of such devotional offerings are called *prashadam* (literally "the Lord's mercy"). The *Bhagavad-Gita* confirms that fruits, vegetables, grain, nuts, and dairy products are fit not only for God, but for human consumption, and that one who lovingly offers food to God according to scriptural guidelines is freed from all sinful reactions and consequent rebirth in the material world: "The devotees of the Lord are released from all kinds of sins because they eat food which is first offered in sacrifice. Others, who prepare food for personal sense enjoyment, verily eat only sin" (3.13). Followers of the *Bhagavad-Gita* thus refrain from meat, fish, poultry, and eggs, since these animal products are not sanctioned either by scriptures or sages. In the modern age, veganism (eliminating dairy products as well) has also become a viable option for those committed to *ahimsa*.[9]

Most temples in India freely distribute sanctified vegetarian food (*prashadam*) daily for the benefit of the multitudes who approach the holy shrines. This food has mystic potency, say Vaishnava stalwarts, such that those who prepare, serve, sell, or eat such foods are purified. Narada Muni, the Vedic sage mentioned earlier, was inspired to embark on the spiritual path merely by tasting such food after it had been offered to the Lord.

Just as Vaishnavas generally promote vegetarianism within the context of *prashadam*, they also acknowledge the benefits of a vegetarian diet as a stepping-stone to spiritual perfection. In the *Bhagavad-Gita* (chapter 17), Lord Krishna himself acknowledges that food can be divided into three categories: goodness, passion, and ignorance. Clearly, eating food in passion and ignorance, which includes the eating of meat, has adverse effects on the human condition. Conversely, say Vaishnava texts, eating food in goodness, such as fruits, nuts, vegetables, whole grains, milk, and so on, sets the stage for transcendence.

Vegetarianism positions us for higher material aspirations and predisposes us to God-consciousness, but without the touch of God we are not likely to achieve the full fruits of a vegetarian diet. "Complete vegetarianism" takes Bhishma's words, as quoted from the *Mahabharata*, into account, and augments this grandsire's teachings, reminding people to offer their vegan or vegetarian food as a sacrifice to God. Which Hindu would deny that it is important to do so? Given a choice between vegetarian foods and vegetarian foods offered to Krishna, which would Grandfather Bhishma prefer? Why not, suggests the *Bhagavad-Gita*, get the most out of our vegetarianism by first offering all that we eat to God?

3

International Society for Krishna Consciousness

Lord Krishna and the Animals

KRISHNA KRIPA DASA AND PETER ALAN MEDLEY

(SARVABHAUMA DAS)

*One should treat deer, camels, asses, monkeys, mice, snakes, birds,
and flies exactly like one's own son. How little difference there actually
is between children and these innocent creatures.*
(Bhagavata Purana 7.14.9)

In the above passage from Vyasa's crowning work, the *Bhagavata Purana*,[1] the sage Narada reveals the compassion and love that a Vaishnava[2] is expected to bestow on animals. In the *Bhagavad-Gita*, or "Song of God," Vyasa recounts Krishna's philosophical teachings to his disciple Arjuna, which profoundly influenced Hinduism (as well as Western transcendentalists such as Walt Whitman, Henry David Thoreau, and Ralph Waldo Emerson).

Lord Krishna, revered by millions of Hindus as God, became incarnate on Earth approximately five thousand years ago in a human-like divine form. Prior to 1965, Krishna devotion or

"Krishna consciousness" was not widely known in the West. In that year, a diminutive sixty-nine year old Chaitanya Vaishnava[3] monk from Calcutta (Kolkata), India, boarded the steamship S.S. *Jaladutta* for America, carrying a box of *Bhagavata Puranas* he had translated into English. A. C. Bhaktivedanta Swami Prabhupada (1896–1977) had only about seven dollars in Indian rupees, and he knew no one in America, but he settled into New York's Greenwich Village and began to lecture, prepare vegetarian feasts for eclectic East Villagers, and publicly chant the Hare Krishna mantra at nearby Tompkins Square Park. Due to his uncommon determination and devotion, and prolific writings, "Hare Krishna" and the International Society for Krishna Consciousness (ISKCON) became known worldwide, establishing temples, vegetarian farms, and vegetarian restaurants on every continent.

Rynn Berry, a historian of vegetarian and vegan diet and cuisine who has been dubbed "the Boswell of vegetarianism," considered Prabhupada's arrival in America to be a landmark event:

> Was this the man who would open Vaishnava temples and vegetarian restaurants in every major city of the world? . . . Yes, this was he, the *dhoti*-clad[4] savior that the Western world had been pining for since the death of Pythagoras and Porphyry. This was the man who would teach them not to kill and eat animals, but to eat the *prashadam*[5] of Lord Krishna. (Berry 1999, 173)

EQUAL VISION: THE PANDITA

Prabhupada's teachings derived from the standard scriptures of India's Vedic culture, and his theological basis for considering animals to be our brothers and sisters lay in Lord Krishna's unambiguous declaration in the *Bhagavad-Gita* (14.4) that all beings, not just humans, share a common divine parentage: "It should be understood that all species of life . . . are made possible by birth in this material nature, and that I am their seed-giving Father." Prabhupada frequently cited Krishna's explanation of how animals should be viewed: "The humble sage, by virtue of true knowledge, sees with equal vision a learned and gentle *brahmana* [a priest or religious scholar], a cow, an elephant, a dog and a dog-eater [a social outcast in Indian society]" (*Bhagavad-Gita* 5.18).

The Sanskrit word translated as "sage" in this verse is *pandita*, adapted into English as "pundit." In commenting on this verse, Prabhupada explains that the *pandita*'s spiritually non-prejudicial "equal vision" is due to his realization that "the Supreme Lord, by His plenary portion as *paramatma* [translated as "Supersoul" by Prabhupada], is present in everyone's heart."[6] Yudhisthira, a key character in the *Mahabharata* and a saintly devotee of Krishna, once demonstrated *pandita*-like compassion for a dog. When the demigod Indra invited him to ascend to heaven, Yudhisthira replied:

> I will only accompany you if you allow [the dog] to also come. . . .
> I will never abandon one who is terrified, who seeks my shelter, who
> is devoted, who is afflicted or weak, or who begs for life. I cannot
> leave this creature here! (Dharma 1999, 905)

Chaitanya Vaishnavism—and any religion unequivocally teaching that God is present within the heart of every living being—demands compassion toward all animals.

Commenting on professional football player Michael Vick's illegal dog-fighting conviction, columnist Crispin Sartwell was unnerved by a blaring inconsistency:

> We write memoirs for our dogs, talk baby-talk to them, let them lick
> our faces. But about other species we are as hard-nosed as possible.
> Essentially, we do whatever we feel like to them, whenever we want.
> . . . If we really believed cruelty to animals debased humans who

participate, we'd have to accept that our massive, industrial-scale systems of cruelty to cows deeply debase all humanity.[7]

Unfortunately, cows are not the only victims: chickens, pigs, turkeys, and other domesticated animals suffer similar terrible fates in animal agriculture. While I doubt that Sartwell is a Hare Krishna follower, his disillusionment with double standards in the treatment of animals was surprisingly akin to that of Joanne Wooding, whose participation in Krishna-consciousness in San Diego arose partly as a response to contradictions: "I used to be an animal rights activist, but I began to feel uncomfortable with people who make political agitation to save the whales and seals, but who are themselves flesh-eaters. I appreciate the Hare Krishna people's policy of protecting all of God's creatures" (Dasa 1985, 34).

In his talks and voluminous writings, Prabhupada expressed similar dismay with human behavior, especially with regard to questionable behavior among followers of the world's religious traditions. In his commentary on the *Bhagavata Purana*, he states:

"Many Hindus, Muslims, Christians, Buddhists and religionists of other cults adhere to their religious principles very nicely but [they do not act] equal to all living entities. Indeed, although they profess to be very religious, they kill poor animals. Such religion has no meaning" (Prabhupada 1987, 8.8.21, 304).

In recorded conversations, Prabhupada expressed disappointment that many prominent spiritual leaders, including popes, were meat eaters, thus setting an example of cruelty and indifference for their followers (Prabhupada 1990, 20:92–93; from a conversation on April 23, 1976, in Melbourne, Australia). Prabhupada argued that Christ's "first commandment is 'Thou shall not kill'. . . . [P]eople should stop killing. So who is Christian? Everyone is violating this first commandment. . . . [I]t is very difficult to find a real Christian" (Prabhupada 1993, 168).

Prabhupada also expected political leaders to protect animals. In Sanskrit, an administrator or warrior is called a *Kshatriya*, "one who protects from harm," related to *ksatra*, "dominion" or "governance." Prabhupada did not consider "dominion" to entail exploitation:

> The King represents . . . aquatics, plants, trees, reptiles, birds, animals and man. . . . Being the representative of the Supreme Lord, [he] is duty-bound to give proper protection to every one of them. This is not the case with [modern] presidents and dictators. (Prabhupada 1987, 1.12.4, 654)

FOOD FOR THE SOUL

Beginning in 1965 (in Greenwich Village), Prabhupada prepared multicourse vegetarian meals, served them to students, hippies, and whoever else showed up, then humbly washed the dishes himself. Since those early days, Prabhupada and his Hare Krishna movement have provided a more animal-friendly diet for many people by cooking and serving millions of vegetarian meals worldwide—most of them free—and disseminating vegetarian cookbooks in scores of languages.[8]

ISKCON's vegetarian food programs have expanded since Prabhupada's death in 1977. According to Gainesville, Florida's ISKCON temple president, Kalakantha Das, in 2009 a Hare Krishna vegetarian lunch program on campus at the University of Florida—which has been going for three decades—served between seventeen and twenty thousand vegetarian or vegan meals a month at peak times, as well as twenty-five thousand vegetarian meals a year to local homeless people.[9] In *Holy Cow: The Hare Krishna Contribution to Vegetarianism and Animal Rights*, Steven Rosen (2004) referred to ISKCON's Hare Krishna Food for Life as the world's largest vegetarian food relief program.[10]

It is impossible to gauge Prabhupada's wide-reaching impact on animal advocacy, touching people such as Steve Jobs (Apple Computer), who reminisced about his college days in a Stanford University commencement address: "I would walk the seven miles across town every Sunday night to get one good meal a week at the Hare Krishna temple. I loved it" (*Stanford Report* 2004, n.p.).

COWS

Vaishnavas love and revere cows for many reasons.[11] The cow is viewed as one of humankind's seven mothers (Prabhupada 1987, 1.11.28, 628), and Hare Krishna devotees use ghee (clarified butter), milk, yogurt, and other dairy products in their temple rituals, as do Hindus in general. *Go-puja*, the worship of a cow, is considered highly auspicious.[12] The sacred Hindu *Rig Veda* (8.101.15) admonishes: "Do not harm the cow, for, in so doing, you harm the earth and all of humanity." In a commentary on *Bhagavata Purana* (1.14.35), Prabhupada stated: "Without cow protection and cultivation of the brahminical qualities[13] . . . no human civilization can prosper" (Prabhupada 1987, 812). Vaishnava scriptures describe how cows, peacocks, and other animals live with Krishna in the kingdom of God (or Goloka, a Sanskrit term that means "divine planet of the cows"). Lord Krishna was himself a cowherd who affectionately cared for cows, lovingly called them by their personal names, and mesmerized these blessed bovines with his enchanting flute music. In fact, Krishna once argued with his father, who was worshipping a demigod, suggesting that his father simply worship the cows of Vrindavan.[14]

In Vrindavan, India, ISKCON devotee Kurma Rupa Dasa operates a *goshala*[15]—a care facility for cattle—that tends sick, injured, or elderly bovines who no longer produce milk or engage in physical labor, allowing them to live out their lives. Kurma Rupa, also an expert in book layout and cover design, was unable to meet a publishing deadline due to an emergency involving cows under his care. Kurma Rupa recognized that caring for the cattle under his protection was more important than publishing. Although our book was delayed, Lord Krishna must have been pleased with Kurma, who recognized that the cows' welfare took precedence over a human project—one of Krishna's names is "Govinda," "one who pleases the cows." ISKCON operates *goshalas* at several other places in India.

According to Prabhupada, "cow's milk is essential for developing the finer tissues of the human brain, so that one can understand the intricacies of transcendental knowledge" (Prabhupada 1987, 3.5.7, 189). But milk in Prabhupada's vision was pure, obtained from beloved cows. Highly processed, chemically treated commercial milk contributes to disease, and modern "dairy" cows are "more or less tortured throughout their lives" (Rosen 2004, 45). Although Hare Krishna devotees have established a number of vegetarian farms where cows are treated lovingly, and are allowed to live out their natural lives, at this time there aren't enough such facilities to yield milk for all ISKCON members. Some devotees buy commercial milk, believing that Lord Krishna will accept and purify the milk if it is offered with love, while other Hare Krishnas have adopted a vegan diet (Rosen 2004, 45).[16] Establishing more ISKCON vegetarian farms would reduce the gap between Prabhupada's ideal and the ugly truth of factory farmed dairy products.

BEYOND PACIFISM: *BHAKTI* AND *AHIMSA*

Prabhupada, a lifetime vegetarian,[17] felt that a teacher should be an *acharya*, one who instructs not just by precept, but—more importantly—by his or her behavior. Prabhupada repeatedly stressed that animals have souls and deserve our compassion. He eschewed leather[18] and advised his disciples to avoid killing insects whenever possible. The epic *Mahabharata*—one of the most important Vaishnava scriptures (of which the *Bhagavad-Gita* forms a single chapter)—declares "*ahimsa paro dharma*": "Nonviolence [*ahimsa*] is the highest duty" (*Mahabharata* 1.11.12). Prabhupada gave even greater stress to the Sanskrit commandment that everyone's "*paro dharma*" (highest duty) is to render devotional service (*bhakti yoga*) to God (*Bhagavata Purana* 1.2.6). For Prabhupada, "violence" was not merely physical harm, but any action that failed to spiritually elevate the actor, or others, to Krishna consciousness—including animals.

According to Prabhupada, *ahimsa* is an automatic byproduct of *bhakti*, which he defined as "devotional service." *Bhakti* fosters *ahimsa*, but nonviolence—especially as practiced by those who believe God and the soul are ultimately illusory[19]—does not automatically lead to *bhakti*. The Vaishnava belief that nonviolence should be supported by devotion shares similarities with the teachings of animal advocate Judy Carman. Carman suggested that *ahimsa*, nonviolence, must include spiritual love.[20] In a similar vein, St. Francis of Assisi's *ahimsa* was fueled by his loving perception of God in all beings. *Ahimsa* is strongest when backed by a love for God.

Because of his devotion to *ahimsa*, Prabhupada deemed it best to intone the Hare Krishna mantra audibly, thereby spiritually benefiting animals and other living beings within hearing range—*ahimsa* combined with *bhakti*. In *Chaitanya Charitamrita* (Prabhupada, 1974), Krishna Das Kaviraja described how Chaitanya Mahaprabhu's (1486–1534) ecstatic chanting of the Hare Krishna *maha-mantra* in an Indian forest inspired wild animals such as deer and tigers—natural enemies—to dance and chant peacefully together (17.1). Prabhupada viewed chanting "*Hare Krishna, Hare Krishna, Krishna Krishna, Hare Hare, Hare Rama, Hare Rama, Rama Rama, Hare Hare*" as the most beneficial prayer for animal or human welfare in our age. In a similar way, Judy Carman notes that she has prayed for the welfare of animals (Carman 2003, 165–259), although likely with less stress on chanting specific mantras or sacred names of God.

According to Vaishnavism, another *yajna* (selfless sacrifice) that benefits animals is the distribution of vegetarian food that has been offered as a sacrifice to God. Such sanctified food is known as *prashad*, "divine mercy,"[21] and can benefit both humans and nonhuman animals. The *Chaitanya Charitamrita* (Madhya 1.140) describes a dog who befriended the Vaishnava saint, Shivananda Sena. The dog ate *prashad* provided by the saint, and heard the chanting of the Hare

Krishna mantra, and as a result, the dog's soul attained the spiritual world after death.

Prabhupada believed that absolute nonviolence cannot be attained in this material world, making *bhakti* absolutely essential:

> When sweeping the floor or igniting a fire, we kill many germs. When we walk on the street we kill many ants and other insects. Consciously or unconsciously, in all our different activities, we are killing. (Prabhupada 1987, 882)

Similarly, in another source, Prabhupada states:

> On the basic principle, *ahimsa paramo dharma* ["nonviolence is the highest duty"], where is *ahimsa*? You have to kill [to eat]; either you kill [a] vegetable or [an] animal, you have to kill. Then, where is the standing of *ahimsa*? (Prabhupada 1990, 19:339–40; recorded conversation, Bombay, April 15, 1976)

The *Bhagavad-Gita* (8.15) characterizes this material world as a place of impermanence and suffering for humans and animals alike, because every creature on Earth has to undergo birth, old age, disease, and death. Kindhearted people may refrain from exploiting or killing other beings, or even go so far as to free animals from laboratories, but such "liberated" animals are only superficially free. Inevitably, living beings will be constrained and pummeled by hostile natural forces—disease, attacks from natural predators, aging, and death. Vegetarians and vegans cause less harm, but they still cause harm. As Prabhupada pointed out, anyone who walks outdoors or drives a car unintentionally kills insects; when we breathe, millions of microbes die. Prabhupada warned that simply committing to a vegetarian or vegan diet, trying to refrain from harming or exploiting animals is laudable, but insufficient, because the goal of a Vaishnava is to stop *all* suffering. This requires blessed release from the impermanent material world.

Lord Krishna glorified *ahimsa* at least three times in the *Bhaga-vad-Gita* (10.5, 13.8, and 16.2), but context should be kept in mind: Krishna was instructing a warrior on a battlefield, and his ultimate message was one of transcendental knowledge and divine love, which must be cultivated even in this violent material world. Because corpo-real existence inevitably entails suffering and death, Krishna taught his great devotee, Arjuna, that the ultimate solution is to escape the cycle of reincarnation and worldly suffering and death through *bhakti yoga.* Krishna's message is as true for animals as it is for people, and our chants can help other animals to reach this ultimate goal. The great sixteenth century Chaitanya Vaishnava, Vasudeva Datta, prayed that the karma of every living entity in the universe—human, animal, aquatic, and insect—would be transferred to him, so that all of these souls could attain the kingdom of God (Kaviraja, *Chaitanya Chari-tamrita*, trans. by Prabhupada, 1974, 15.169).

Prabhupada frequently quoted the sage Chanakya Pandita (c. 350–275 B.C.E.), who stated unequivocally: "Meat-eating is improper for everyone" (Subramanian 1990, 85). The *Bhagavad-Gita* teaches that good or pious actions are preferable to sinful ones, but even good karma is binding, leading to reincarnation (though in a relatively "good" birth, which still entails a certain amount of suffering and death). However, *yajna*—non-karma-producing sacrifice in the ser-vice of the divine, done without selfish attachment to personal fruits or rewards—frees a soul from bondage.[22] Although he considered eschewing meat to be extremely important, Prabhupada sometimes chided vegetarians who were arrogant, pointing out that monkeys and pigeons—who were all vegetarians or vegans—are not enlight-ened. Ignorant creatures, like ignorant humans, are vulnerable to the ongoing pain and suffering of material life. Prabhupada stressed that humans should not merely refrain from eating animals, but should help animals to attain spiritual liberation. In his view, anything short of such spiritual or transcendental compassion is inadequate, how-ever well-meaning. He repeatedly cited scriptural injunctions recommending that we chant God's holy names, especially the Hare Krishna *maha-mantra*, to elevate both human and animal souls to the kingdom of God, and to transcend the threefold miseries of material existence.[23]

As a seven year old boy in Southern California, I once spied a hawk swooping down, attacking a rat. I foolishly grabbed the rodent to protect him or her from the hawk, and the terrified rat bit my hand. Later, it dawned on me that even if I could save the rat from the hawk, I couldn't save my rodent friend from the cruel certainty of death any more than I could save myself from this same end. Much later, in Texas, after reading the *Bhagavata Purana*'s account of a Hindu king who rendered material care to a baby deer, but neglected his own spiritual practices, I encountered a small bird lying under a tree with a broken neck. Seeing anxiety and fear in his or her eyes, realizing that medical care couldn't save the little bird—and fearing that his or her death was fast approaching—I offered my feathered friend spiritual compassion and eternal benefit by chanting the Hare Krishna mantra with the understanding that the spiritual sound vibration would profoundly benefit the dying bird's soul in preparation for the afterlife.

Prabhupada's teachings reflect the Indian culture's intimate intertwining of nonhumans and humans, and the importance of *ahimsa* rooted in *bhakti*. King Yudhisthira's desire to help the dog escape from worldly suffering, and Chaitanya Mahaprabhu's compassionate deliverance of Shivananda Sena's dog to *Vaikuntha* (the spiritual world), both exemplify the Hare Krishna understanding of the highest compassion for animals, as taught by the movement's founder (*acharya*), A. C. Bhaktivedanta Swami Prabhupada.

4

The Jain Center
of Southern California

Theory and Practice across Continents

CHARLOTTE LAWS

An ornate, tangerine colored building nudges the sidewalk; it appears to have been chiseled by a thousand patient hands. The carved superstructure towers over unassuming eateries, gas stations, banks, pocket parks, and simple churches in Buena Park, California.

This queen-like edifice is officially called the Jain Center of Southern California, housing a temple, classrooms, a library, a cafeteria, a marble atrium, and a resplendent staircase. Once every few weeks, about a thousand Jains socialize and practice the Jain tradition here; there are over fifty such centers around the United States, and hundreds throughout the world. I was visiting merely to question adherents as to how they reconcile Jainism's demanding, ascetic principles with their personal belief and practice, as well as with the temptations of modern society. As I stepped inside the complex, I sensed that the huge, circular window above me was eyeing my every move, like a guardian commissioned to preserve both this sacred space and the unity of all things.

At its core, the Jain tradition is an ideological ally of animal rights/ liberation philosophy, advancing the view that nonhumans are of equal value to humans, and are worthy of equal consideration. Jain religious texts estimate that there are 8.4 million different species (Tatia 1994, 53), each one deserving of love and respect. Jainism, which originated in India, is arguably the most demanding religion in the world. *Ahimsa*, defined as nonviolence toward all living beings, is the dominant tenet of the Jain faith. Adherents are expected to be vegetarian, and to refrain from violence in word, thought, and deed.

Jain monks and ascetics, who lead a markedly more austere and arduous life than the laity, are prohibited from eating animal products and root vegetables. They cannot even pull fruit from a tree because this is deemed an act of violence. Eating is always a risky undertaking for a Jain ascetic, and "producing and preparing food inevitably results in the sin of violence" (Babb 1996, 58). (Jain laity are permitted to pluck fruit, and they feed Jain ascetics so that these rigorous ascetics will have something to eat.) Jain ascetics often wear mouth shields in order to protect minute organisms in the air, gently sweep the ground as they walk so as to avoid inadvertently crushing insects, avoid sex (in part, because it kills sperm), and may eventually choose to starve themselves to death in a journey toward spiritual perfection. Ascetics fast, meditate, and wear white robes (Shvetambara sect) or nothing at all (Digambara sect)—often enduring frigid temperatures. They own virtually nothing, do not point (because pointing could frighten animals) (Jacobi 1884, 145), refrain from touching leaves, and tend to stay in the desert to avoid disturbing "natural life forms" (Chapple 1993, 63).

Lord Mahavira, the founder of modern Jainism, lived from 599 to 529 B.C.E., and was a wandering ascetic for most of his life. He is the subject of Jain books, classes, and discussions, and his image can be found in Jain temples, including the one I visited in California.

Because Mahavira did not wish to injure or step on any living thing, legend has it that "many sorts of living beings gathered on his body, crawled about it and caused pain there. (He did not scratch himself.) Without ceasing in his reflections, . . . [he] slowly wandered about, and, killing no creatures, he begged for his food" (Jacobi 1884a, 79–90, 82).

Ascetics such as Lord Mahavira have been the focus of scholarly study for centuries, in part because their lives of assiduous self-restraint are so incredible. But how do ascetic teachings affect the ideals and practices of the hundreds of ordinary Jains who brushed past me at the Jain Center, as well as the estimated ten million who live elsewhere in the world (Shah 2001, 7)? Do they strive to emulate ascetics, Do they routinely compromise Jain ideals—are they trapped in a spiritual quagmire? How do they safeguard—or actively fight for—nonhuman beings in contemporary society, where animals are viewed as expendable, as mere means to human ends?

I shoved my sneakers into storage bin 143 in the Jain Center's shoe room (footwear is prohibited beyond the lobby). The wooden cubbyholes, which spanned from corner to corner and ceiling to the floor, contained flip-flops, plastic sandals, and other nonleather footwear. Inside, a cabinet housed purses and bags and a table displayed a Jain newsletter, which contained sixteen articles, all spotlighting the importance of vegetarianism and compassion toward animals.

After ascending the slippery marble staircase, I came upon Yogesh, my first interviewee. He wore trousers and a button-down shirt, as did a majority of males in the facility; other men were wrapped in sheet-like garments. Females were largely draped in saris. Everyone appeared to be Indian.

Like most ordinary Jains, Yogesh is a vegetarian and regularly assists animal organizations, such as People for the Ethical Treatment of Animals (PETA) and Purple Cow, a facility that rescues aged farm animals. He heats water prior to drinking so as to kill as few germs as possible (which I would have expected only from an ascetic). He explained: Boiling water kills germs immediately, thus ultimately resulting in fewer germ deaths. Without heating, bacteria multiply in the stomach and later perish in greater numbers.

Yogesh told me about Jain retreats, which last forty-five days, during which time people sleep on the ground, fast, or eat only for survival, and generally give up every luxury. He added: "I am from Gujarat, where the age-old ritual of goat sacrifice is common. So Jains buy goats from the killers and take them to animal shelters so they do not die." It is also common for Jains to rescue animals by purchasing them from butchers. Yogesh pointed out a temple donation box, noting that all funds are used to promote *ahimsa* in India, usually in the form of aid to facilities that rescue dogs, cats, sheep, camels, water buffalo, goats, oxen, cows, rats, mice, rabbits, and birds, among other species.

In 1955, there were three thousand Jain animal shelters and hospitals in India (Lodrick 1981, 13); and there are no doubt more today, especially since Jains often convert sections of their homes into sanctuaries, hospitals, or refuges for sick and deformed animals. I learned that the Jain Charity Hospital for Birds, founded in 1956 near India's capital (Delhi), takes in over fifteen thousand feathered friends per year, mostly pigeons, who are treated for cancer and other ailments, then released. The facility does not take in predatory birds because these animals violate the principle of nonviolence (Lodrick 1981, 17). Some Jains provide rooms where insects dwell, especially in Yogesh's home state of Gujarat (Chapple 2006, 246). Some Jains "carefully remove bugs from the streets and feed them gently" (Nevaskar 1971, 186).

Unlike American factory farms and vivisection labs, which hide atrocities and therefore prohibit public inspection, the largest Jain animal hospital in Bombay is always open to visitors. Veterinarians and their assistants "heal the sick and lame, and bring the blind and paralyzed their food" (Lodrick 1981, 69). One visitor observed "rescued cows with gauze pads affixed to injuries . . . a hobbling camel with a splint on one leg . . . a little girl kissing a bull . . . [and] an old woman with a bucket of grain for stray egrets" (Tobias 1991, 34). Another visitor remembered a heron who was "proud of his wooden leg" and added that the facility is "an example of the kindness and humanity of [the Jains], whose charity would not allow any being . . . to suffer" (Rousselet and Buckle 1876, 12).

When I asked if the Jain Center sold books on Jain animal hospitals, Yogesh directed me to a humble room, where I found a twiggy grasshopper of a man, wrapped in a light-green cotton sheet. He explained in rudimentary English that there were no items for sale; books were only available for checkout. He pointed to ten books on a shelf.

"Only ten books?" I asked. He nodded. "Could I check out . . . eight?" (I didn't think it was right to walk off with the entire library. After all, what if someone else needed a reference?) I offered him my driver's license in exchange, but he refused, instructing me to "just write name and phone number on paper." I thought about the honesty, and consequent trusting nature, of these Jains. Purses and valuables were housed in an unlocked cabinet, mountains of unattended plastic shoes were piled nearby, and this man was willing to give a complete stranger eighty percent of the Center's library without even asking for my ID!

Being less trustful than a Jain, I safeguarded the eight books in my car before returning to find Gom, a spindly Indian man with glasses and a ritual smudge on his forehead. He was a vegetarian, a warm-water germ protectionist, and an opponent of pets, vivisection, and zoos, although he said some Jains, out of politeness, might visit a zoo when entertaining out-of-town guests. He explained: "A zoo is a commercial enterprise that causes animal suffering." He continued: "Zoos do not value animals' lives. And Jains are against vivisection. We might find ourselves in an animal body in the next life."

I asked him why Jains would oppose keeping companion animals when five million homeless dogs and cats are killed in U.S. shelters, and millions more throughout the world each year. Without adoptions, the number of deaths would climb. Again Gom patiently explained: "Keeping pets deprives them of the right to be free. The solution is to outlaw pet shops and breeders. We don't have many homeless dogs and cats in India because most people don't believe in keeping pets in the first place." I asked whether he and other Jains were politically active, working to outlaw breeding facilities and pet shops, but he said, "No, we Jains simply set an example for others." I nodded; setting an example is important.

I did not meet a single Jain who expressed willingness to advocate for nonhumans actively, beyond setting an example in their daily life, tending needy animals themselves, and buying animals from researchers, butchers, and others who might kill or harm these creatures. Withdrawal from the world, and the non-confrontational Jain philosophy and practice, crept into conversations again and again in my visit to the Jain Center of Southern California. From the perspective of a goal-oriented American, and a passionate animal rights advocate, Jains seemed like a work of art. They were beautiful, inspiring, and carefree, but mere decorations, dancing on the sidelines—focusing on their own salvation and enlightenment, while leaving others to fight for social and political change. One might imagine a glass cover insulating a piece of art from the cruelty and suffering of the world, its frame outlining traditional ascetic parameters. Perhaps these self-imposed parameters decrease overall violence, since every human movement necessarily means death for smaller beings. I probed further.

"What do Jains do if a goat killer or butcher refuses to sell an animal?" I asked a Jain.

"We must watch the animal die," Gom replied.

In general, Jain laity—as opposed to more disciplined ascetics— seem to have four aims: set a good example, lead the most ascetic lifestyle that's pragmatically possible, maintain a nonviolent mindset, and refrain from personally causing harm to living beings whenever you can. These practices, when maintained, assure a positive rebirth, which brings the individual closer to salvation: "The ultimate goal of Jainism is for the soul to achieve liberation" (Shah 2001, 10), and liberation only becomes possible when one sheds karma, which requires that we refrain from harming other beings, and resist negative thoughts. Anger, or even the unintentional killing of a sentient creature, large or small, will result in negative karma (Shah 1994, 5). Some Jain sources indicate that intention is everything. If a Jain crushes a small being by mistake, he or she "will not attract even the slightest karmic bondage" (Narvi 1993, 147).

In addition to practical difficulties, karma helps explain why Jains don't feel compelled to desperately strive to rescue every living being who is in need. In their view, those who suffer have brought misfortune upon themselves, in previous lives. Beings have lived innumerable former lives as an insect, dog, human, tree, microbe, and so on. These lives may have been far from perfect—they may have been a carnivore or harbored hatred, for example, which later resulted in an unfavorable rebirth. Karma must play out. The Jain goal is to escape reincarnation and attain enlightenment, following in the footsteps of enlightened beings, such as Mahavira, a man who overcame attachments and escaped the cycle of birth, death, and rebirth (Babb 1996, 5).

Gom threw open a door to reveal statues of Mahavira (and two other gurus) in the meditation area. The images wore gold and red headdresses, held orange flowers, and were positioned under a full-size, white gazebo. Entering visitors smudged a gray concoction on their foreheads and rang a golden bell on leaving. Incense filled the air, a lone candle burned on an oblong, silver table, and solemn Jains meditated cross-legged on floor mats.

Gom complained about how challenging it is to live as a Jain in America, and how today's youth too often embrace only the outward rituals rather than Jain principles, a comment that surprised me, since there were no youngsters in the temple meditation room. Gom felt that teenage Jains succumb to Western peer pressure more than their adult counterparts. He continued: "Concessions are made for those who live in this country, where it is more difficult to resist consumerism, and to maintain a vegetarian lifestyle. It is even harder to be vegan."

When Gom settled in to meditate, I went in search of a few Jain tempted teen consumers. I found four seventeen year olds snacking on tortilla chips outside the facility, and joined them.

"It's hard being observant in America," a brunette named Trish told me. "But I think we follow the principles as much as our parents. It's not just about ritual. We come here every two weeks, partly to please our parents and to see our friends, but also because we like the religion."

Like Gom and Yogesh, Trish and her friends were vegetarian, warm-water germ protectionists, who also tried not to eat turnips, onions, potatoes, and other tubers. Jains believe that root vegetables are "teeming with life-forms" (Babb 1996, 23) and contain many souls (Babb 1996, 138). Numerous Jains told me that they refrain from root vegetables because eating roots is "killing many souls." Trish explained further: "If you place a tomato in water, nothing happens, but if you put a piece of potato in water, it grows [and produces many potato plants]. This means it has lots of souls. Plus we don't want to kill insects that live inside."

"Do humans have one soul?" I asked. She and her friends nodded in the affirmative.

"Does this mean it is better to kill a human with one soul than a root vegetable with many souls?"

The teenagers giggled. Trish explained that even though all beings suffer equally and should be treated with respect, the Jain tradition is hierarchical. It is especially important to preserve living beings with five senses, such as humans, rabbits, pigs, mice, and other sentient creatures (Von Glasenapp 1942, 55). One-sensed beings, such as microorganisms, are on the "lowest" level of the Jain hierarchy. They have only the sense of touch, and are so small and "undifferentiated that they lack even individual bodies" (Jaini 1979, 109). (Of course, they will have lived previously as five-sensed beings at some point in their many-bodied existence.) The next highest level holds those with a sense of taste and touch, such as worms, snails, leeches, and oysters. The third level adds smell, and includes ants and spiders; the fourth adds sight, and includes bees, flies, mosquitoes, and butterflies (Von Glasenapp 1942, 52–55).

These young Jains seemed to know quite a bit about their religion, so I asked another question: "Why are Jains vegetarian rather than vegan?"

"Because where I come from in India—a small town—getting milk and eggs doesn't harm animals," Trish replied. "Cows and chickens are treated like family members and die natural deaths. But with modern factory farms, it's different, and Jains need to be vegan." There are Jains in India—mostly the younger generation—who have adopted a vegan lifestyle as their ethical obligation (Chapple 2006, 205).

Trish told me that she and her friends transport bugs outside of buildings rather than kill them; they refuse to build fires when on camping trips (in order to protect flying insects), don't wear leather or animal products, and (like ascetics) don't eat after sunset (to avoid accidentally harming small beings) (Navaskar 1971, 158). Additionally, Trish volunteers for animal organizations as well as human organizations, specifically the Midnight Mission and a local hospital.

Trish suggested that I attend one of the many temple classes that were about to begin, so I headed back inside the temple. The gathering that I joined resembled a middle-school classroom, and I was an unexpected visitor who seemed to startle the regular students; I triggered a lively debate with my inquiries: "Stealing and violence against living beings are both sinful deeds. What happens when these principles conflict with each other? Should a Jain, for example, steal to rescue an animal from a factory farm or vivisection lab in order to protect that animal from torture and certain premature death? What do you think of underground activists, such as the Animal Liberation Front?"

Prior to my question, nineteen students sat obediently on the floor with books on laps, spellbound by three, sedate instructors. After my question, the room seemed more like a lively school cafeteria—but the teachers did not seem to notice. "There are many gray areas," one of the teachers quietly explained. "Rescuing an animal has consequences if the animal is someone's property. There is no practical way to save all animals. Plus, no one can really change anyone else's mind." I asked what Jains would do if they stood face-to-face with human slavery or the extermination of Jews in Nazi Germany, but the more I tried to dig Jains out of their ascetic caves, the more my shovel crashed into impenetrable rock. No Jain that I met was willing to abandon their composed inner world for direct action. No one suggested that certain laws be ignored, or that revolutionary action must sometimes be taken. One of the teachers even noted that a Jain activist, fighting for a cause, is relegated to the bottom rung of the enlightenment ladder. A more advanced Jain is devoid of emotion, withdraws from the world, and focuses on an inward life. A second instructor added: "It is best to buy an animal from a research lab. We are not in favor of illegal acts, but we would not criticize animal activists either." Although these teachers expressed pessimism with regard to changing humanity, there was a distinct optimism in the way they refrained from judging and hating others.

Still, they were willing to take a stand against contributing to suffering and premature death: "Although a Jain would not rescue cows from slaughter," a Jain teacher concluded, "a Jain must never work as a slaughterhouse operator." This made me wonder whether there's a difference between killing and letting an individual die. The oldest extant Jain canonical work, the *Acaranga Sutra*, says: "A wise man should not act sinfully towards animals, nor cause others to act so, nor *allow* others to act so" (emphasis added; Chatterjee 1978, 229). The word *allow* seemed to suggest that Jains should be active in the same way as the Animal Liberation Front, but those I met at the center interpreted *allow* only to include legal acts.

"Besides working in a slaughterhouse, what professions are unacceptable for Jains?" I asked one of the teachers.

"India is largely agricultural," one of the teachers noted, "but working in this capacity is forbidden because moving soil injures insects and worms. Also, a Jain should not work as a fisherman, soldier, logger, butcher, brewer, or making ammunitions." It turns out that there are fifteen jobs deemed cruel and unacceptable, including handling animal byproducts, charcoal, wood, or insect secretions, and trading in animals or humans (Mehta 1969, 113–14). Jain texts discourage people from taking jobs that require castrating animals, clearing trees, drying up lakes or rivers, or using fire in an extensive way (Rampuria 1947, 22). Some lay Jains engage in these professions out of necessity, and they know that they will suffer karmic repercussions.

By avoiding objectionable professions, as chance would have it, Jains have become a wealthy and influential minority. They tend to enter well-paying, white-collar professions, for example as bankers, jewelers, lawyers, computer technicians, physicists, property owners, and merchants (Navaskar 1971, 158). Jain affluence may have something to do with their preference for buying animals from killers rather than taking on the tactics of the Animal Liberation Front. On special religious days they are sometimes so "zealous in preventing anyone from taking the life of an animal that they request the authorities to prohibit the slaughter of animals, and offer to repay the loss incurred with large sums of money" (Navaskar 1971, 172). In contrast, animal activists often lack the ability to rescue animals with their wallets, and may see civil disobedience (and other less sanctioned tactics) as their only means of bringing much needed change. It is paradoxical that the Jain renunciation of the world has "secured their economic advantage among the struggling masses of India" (Noss 1956, 1954). Furthermore, their devotion to nonviolence—as well as their abstinence from gambling and drinking—has earned them respect around the world (Noss 1956, 152).

Even though they tend to have well-paying jobs, Jains are not greedy consumers. They limit their possessions to what is necessary for survival, and aspire to transcend worldly entanglements altogether. The Jain religion "has advanced systematic and integral thought regarding the preservation and protection of the [natural sur-roundings]" (Glera 2002, 6); more specifically, Jains have "achieved what is normally called progress without making a mess of [the] envi-ronment" (Tobias 1991, 59). Surplus income is often given to the temple or used to help finance animal protection. A mere 970 families funded the multi-million dollar Jain Center (which was still under construction during my visit), indicating that American Jains, like their Indian counterparts, are prosperous and generous.

Outside, on the temple lawn (after feeding my granola bar crumbs to whatever insects might live nearby), I reflected on my visit. There are distinct differences between Jain practice and the animal rights/ liberation movement. It seemed ironic that "higher" Jains are less likely to work for change in this world—to impart wisdom, or make a positive impact on others—except by setting an example with their own lives. In contrast, a more "advanced" animal activist is likely to purposefully work for change. He or she tends to make a meaningful contribution to the cause, changing minds, hearts, and habits, and ultimately saving untold animals from misery and premature death.

Jains and animal liberationists share the same goal: both hope for a nonviolent world where the interests of nonhuman animals matter; both hope to trigger change, whether by example or action; and both have immeasurable empathy for the truly powerless, abused, and for-gotten of this world—nonhuman animals. A sixteenth century Jain text (*Uttaradhyayana Sutra*) expresses deep commonality between Jains and animal advocates. The author, a young prince named Mrga-putra, expresses his understanding of the sufferings of nonhuman animals at the hands of exploitative humans: "By sharpened razors and knives and spears have I these many times been drawn and quar-tered, torn apart and skinned. As a deer held in helpless snares and traps, I have been bound and fastened, even killed. As a helpless fish, I have been caught with hooks and nets, scaled and scraped, split and gutted, and killed a million times" (Koller 2006, 32).

5

Buddhism and Animal Liberation

The Family of Sentient Beings

NORM PHELPS

When I first attended Buddhist teachings—nearly twenty-five years ago—something struck me as peculiar. Whenever our teacher was speaking about the beings to whom we ought to show kindness, compassion, and respect, he never said "people" or "human beings." He always said "living beings" or "sentient beings" (which he used interchangeably). Since I was just becoming active in the animal rights movement, this raised hopes in me that I hardly dared entertain, for fear of disappointment. But finally, my urge to understand more fully triumphed over fear, and during the question and answer period at the end of a Sunday morning teaching, I raised my hand: "When you say 'living beings,'" I asked, "does that mean just human beings or does it include animals as well?"

Since Lama Kalsang had taught for a number of years in the United States, he was past being surprised at such ignorance from North American Buddhist students. "It means all sentient beings," he explained, "all beings who are able to experience suffering—of course it includes animals."

"Does it include plants, like flowers and trees?"

Lama was very patient. "No," he said, "because they aren't sentient; they cannot suffer. Still, we must protect our environment for the sake of all sentient beings, including ourselves."

That sounded good, but I was still uncertain, and so I took the final step: "The first precept, 'Do not kill': does that apply to animals or only to human beings?"

"It applies to both animals and human beings," he assured me. "We should not kill, or cause to be killed, any sentient being."

I felt a surge of joy go through me like I have experienced only a few times in my life. If there was a moment when I was "converted" to Buddhism, that was it. My search was over. I had found my religious tradition.

THE MEANING OF GOOD AND EVIL

Buddhist morality, I would soon learn, is based on sentience. In Buddhism, joy and suffering are the definition of good and evil. We know directly, immediately, and to the depth of our being that our own joy is good, and our own suffering is evil. We know this even as infants, before we have acquired language. We need no rational arguments or empirical studies to explain our pain or joy; and no rational arguments or empirical studies can falsify this knowledge, or call our feelings into question. Knowing pain as evil and joy as good is a fundamental category of awareness, prior to rationality and structured empiricism alike. It is the primary axiom from which our moral geometry proceeds.

The Buddha taught that if this sense experience is true for us— as it unquestionably is—then it must be true for all other sentient beings; the Buddha's intuition is confirmed by animal behavior. From the smallest and simplest to the largest and most complex organisms, all beings seek pleasure and shun pain, just as we do. In this way, the most profoundly, intimately subjective experience possible—our experience of pleasure and pain—forms the basis for an interpersonal ethic that can guide our treatment of all sentient beings. It is good to ease the suffering of others, and promote their joy, and it is evil to inflict suffering on others, or deprive them of joy.

In a similar way, most of us are born with a profound love of life and dread of death. Again, this is a fundamental quality of our consciousness that does not depend on rational argument—this understanding exists at the core of our awareness, at the heart of our subjectivity. This understanding is prior to reason, and "objective" systems of evaluation are meaningless in the face of such core knowledge. In fact, attempts to apply an "objective" standard to this fundamental fact of subjective consciousness never fail to lead us dreadfully astray. For example, Western philosophers (such as Jeremy Bentham) sometimes indicate that killing an animal instantly and painlessly is ethical because animals have no sense of the future, and therefore lose nothing through death. This is a prime example of the trouble that abstract thought can lead us to when disengaged from our most urgent subjective experiences. So far as I know, no one ever asked Bentham whether he would prefer to continue living or to die instantly, painlessly, and without foreknowledge. Most of us know what our response would be, how urgently we wish to remain alive. Generally, only those who suffer unbearable pain or severe depression might choose death over life.

Philosophical claims that animals don't share this most powerful of urges, the urge to live, are sophistry in the service of human convenience, appetite, and arrogance. We enjoy the taste of animal's flesh, we like the look and feel of their skin on our feet, and so we salve our consciences by telling ourselves that they have no sense of the future and no concept of death, and that we can therefore kill them with impunity—we take nothing of value from them by taking their lives.

The Buddha engaged in no such self-serving rationalizations. The *Dhammapada* (*Dharma Path*), the most beloved scripture in the Buddhist canon, says:

All beings tremble before danger; all fear death. When a man considers this, he does not kill or cause to kill. All beings fear before danger; life is dear to all. When a man considers this, he does not kill or cause to kill. (*Dhammapada* 1973, 129–30)

Just as it is evil to deprive others of joy or cause them to suffer, it is evil to take life, which is the most precious possession of every living being, and to which every living being clings desperately when threatened.

THEY ARE US

Western philosophy typically divides the world into human and nonhuman. Westerners envision a great divide that separates humans from other animals. Darwin's theory of evolution by natural selection offered a scientific basis for breaking down this dualistic notion—showing continuous, unbroken lines of gradual step-by-step development from the simplest organisms to the most complex beings, including human beings. But the residue of our earlier convictions is still with us, especially in the ethical sphere. Many people still believe that it is appropriate to have one ethical code for dealing with fellow human beings, and another ethical code for dealing with nonhuman animals. For most people, including most philosophers, it's perfectly acceptable to treat other animals in ways that we would find horrifying for human beings—enslaving them for entertainment and imprisoning and killing them for food, for instance. Buddhism considers such separate ethical codes both unnecessary and inappropriate, because there is no morally significant difference between human beings and nonhuman animals. All are sentient, and sentience is all that matters.

For ontological reasons that need not concern us here, Buddhist texts do not discuss "souls." Some Buddhist schools decline to name the functional equivalent of the Western "soul," while others make reference to "Buddha nature," "the true nature of mind," "the clear light of awareness," or other terms that point toward the ineffable, without concrete definition. But whatever Buddhists call "soul"—or decline to call it—all schools agree that "it"—"Buddha nature"—is identical in all sentient beings. As my spiritual teacher told me: "There is no difference between the Buddha nature of the most unfortunate homeless dog on the street, and the Buddha nature of the Dalai Lama." Geshe Rabten (1920–1986), a highly respected Tibetan lama who taught widely in the West, expressed this same idea differently: "We may think that animals are a separate category of beings from us. . . . This is a mistake" (1984, 103).

Thus, while Western thought often stresses differences between human beings and other animals, Buddhism stresses not merely the similarities, but the *shared identity* of human and nonhuman animals. To paraphrase a wise old nonhuman, Pogo Possum: "We have met the animals, and they are us." And we are them. This creates an imperative to treat other animals just as we would want them to treat us, if circumstances were reversed—which someday, given Buddhist teachings on reincarnation, they will be.

This identity extends to all sentient beings, not merely to the cuddly, charismatic, or more complex beings, with whom we more readily form relationships. One day, when my teacher and I were leaving the meditation center after a thunderstorm, we came upon a dozen or more earthworms who had come up out of the ground to avoid drowning in water-filled tunnels, and were marooned on a concrete driveway, thrashing about blindly, with no hope of survival. Lama Kalsang began picking them up one at a time, carrying them to the safety of the lawn. I, of course, followed suit. All he said was: "They want to live as much as we do." No further explanation was necessary. No ant, no spider, no living being whatsoever is purposefully harmed or killed in any Buddhist center with which I am familiar.

Buddhist morality firmly grasps this crucial point: Purely subjective experiences cannot be measured on any objective scale. Consequently, there is no question of ranking sentient beings according to some supposedly "objective" scale of consciousness, or thereby deciding that some beings have moral priority over others because they are puta-tively "more aware," or have a richer interior life. Joy and suffering are entirely subjective—they are individual experiences. The chicken's pain is as agonizing to the chicken as my pain is to me. Her extreme pain fills her consciousness, hijacks her life, and destroys her peace in the same way, and to the same degree, that my extreme pain fills my consciousness, hijacks my life, and destroys my peace. For this reason, avian pain must be accorded the same level of moral concern as human pain. Similarly, the life of the lobster is the only life he or she has—and so that life is everything to him or her. That life is as precious to him or her as my life is to me. And for that reason, crustacean lives must be accorded the same level of moral concern as human lives.

Buddhist morality is absolutely egalitarian. The object of Buddhist ethics is to ease the suffering and extend the lives of others, with-out regard for race, nationality, gender, wealth, social standing, spe-cies, ability to use language, ability to make tools, or possession of an endo- or exoskeleton, development of a centralized or decentral-ized nervous system, or any other characteristic apart from their sen-tience. In the Buddhist tradition no sentient being is more important than any other sentient being.

COMPASSION IN THE WORLD

As a sentient being, I know directly and urgently the agony of suf-fering and the dread of death. I can safely conclude that all sentient beings share this agony and dread. Just as I am determined to ease my own suffering and extend my own life, empathy compels me to an equally strong determination to ease the suffering and extend the lives of others. This determination stems from and is an expression of compassion, on which all Buddhist morality is based.

It is one thing to generate compassion for all living beings while sit-ting comfortably at home on a meditation cushion. It is quite another to put that compassion to work in the world, helping living beings, perhaps at considerable inconvenience to ourselves. But that's what Buddhists must do—that's what Buddhism calls us to do. If our compassion does not benefit others, it is a delusion. The Buddha tells us:

> He who for the sake of happiness hurts others who also want happiness shall not hereafter find happiness [because of karma]. He who for the sake of happiness does not hurt others who also want happiness shall hereafter find happiness. (*Dhammapada* 1973, 130)

Similarly, Sri Lankan Buddhist teacher Mahathera Narada tells us that compassion:

> has the characteristic of a loving mother whose thoughts, words, and deeds always tend to relieve the distress of her sick child. It has the quality of not being able to tolerate the sufferings of others. Its manifestation is perfect nonviolence and harmlessness—that is, a compassionate person always appears to be perfectly nonviolent and harmless. (Narada 1988, 182–83)

DO NOT KILL *ANY* LIVING BEING

As Lama Kalsang told me that Sunday morning many years ago, at the beginning of my Buddhist education, Buddhism's first—and most important—precept, "Do not kill," applies to all sentient beings. This is not, and has never been, a matter of dispute within Buddhism. All schools agree on this point. As Buddhist scholar and author Peter Harvey explains: "The first precept, regarded as the most important, is the resolution not to kill or injure any human, animal, bird, fish, or insect" (Harvey 1990, 202). Thich Nhat Hanh, the Vietnamese Zen monk who is among the most revered Buddhist teachers in the West, tells us: "In every country in the world, killing humans is condemned. The Buddhist precept of non-killing extends even further, to include all living beings" (Hanh 1997, 42).

In applying this first Buddhist precept to nonhuman animals, the Buddha forbade all forms of animal agriculture—all buying and selling of living animals—and all forms of hunting, trapping, and fishing, as well as snake charming—a prohibition that today should be understood to condemn all use of animals for entertainment (including rodeos, circuses, zoos, and theme parks). All of these activities are absolutely forbidden to Buddhists. So far as we know, the Buddha did not object to the use of animals for labor and transportation, but this is probably because he believed that animals undertaking these tasks could be happy so long as they were not overworked, were well fed and watered, and were able to live out their later years in peaceful retirement. The Buddha's ethics, we must remember, are based on the real suffering of living beings, not on abstract principles. Therefore, theoretical consistency is not important. What matters is the actual reduction of suffering, and the preservation of life.

The Buddha repeatedly and unequivocally instructed his followers to adhere to a lacto-vegetarian diet. (He allowed the consumption of dairy products because cows, being objects of veneration, were rarely mistreated or slaughtered in ancient India.) When a disciple named Mahamati asked if it was permissible to eat meat, the Buddha answered:

> How can I permit my disciples, Mahamati, to eat food consisting of flesh and blood, which is gratifying to the unwise but abhorred by the wise, which brings many evils and keeps away many merits, and which was not offered to the *rishis* [ancient sages] and is altogether unsuitable. (*Lankavatara Sutra* 1999, 212)

He goes on:

> Thus, Mahamati, wherever there is the evolution of living beings, let people cherish the thought of kinship with them and thinking that

all beings are [to be loved as if each animal were their] only child, let them refrain from eating meat. (212)

The Buddha becomes even more emphatic in his conclusion: "Thus, Mahamati, meat eating I have not permitted to anyone, I do not permit [it], I will not permit [it]" (219).

The reason for this absolute prohibition is simple. Eating meat violates the first precept: "If, Mahamati, meat is not eaten by anybody for any reason, there will be no destroyer of life" (217). If no one ate meat, no one would kill animals for human consumption. When we eat meat, we kill the animal whose flesh we consume just as surely as if we wield the knife. Likewise, when we in the modern world eat eggs, drink milk, or eat cheese and ice cream, we are responsible for the unspeakable suffering of the chickens and cows on factory farms, and we are equally responsible for their early death. Animals in contemporary animal industries are killed as soon as they are too old, tired, or sick to bring profit. Eggs and dairy—even so-called free-range eggs and dairy—are as much the product of slaughter as is meat. If the Buddha were alive today and could see the practices of modern factory farming—including the dairy and egg industries—he would call for a vegan diet to reduce suffering and loss of life. As it is, his teachings on compassion and *ahimsa* mandate a vegan diet because we live in a world where laying hens spend their lives imprisoned in battery cages so small they cannot spread their wings or turn around, and male calves born of "dairy" cows are locked into crates so tiny they cannot move, until they are sent to slaughter while still calves, for the sake of veal.

A LITTLE LOOPHOLE, MAYBE?

Human nature is human nature; it's the same in all of us, whether we are Buddhists, Hindus, Christians, Jews, Muslims, Wiccans, shamanists, agnostics, or atheists. The temptation to eat meat is strong, and over the centuries all too many Buddhists have gone looking for loopholes in the Buddha's instructions to justify their habit of eating meat. By far the most popular justification is the claim that the Buddha allowed his monks, when they were begging for their daily meal, to accept and eat meat offered by householders, provided they had no reason to suspect that the animal might have been slaughtered specifically to provide them with food.

Whether the Buddha actually gave this instruction and, if he did, whether he later rescinded these words, are matters of considerable controversy within the Buddhist community.[1] Space does not permit me to delve into this controversy, but even if the Buddha did offer this teaching, it cannot be used to justify eating meat that we buy from restaurants and supermarkets. The reason it cannot be used for this purpose is simple. When we buy meat at a supermarket or restaurant we place an order for an animal to be killed. Someone must slaughter an animal if we are to eat meat. Therefore, if we purchase meat we create the need for an animal to be killed. The fact that the animal was slaughtered "on spec," so to speak, and the order was placed long after the animal was killed, is merely a quirk of modern marketing. Morally, this delay changes nothing. "Food" animals are killed specifically for those who buy meat; if no one buys meat, no one will kill animals for consumption.

Whatever the Buddha may or may not have said to begging monks about eating meat offered to them when they were begging, so long as it was not killed specifically for them, Buddhist ethics are fundamentally about compassion. Buddhist ethics are not about personal purity or adhering to the letter of a legalistic set of regulations. It is not compassionate to eat the flesh of slaughtered animals, thereby creating an economic demand that will result in yet more slaughter.

CONCLUSION

There's a popular Buddhist teaching that each of us has been traveling through the cycle of birth, death, and rebirth for so many endless eons that every living being, human and nonhuman alike, has at some time been our mother at least once, and has therefore given us life, cared for our needs, and likely extended great love and kindness. Alluding to this teaching, Buddhist teachers often refer to all living beings as "mother beings." The Buddha's voluminous teachings on morality can all be summed up in one sentence: Love your mothers—every single one.

6

Buddhist Reflections on Animal Advocacy

Intention and Liberation

MATTHEW J. WALTON

The street that encircles Sule Pagoda in downtown Rangoon (Yangon), Burma (Myanmar), is crowded with merchants selling goods that assist pious Buddhists in their religious duties: garlands, incense, baskets of fruit for offerings, and gold leaf to rub on Buddha statues while saying prayers. However, one of the offerings is decidedly different: live birds kept in cages, sold to people for release, thus bringing the liberator karmic benefits in the future, and good luck in general.

This practice (including the liberation of other nonhuman animals such as fish, pigs, and cows) has been common in Asia for centuries, but to an outsider it can appear confusing, even contradictory. Good karma may follow from the act of liberation, but aren't Buddhists also encouraging people to catch, cage, and sell birds? Can the people who buy and liberate these animals be held responsible (from a karmic perspective, at least) for complicity in this practice? What about motivation? Are those who release birds concerned only with personal benefit? Or do they care about the well-being of the birds, who are caged for long periods of time, waiting for a potential savior? For that matter, do they consider the consequences for merchants, who are performing a delicate karmic dance: collecting demerits for catching and caging birds, but also rewards for providing opportunities that will benefit others?

The liberation of animals in Asia has a long, many-layered history, and my purpose here is not to deconstruct or critique this practice.[1] Rather, I begin with this example to introduce the Buddhist notion of the importance of *intention* with regard to action. I will use this framework of intentionality to evaluate the practices of the animal liberation movement in the West, hopefully drawing insights from Buddhist teachings that can inform advocacy and action on behalf of animals. The purpose of this chapter is to see what a Buddhist interpretation of intentionality offers people in the West who support the practice of animal liberation.[2]

I begin with an explanation of a variety of Buddhist views on non-human animals. I also review some basic points of Buddhist doctrine, to provide a framework for understanding these views. I then move to a brief explanation of the doctrine of karma, contrasting the Buddhist emphasis on intention with other understandings of karma. Finally, I analyze animal liberation in the West in terms of a Buddhist doctrine of intention, offering a reflective model for activists to evaluate their own motivations. In the process, multiple interconnected meanings of the term *liberation* emerge for consideration.

BUDDHISM AND ANIMALS

First, as with any religious tradition, it's important to note the wide gap that often exists between religious doctrine and religious practice.[3] In the case of Buddhism, this difference is particularly pronounced in the ritual-based practice of laity versus the scriptural knowledge of monks. To complicate matters further, Western Buddhists tend toward Buddhist practice that is less ritualistic, and which is based more on textual study, thus further distinguishing their experience and understanding of Buddhism from that of other Buddhist laity. Nonetheless, it is valuable to look at some basic Buddhist ideas about animals in order to inform our understanding of how the practice of animal liberation fits into a Buddhist worldview.

The Buddhist system of ethics is founded on five basic principles, by which monks must always abide, and which laity often undertake both on special days and before a period of meditation. These five precepts include vows to abstain from killing, taking what has not been given, sexual misconduct, telling lies, and taking intoxicants.[4] Unlike most other religions, the Buddhist prohibition against killing is extended to all living beings, not just humans. The reason for this is linked to Buddhist understandings of karma and rebirth.

In brief, Buddhists believe that all of our actions have consequences that affect our future. There can be no action without a prior cause, and no action takes place without a corresponding effect. Of course, the exact workings of this system are complex, but the important point is that this process does not take place only over the course of one lifetime.

According to Buddhist beliefs, the source of existence is craving, an overwhelming desire to continue to be. This craving manifests itself daily in our lives, such as our desire to have pleasant things and pleasant experiences, and our desire to avoid unpleasant things and unpleasant experiences. But in a broader context, this craving situates us in an infinite cycle of rebirth; we are repeatedly born until we finally overcome all desire and attachment.[5]

The time spectrum of cause and effect, then, is expansive. Our actions in this life affect our circumstances in future lives, just as the circumstances of our present life have been conditioned by our actions in previous lives.[6] Our actions affect the form in which we are born. Good actions can lead to human rebirth, or in a higher realm, while bad actions can lead to rebirth as an animal, or even in a hell realm.[7] The important point to draw from this brief explanation is that, with an infinite number of past existences in many different forms, we must assume that every other being was at some point related to us. The implication is that, just as we would never consider killing and eating our mother, we should avoid killing or eating *any* living being; all beings have been closely related to us at some time in the past.[8]

In fact, Buddhist doctrine takes this point even further, teaching that we should cultivate *nondiscriminating* compassion for all beings. That is, we should strive to love everyone equally, ideally without distinction between family and strangers, friends and enemies, or humans and nonhuman animals. From a Buddhist perspective, only nondiscriminating compassion is true compassion because only this form of compassion remains unclouded by false distinctions between self and other.

Finally, the Buddha taught that we should not harm animals because the circumstances of our future lives are dependent on actions in this present life. Just as the desire to eat meat in this present life is the result of having existed as a carnivore in previous lives, harm done to animals in this life can result in a lower future birth, perhaps as a factory farmed animal, or as a human who must endure similar suffering. Thus, the doctrine of cause and effect suggests that one should avoid harming any living being in any way.

In practice, Buddhists don't always interpret the first precept as protecting all animals. There are occasional restrictions on meat eating, particularly on important festival days or during certain months of the year, but vegetarianism remains rare in Asian Buddhist countries, and is often treated as an *ideal* guideline, rather than a philosophy for everyday life.[9] Still, the Buddhist doctrine on nonharming, particularly when viewed in connection with notions of karma and intention, can (and ideally should) inform practices of animal liberation.

INTENTION AND THE BUDDHIST DOCTRINE OF KARMA

Whereas the earlier Hindu understanding of karma focused on action and results; Buddhism focused on *intentional* action, making intention central to the karmic effect of a deed.[11] The Buddhist concept of action is broad. Buddhists went so far as to suggest that even thoughts have consequences (which come into play later in this essay, in considering animal liberation in the West).

Of course, committing a deed, rather than just thinking about a deed, magnifies karmic effects. The importance of intention, however, requires that Buddhists consider the motivation and mind-set of the individual who performs an act. Thus, an important aspect of the Buddhist theory of cause and effect is that karmic affect differs for actions in general (which are not necessarily karmically fruitful) and *intentional* actions (which bear karmic consequences).

INTENTION AND ANIMAL LIBERATION IN THE WEST

Having established the critical importance of intention in Buddhist understandings of karma, we turn to animal liberation in the West. The first question to ask might be "*Why* are people liberating animals?" The most common responses would include "because they are suffering," "because it is cruel to keep them caged," or "because their natural state is to be free." All of these responses appear to reflect positive motivation from a Buddhist perspective; indeed, alleviating suffering was the Buddha's primary motivation in his quest for enlightenment.

An analysis of intention, however, requires us to dig deeper into an individual's mindset and motivation. The rage that we often find directed by animal liberation activists toward those who imprison, torture, and kill animals is understandable, because such people are responsible for an appalling amount of suffering. But from a Buddhist perspective, this anger actually limits the effectiveness of animal liberation.

Buddhists divide action into two categories: wholesome and unwholesome.[12] Unwholesome acts are rooted in greed, hatred, and delusion; they not only cause harm to oneself and others, but also condition future circumstances, leading to unfortunate rebirths. Thus, the act of animal liberation, which ought to be motivated by compassion and a desire to alleviate the suffering of another being, might be "tainted" by feelings of rage or hatred directed toward those who exploit animals.

Additionally, animal liberation activists sometimes express an inclination to care more about the welfare of nonhuman animals than about human animals. Again, this is not surprising, given that humans are the source of so much suffering in the world, and given that many view animals as innocent victims who deserve help and protection. But Buddhist teachings of nondiscriminating love and compassion caution against this sort of distinction. Pure compassion cannot be accompanied by a mind-set that discriminates between the well-being of different species. From the Buddhist point of view, animal liberation activists who see the welfare of nonhuman animals as more important than human welfare are misguided.

MULTIPLE MEANINGS OF "LIBERATION"

The end goal of Buddhist practice is liberation. But this liberation is both more complex and fundamental than the act of liberating an individual from bondage or suffering. The Buddha's primary insight was to realize that suffering comes from attachment and desire. We desire things that are pleasant, and when we don't get them we are unhappy. Similarly, we want to avoid things that are unpleasant, yet we cannot. The Buddha also came to see that the impermanence of existence compounds suffering because we desire to hang onto things that come and go from our lives. The Buddha's response to the world's pervasive suffering was to free himself from attachment, from desire. This enlightenment brings liberation.

Several other aspects of Buddhist liberation are also key to understanding this fundamental Buddhist concept. First, one can only liberate oneself. While teachers, guides, and supporters are likely to be an essential part of the path, liberation can only be gained through one's own efforts. Second, Buddhist liberation is an internal process, not necessarily connected to external circumstances. One can imagine a situation where an enlightened person is in prison yet remains liberated because she is not attached to desire and does not wish her situation to be different. Finally, Buddhist liberation is quintessentially *moral*. One cultivates moral behavior along the path to enlightenment until one reaches the point where one can behave in no other way. One is no longer good for the sake of karma, or good merit, or because of an externally imposed ethical code, but simply because one is incapable of causing suffering.

From a Buddhist perspective then, animal liberation is just one form of moral and ethical practice that leads to the ultimate liberation of oneself from the chains of attachment. Yet this noble practice is only effectively part of the Buddhist path to ultimate liberation if activism is conducted with right views and right intentions, that is, with pure compassion, untainted by anger or hatred, seeking only to alleviate the suffering of others.

Let me be clear. My intention is not to discourage people from acting to liberate animals, nor is it to critique liberationists. I do believe, however, that action undertaken on behalf of animals can benefit from an understanding of the Buddhist doctrine of intention and from exploring motivation. Activists would do well to adopt this reflective process. The rhetoric of the animal liberation movement often privileges action over reflection on the assumption that only action can liberate animals. This is true in an immediate sense, but activists should not equate reflection—particularly the type of reflection that I'm advocating here—with an unwillingness to act.

Presumably, the goal of animal liberation is to end the confinement, torture, and killing of nonhuman animals (which liberates humans as well). This is an admirable goal, not only for the sake of animals, but also on behalf of humans who mistreat other animals. While this may sound strange at first, Buddhists consider occupations that involve harming other beings to be examples of "wrong livelihood."[13] Therefore, if animal liberation activists are acting to change these practices, they're also helping to liberate people from "wrong views"—in this case, the belief that humans are fundamentally superior to animals and are therefore justified in hurting and killing them. However, it is difficult to see how actions on behalf of animals can serve this dual purpose when they are undertaken with hatred and anger toward those who are cruel to animals. While in no sense condoning cruel exploitation of nonhuman animals, Buddhist teachings require activists to be just as compassionate toward those who cause harm as those who are harmed.

This is yet another manifestation of the Buddhist ideal of nondiscriminating compassion, which seems beneficial to long-term animal liberation goals. Too often, anger directed toward humans who mistreat animals obscures compassionate motivation. If we truly wish to change the hearts of others and awaken compassion within, our actions need to be motivated by compassion.

IMPLICATIONS FOR ANIMAL LIBERATION PRACTICES

Some of the implications of this analysis for animal liberation should already be apparent. We can draw conclusions as to what types of actions might be appropriate or inappropriate, but only the acting individual can know her or his intentions, so the application of this principle can only be personal. For example, any action that specifically seeks to harm others is clearly antithetical to the Buddhist notion of compassion, yet an action that causes no specific harm can be considered counterproductive, from a Buddhist point of view, if one acts with malice. In the Buddhist worldview, animal liberation carried out with feelings of hatred or anger will have negative repercussions. In the words of the Buddha: "Through hatred, hatreds are never appeased; through non-hatred are hatreds always appeased— and this is a law eternal" (*Dhammapada* 1-5).

Groups like the Animal Liberation Front (ALF) have nonharming written into their guidelines, yet the words and actions of activists often run counter to the spirit of nonharming. Indeed, a Buddhist framework might lead ALF activists to reflect on the idea of "militant" action on behalf of animals. (Some people even question the violent roots of this term, and whether or not "militancy" ought to be applied to acts of animal liberation rooted in compassion.)

It is reasonable to assume that animal liberation can be carried out guided by compassionate motivation. Even monkey-wrenching and sabotage can remain under this critical framework. More challenging, however, are techniques like home demonstrations, where activists deliberately disrupt the personal lives of certain individuals in the hope of making the lives of animal exploiters miserable enough that they will change their behavior. Again, my purpose is not to suggest that activists abandon these techniques, merely that they critically analyze such acts through a Buddhist lens of intention. Whether or not such acts manifest Buddhist compassion is a question that activists must answer for themselves.[14]

Finally, an essential part of analyzing intention is to honestly consider possible results.[15] One must not only ask the practical question of whether potential results align with one's goals, but also whether one's actions might indirectly cause harm. Animal activists are often criticized for indirect negative results (the death of animals that are being liberated, the loss of livelihood for those involved in professions like fur trading, etc.). Honestly appraising intentions, motivation, and potential results can lead to more cooperative action, and perhaps even societal changes, particularly if liberationists are understood to be motivated by compassion rather than anger.

I have noted the importance of intention in Buddhist teachings and why animal liberationists might benefit from analyzing their actions through the reflective lens of intention. The compassionate roots of animal liberation must be apparent not only in one's motivation, but throughout any liberation action. If we wish to create a society that acts compassionately toward all living beings, we must reflect compassion first and foremost in our own actions.

7

Daoism

From Meat Avoidance to
Compassion-Based Vegetarianism

LOUIS KOMJATHY

"Animal advocacy" and "animal liberation" have never existed in the Daoist tradition.[1] These are largely modern concerns and commitments that have emerged from industrialized contexts of alienation, dehumanization, depersonalization, objectification, and so forth. They derive from cruelty and violence inflicted on sentient beings, most noticeably on the part of certain humans and institutions in the name of "human benefit" and "progress." For some, this situation evokes a feeling of compassion for nonhuman sentient beings. A traditional Daoist response involves investigating the ways in which humans have created these patterns of disruption—whether by placing constructs onto reality, including concrete pavement and "virtual realities," or by distorting our own nature through nationalism, legalism, and/or "morality."

Contemporary social problems are ecological in every sense of the word. In modern, industrialized nations, suffering and violence—not simply physical violence—are pervasive. While many people have become deaf or anesthetized to violence, the veils of "ignore-ance" (ignoring what is happening) cannot remain forever: "One day there will be a great awakening when we realize that all of this is a great dream" (*Zhuangzi*, chap. 2; DZ 670, 2.12b–13a). The various dimensions of this dream deserve inquiry and reflection.

With respect to "*reflections on animal advocacy and world religions*," the current "great dream" is that animals are "less than human" and that nonhuman animal suffering is acceptable for human "benefit." The subtitle of this paper thus should not be taken to imply that the subject of "animals" can be reduced to "meat." I have included "meat avoidance" in the subtitle for two principal reasons. First, throughout Chinese history animals have been understood principally in anthropocentric and sociocentric ways, especially as substances for human use. Second, "animal advocacy" in this historic context was most often expressed as compassion for sentient beings (especially in light of a Buddhist commitment to the alleviation of suffering), through a commitment to a vegetarian diet. However, the historic reasons for vegetarianism among Daoists, only some of which involve ethical commitments to other species, are complex. Thus, early Daoist forms of "meat avoidance" stand in contrast to later, fully developed Daoist vegetarian commitments. Vegetarianism may, in turn, be understood as one of the clearest ways to express a commitment to "animal advocacy."

In the pages that follow, I trace the historical development of Daoist vegetarianism and then provide a normative Daoist perspective on the necessity of embracing a conservationist ethic. Such an ethical practice involves inclusive compassion, energetic attentiveness, and the recovery of our innate goodness.

ANIMALS, BLOOD, AND MEAT IN EARLY DAOISM

Throughout Chinese history, animal slaughter, blood sacrifice, and meat consumption have been the norm. In this context, animals were viewed, first and foremost, as materials for human exploitation: meat for human sustenance, medicine for curing disease, and sacrificial offerings for efficacious communication with gods.[2]

One of the primary rituals, both on a state and local level, involved killing animals in order to supply sustenance for gods and ancestors. Celestial entities, like terrestrial beings, were believed to need blood to survive. This normative, ritual use of blood sacrifice extends from the ancient state religious rituals of the Shang and Zhou dynasties (Lewis 1990), through contemporary popular practices (Kleeman 1994).[3] Animal sacrifice is a central, defining feature of Chinese religions (Kleeman 1994).

Similarly, the dominant diet included slaughtered animals in traditional Chinese society, at least when meat was available. One ate meat if and when possible. While members of the cultural elite frequently had the opportunity to consume large amounts of meat,[4] such foods supplemented a diet of vegetables and grains for the ordinary person. Historically, the Chinese diet thus tended to center on vegetables and grains, with only a little meat on occasion (see Xu 1999).

Animal flesh was viewed not only as necessary for personal survival, health, and vitality, but also as offering medicinal qualities.[5] In the context of classical Chinese medicine, which incorporated a system of correlative cosmology (yin-yang and the Five Phases [*wuxing*]), animals and their flesh were categorized as follows: wood/mutton, fire/chicken, earth/beef, metal/dog, and water/pork (see, e.g., *Huangdi neijing suwen*, chap. 22; DZ 1018; Veith 1949, 205–6).[6] In this cosmological system, a diet without meat was and is seen as leading to potential deficiencies; simultaneously, the consumption of specific kinds of meat was believed to have curative properties (see also Kieschnick 2005, 189).

These details are necessary for understanding the overall cultural context in which Daoism developed—a world in which animal slaughter, blood sacrifice, and meat consumption were the norm. To follow a religious lifeway that omitted these religious/societal norms, was considered a rejection of fundamental Chinese cultural values and standard social activities. Such a choice had the potential to create social disharmony, one of the greatest fears in Chinese society.

In the earliest moments of organized Daoism, namely, the emergence of the Tianshi (Celestial Masters) movement in the Later Han dynasty (25–220 C.E.), Daoism began a theological and ritual shift that would forever change the Chinese religious landscape. The Celestial Masters superimposed a higher and purer pantheon of deities onto the hierarchy of gods and spirits that then dominated the Chinese theological landscape of state rituals and popular deity worship. Daoist priests and religious communities in the early medieval periods (Later Han and Period of Disunity) that followed the Han Dynasty defined their pantheon in contrast to those of imperial households, administrative elites, and the populace at large. Consequently, Daoist deities were defined as pure emanations of the Dao, who did not require meat or blood for sustenance; early Daoist communities rejected blood sacrifice and meat offerings in ritual activities (Kleeman 1994; see also Kleeman 2005; Kohn 2004, 44–45).

Daoist cosmology includes Three Heavens (*santian*) populated by specifically Daoist gods, gods defined as pure emanations of the Dao (Kleeman 1994, 201). These celestial beings, it was believed, did not eat meat, consume blood, or drink alcohol; they only responded to written petitions (*zhang*) issued by legitimate authorities—specifically ordained Daoist priests (*daoshi*) (Kleeman 1994). Daoist deities were nourished by cosmic ethers and astral palaces, and "orthodox" Daoist rituals centered on bloodless and meatless offerings. Animals were freed from sacrificial servitude. In addition to asserting superiority through theological claims regarding their nearness to the primordial undifferentiation of the Dao, the rejection of standard Chinese ritual activity also served a political function: because Daoist deities were higher, and thus more powerful than non-Daoist gods, and because only ordained Daoist priests could issue petitions to these powerful beings, rulers, officials, and people in general were dependent on Daoist ritual experts for assistance.

While such was the "orthodox" view of Daoist deities and sacred realms, concessions and accommodations were (and are) common (see, e.g., Lagerwey 1987; Saso 1972, 1978; Schipper 1993). Although meat and blood were not included in Daoist rituals, meat consumption continued. That is, Daoist deities did not need meat to survive, but human beings did. Thus, Celestial Masters did not extend their ideas of "purity" (see Douglas 2002 [1966]) to a vegetarian diet; life was compartmentalized into "celestial realms," "ritual occasions," and "daily life." Historical sources indicate that animal slaughter, blood sacrifice, and meat consumption were excluded from early Daoist ritual contexts, but that daily communal life still involved eating slaughtered animals.

One gains insight into early Daoist views of animals and meat consumption by reading the fourth century C.E. *Laojun shuo yibai bashi jie* (*180 Precepts of Lord Lao*; DH 78; DZ 786, 2a–20b).[7] With respect to animals and meat consumption, the relevant precepts are as follows:

4. Do not kill or harm any being.
24. Do not drink alcohol or eat meat.
39. Do not engage in killing.
40. Do not encourage others to kill.
49. Do not step on or kick the six domestic animals.
79. Do not fish or hunt and thereby harm and kill the host of living beings.
98. Do not catch birds or animals in cages or nets.
132. Do not startle birds or animals.
176. To be able to cut out all meat and living beings and the six domestic animals is best; without doing this, you will violate the precepts.
177. To be able to eat only vegetables is best; should it be impossible, match [your food to] the ruling constellation.[8] (Adapted from Kohn 2004, 136–44)

These Daoist precepts suggest a "bioregional ethic" among Celestial Masters communities. They were concerned for place and community, including the potentially harmful effects of human activities on nonhuman inhabitants.

Two points must be emphasized. First, it seems that the *180 Precepts of Lord Lao* was intended for libationers (*jijiu*), high-ranking members and leaders of the Celestial Masters community (see Schipper 2001, 89–90). Second, a distinction must be made between killing animals and eating meat. While libationers probably avoided killing animals with their own hands, it's unlikely that they were strict vegetarians. Rather, references to meat avoidance probably relate to ritual purification and ritual performance at certain prescribed times.[9] In this way, vegetarianism is best seen as an extension of personal conduct requirements with respect to traditional Chinese mourning rites. The *180 Precepts of Lord Lao* is a disparate text and probably served more as a set of conduct guidelines than authoritarian rules.

Members of early Daoist communities, specifically the Celestial Masters and their spiritual heirs, the Shangqing (Highest Clarity) and Lingbao (Numinous Treasure) movements, abstained from consuming meat and alcohol to purify themselves. In preparation for ritual activity, and in order to ensure efficacious relations with gods who were "vegetarian" in some sense of the word, priests and community members avoided meat—making their personal diet correspond to the "diet" of celestial beings. These Daoists did not refrain from slaughtering animals and consuming their flesh out of compassion; they avoided meat consumption (for limited durations) because ritual and theology required them to do so. Their informing worldview was theological, rather than ecological. One finds a similar pattern in contemporary Zhengyi (Orthodox Unity) Daoism, a householder and village-based ritual tradition with at least some connections to Tang-dynasty Celestial Master Daoism (see Kohn and Kirkland 2000, 349). Modern priests and ritual assistants in the Orthodox Unity tradition abstain from meat and alcohol as part of a purification process in preparation for formal ritual activity, while at the same time consuming large quantities of meat and alcohol in daily life (see, e.g., Saso 1978).

In the earliest historical moments of Daoism, however, certain adepts completely abandoned ordinary Chinese diets and consumption patterns. These individuals were immortality seekers, people who sought to complete a process of self-divinization (see Puett 2002). There's a discernable logic here. If the highest gods reject meat and blood offerings, and if one wanted to ascend to their sacred realms and/or to godhood, one must abstain from conventional terrestrial consumption. To become a god, one must "eat" like a god, or at least consume substances that might confer immortality.

In the early medieval period, some Daoists turned their attention from communal ritual activity to search for personal postmortem survival. In terms of meat consumption, this included "alchemical diets" or "cuisines of immortality." Here there was a hierarchy of ingestible substances, with ordinary foodstuffs on the bottom, and cosmic ethers on top. Some external alchemy (*waidan*) practitioners endeavored to "ingest the marvelous," that is, vegetal and mineral substances that would confer longevity and immortality (Campany 2001; 2002, especially 18–97; 2005).[10] In concert, many medieval Daoists practiced "abstention from grains" or "cereal avoidance" (*bigu*) (Lévi 1983), which aimed at extinguishing the Three Death-Bringers (*sanshi*)— biospiritual parasites seeking to bring about a premature death for human beings. Although conventionally interpreted as the abandonment of grains in particular, recent research suggests that *bigu* often referred to complete fasting (Campany 2002, 22–24; Eskildsen 1998, 43–44, 153–54).

Another dimension of these early medieval culinary disciplines included ingesting astral effulgence and cosmic ethers, sometimes referred to as "*qi* ingestion" (*fuqi*). This form of Daoist practice was especially prominent in the Highest Clarity movement (Robinet 1989, 1993). Daoist dietetics are thus far more complex than mere "food consumption." In addition to the ingestion of food, Daoist dietetics includes herbology and mineralogy, fasting regimens, ingestion of seasonal and locality influences, and absorption of astral effulgence.

There were three distinct religious dietary practices in early medieval Daoism: divine vegetarianism for deities, ritual vegetarianism (occasional vegetarianism) for priests and community leaders, and complete vegetarianism for immortality seekers.

TOWARD A VEGETARIAN COMMITMENT IN LATER DAOISM

As we have seen, meat avoidance played some role in early and early medieval Daoism, though for what are likely to seem unfamiliar spiritual reasons. It was not until the steadily increasing influence of Buddhism, after the fourth century C.E., that an "ethical" or "soteriological" view of sentient life began influencing Daoist communities. In Chinese culture and society, the association of vegetarianism with Buddhism is so strong that "eating purely" (*chisu*; *sushi*) is most often interpreted as "believing in Buddhism" (*xin fojiao*). Nonetheless, one also finds a tendency toward vegetarianism in Daoist monastic communities.

Daoist dietary matters are complicated by a dearth of texts providing explicit arguments or explanations for vegetarianism. When or if vegetarianism ever was completely institutionalized and thoroughly embraced by Daoists is unclear. There are hints of early adherents and proponents of vegetarianism, but it is unclear if vegetarianism was ever fully required for Daoist monastic participation.[11] It is clear, however, that in contemporary China "Daoist vegetarianism" is principally practiced by monastics of the Quanzhen (Complete Perfection) order.

In this section, I briefly discuss the influence of Buddhism, then examine early and later Quanzhen views of animals and meat consumption.

In Chinese Buddhism, among both monastics and laity, vegetarianism became increasingly normative from the seventh century onward. As John Kieschnick (2005) has suggested: "While, in the sixth century, for a monk to renounce meat was considered a sign of eminence, by the tenth [century] it was considered a minimum requirement for any monk or nun" (201). Kieschnick traces the formation of Buddhist vegetarianism in China, noting that "vegetarianism is perhaps the most important contribution Buddhism has made to Chinese cuisine" (Kieschnick 2005, 186). (One might reverse this to note that vegetarianism is perhaps one of the most important contributions of Chinese Buddhism to Buddhism as a whole, since most Buddhists around the world continue to eat meat.)

Buddhist views on animals and the Buddhist rationale for vegetarianism are important to an understanding of Daoist vegetarianism. Briefly stated, in some Indian sources (and thus in some influential Chinese sources), the Buddhist precept against killing was not interpreted as a prohibition against eating the meat of slaughtered animals; as long as Buddhists did not witness, participate in, or personally influence the killing of animals, it was often considered acceptable to consume flesh (Kieschnick 2005, 188, 192–93, 195). Such Buddhists, like most modern "consumers" in industrialized nations, may have found the actual practice of slaughtering animals abhorrent, but they often did not notice their implicit collaboration and participation in meat consumption. As Chinese Buddhists reflected on the insights and prohibitions mentioned in Mahayana sutras, and began creating distinctively Chinese forms of Buddhism, monastics and laity recognized vegetarianism as a clear requirement.

This Chinese dietary shift involved a more complete adherence to Buddhist views on karma, reincarnation, and the Mahayana ideal of the *bodhisattva*—the being of limitless wisdom and compassion committed to the universal salvation of all sentient beings. From this perspective, meat consumption had negative karmic consequences. By consuming the flesh of slaughtered animals, one was participating in suffering and death. The karmic consequence might be a less soteriologically opportune incarnation, including potential rebirth as an animal (Kieschnick 2005, 201–5). Furthermore, slaughtered animals might be one's former relatives. In a characteristically Chinese move,

the act of eating animals was therefore tantamount to filial impiety.
Just as important, Buddhists applying and embodying Mahayana views
of interconnection and universal salvation saw suffering *as suffering*,
without distinctions between "human" and "nonhuman." Vegetarianism, rooted in a pervasive concern for all sentient life, was the natural
culmination of Buddhist cosmology, philosophy, and soteriology.[12]

In the initial stages of communal and institutionalized Daoist vegetarianism, it appears that a meatless diet was understood as an extension of earlier "alchemical diets," mentioned above. Some members
of late-medieval Daoist monastic communities thus began to embrace
vegetarian diets. For example, according to the seventh century *Fashi
jinjie jing* (*Scripture on Prohibitions and Precepts Regarding Ceremonial Food*; DH 80), the "five food groups" are identified as vegetables,
grains, vegetal substances, minerals, and *qi* (*ch'i*):

> Eating vegetables is not as good as eating grains; eating grains is not as
> good as eating fungi and excrescences; eating fungi is not as good as
> eating gold and jade; eating gold and jade is not as good as eating pri-
> mordial *qi*; and eating primordial *qi* is not as good as not eating at all. By
> not eating at all, even though the heavens and earth may collapse, the
> self will remain eternally. (Adapted from Kohn 2004, 51; italics mine)

In this succession we see that the aspiring adept endeavors to move
from a yin (terrestrial) condition to a yang (celestial) condition. From
a soteriological perspective, one endeavors to attain and/or create self-
transcendence through a dietary shift. While meat avoidance became
central to Daoist diets aimed at immortality, they were not maintained
out of concern for animals. Instead, vegetarian Daoists believed that
ordinary consumption patterns, whether animal flesh, grains, or food
in general, bound the adept to the mundane.

While vegetarianism seems to have had some place among early
Daoist monastics (see Kohn 2003, 112–32; 2004, 44–47, 50–53), it is
unclear if this diet became normative. Currently, no evidence exists

that Daoists ever required lay believers to renounce animal slaughter or meat consumption; when vegetarianism was practiced, it was practiced by the Daoist clerical elite.

As mentioned, the Daoist movement most often associated with vegetarianism is the Complete Perfection monastic order. In the earliest historical phases of the movement, when Complete Perfection was a small renunciant community (see Eskildsen 2004; Komjathy 2007), there is little evidence that vegetarianism was required.[13] Generally speaking, the writings of the first-generation adepts, most commonly known as the Seven Perfected, provide few explicit discussions of animals or dietetics. For example, the Ten Admonitions of Liu Changsheng (1147–1203) and Ma Danyang (1123–1184) make no mention of vegetarianism (Komjathy 2007, 148–57).

Although early adepts seem to have accepted the five basic Buddhist precepts, we must again keep in mind that avoidance of killing was not necessarily understood to be equivalent to meat avoidance. Nonetheless, we do find some hints that early Complete Perfection adherents, and leaders of this regional and national religious movement such as Ma Danyang, expressed concern for the plight of non-human animals; Ma Danyang was especially committed to an ethic that reached across species (Marsone 2001, 103).

The fact that early adepts lived in seclusion in the mountains of Shandong and Shaanxi not only suggests a commitment to intensive religious training, but also an appreciation of natural and secluded environments. Some of their extant poetry expresses just such sentiments. Qiu Changchun (1148–1227), for example, writes:

> The landscape of this place is truly beautiful;
> Humans and animals respond to each other.
> Water and bamboo surround a few dozen houses;
> Each household understands the Mandate of Heaven.
> I love the clear and empty scenery of nature;
> Holding my walking-stick, I explore the dark paths.

93

Every day I walk around the village one time;
Wandering aimlessly, I sing and chant at leisure. (*Panxi ji*, DZ 1159,
  6.5a)

And from the same source, a reference to karma and reincarnation:

When a dog gets sick, there is no one who will cook porridge for it;
When a donkey falls to the ground out of cold, its limbs become
  stiff [from neglect].
This is because people do not know how to cultivate hidden virtue
  (*yinde*);
Changing husks, how could they avoid calamity and retribution?
  (ibid., 2.6b)

In these and similar poems, Qiu expresses a sense of reverence for secluded places, places that are filled with natural beauty, places that support self-cultivation. He also conveys compassion for domestic animals who are dependent on the kindness of humans to survive and flourish. From Qiu's perspective, people who don't show concern *through their actions* will accrue negative karma in one form or another.[14] Daoist adherents must, therefore, "cultivate hidden virtue." Viewing the world and sentient beings from a more encompassing, transpersonal perspective, Daoists aim to relieve suffering, nourish existential flourishing, and adhere to an ethical code that is likely to go unnoticed and unrecognized by others.

As Quanzhen began to be transformed from a local religious community and regional religious movement to a nationwide monastic order under Qiu Changchun and the second-generation adherents, a corresponding shift occurred from ascetic and eremitic training to institutionalized monasticism. Earlier Quanzhen commitments to celibacy and abstention from intoxicants became requirements for entrance into, and continued association with, the monastic order. Monastic manuals provide guidance and explain the expected daily routine.

In texts such as the fourteenth century *Quanzhen qinggui* (*Pure Rules of Complete Perfection*; DZ 1235; cf. Yifa 2002), there is no mention of meat avoidance or vegetarianism. The only relevant dietary proscription found among monastic rules is as follows: "Those who drink alcohol, indulge in sex, seek wealth, lose their temper, or eat strong-smelling vegetables will be expelled [from the monastic order]" (12a).[15] It is noteworthy that a meatless diet is not required. While one might argue that vegetarianism was already normative in fourteenth century Complete Perfection monasteries, it is unclear to what extent vegetarianism was a central feature of late-medieval and late-imperial Daoist monastic life.[16]

Complete Perfection Daoism lost its place of supremacy in the Daoist tradition during the Ming dynasty (1368–1644), but again came to prominence during the Qing dynasty (1644–1911).[17] In particular, there was a resurgence of Complete Perfection under the leadership of Wang Changyue (Kunyang [Paradisiacal Yang]; 1594?–1680). Today Wang Changyue is identified as the principal architect of the formal Longmen (Dragon Gate) lineage of Complete Perfection, with its headquarters located at Baiyun guan (White Cloud Temple, Beijing). He composed/compiled monastic manuals and precept texts that continue to provide the foundation for ordination and the standard for daily monastic life.

In two of these texts, the seventeenth century *Chuzhen jie* (*Precepts of Initial Perfection*; JY 292; ZW 404) and *Zhongji jie* (*Precepts of Medium Ultimate*; JY 293; ZW 405), there is strong evidence that vegetarianism was part of daily Complete Perfection monastic life. As expressed in the seventh of the "Ten Precepts of Initial Perfection": "Do not drink alcohol or eat meat in violation of the prohibitions. Always harmonize *qi* and innate nature, remaining attentive to clarity and emptiness" (ZW 404, 9b; also 32a). Similarly, according to precept two of the "Three Hundred Precepts of Medium Ultimate": "Do not eat the blood and flesh of living beings" (ZW 405, 2a). The latter precept, in particular, suggests strict vegetarianism.

It is important to note, however, that a later section of the *Precepts of Initial Perfection*, specifically precept four of the "Nine Precepts for Female Perfected," reads as follows: "During rituals and recitations, be diligent and circumspect, give up all eating of meat and drinking of alcohol" (32a). Thus, it would seem that certain members of the monastic community were only practicing occasional vegetarianism, or semi-vegetarianism, in ways that paralleled earlier Daoist views of temporary ritual purification. The Qing-dynasty Complete Perfection ordination system offers one interpretation of these discrepancies: there were three levels of practice corresponding to three texts. The *Precepts of Initial Perfection* corresponded to the first level, and was thus intended for initiates or novices, while the *Precepts of Medium Ultimate* corresponded to the middle level, and was thus intended for confirmed members of the monastic community. Perhaps only fully committed monastics were required to maintain a strict vegetarian diet. However, it is unclear to what extent this was realized, rather than a mere ideal, and the texts also lack explicit rationales for meat avoidance.

Perhaps for those who followed such monastic guidelines, there were at least three underlying principles: (1) earlier Daoist views of ritual purity (now extended to all-encompassing existential commitments); (2) earlier Daoist alchemical diets, in which meat consumption bound one to the mundane world and inhibited the complete alchemical transformation required for immortality; and (3) Buddhist influence concerning karma and the suffering. Only the third suggests concern for animal welfare. Interestingly, the highest of the three precept texts, the *Tianxian jie* (*Precepts of Celestial Immortality*; JY 291; ZW 403), suggests that "celestial immortals" are also Buddhist *bodhisattvas* (see Kohn 2004, 111–13). A similar trend is found in much Daoist alchemical literature of the Qing dynasty.

PERSONAL OBSERVATIONS AND REFLECTIONS

As a final point regarding daily Complete Perfection monastic life, I will mention some relevant information from my fieldwork in mainland China, which included living as a visiting Daoist monk (*yang daoshi*) at contemporary Daoist monasteries in Shandong and Shaanxi.[18] (The contemporary situation for Daoist monastics in mainland China may also be instructive regarding earlier moments in Daoist history.)

In accordance with modern Complete Perfection religious rules, monastics are prohibited from eating meat or taking intoxicants. This means that all meals within the monasteries are vegetarian. Generally speaking, monastic dishes tend to be simple combinations of vegetables with minimal amounts of seasoning, supplemented with rice, millet, or *mantou* (steamed buns). At times, one also finds *doufu* (tofu). Generally speaking, monastic meals go beyond modern conceptions of "vegetarianism"; they are vegan (no eggs or dairy products). Until quite recently, dairy products were not consumed in China, so the avoidance of eggs is most noteworthy.[19]

My experiences behind monastic walls in China reveal two discrepancies. First, within the refectory of Mount Lao near Qingdao, monks are currently offered milk, yogurt, and eggs. Second, the majority of contemporary Daoist monastics are only vegetarian while "inside the gates." When outside temple compounds with fellow monastics, family, officials, visitors, and so forth, they eat meat and consume alcohol. When I refused such products, even when "given permission," most monks inquired as to how long I had been vegetarian, abstaining also from intoxicants. When I replied sixteen and fourteen years respectively, most expressed surprise. Quanzhen monastics offer a variety of reasons for consuming meat: nutrition, personal health problems, lack of dedication, and so forth. When asked about the importance of vegetarianism from a Daoist perspective, most simply recalled monastic rules and did not seem to understand (or had not considered) deeper motivations. These details expose the contextual meaning of vegetarianism in contemporary Daoist monasteries, as well as contemporary Chinese dietary habits and health views. Moreover, most Chinese Daoists are living in local communities where "livestock" is raised in a bioregional manner, which is very different from factory farming in industrialized countries.

While most contemporary Complete Perfection monastics may not be considered strict or lifelong vegetarians, some show clear concern for nonhumans. For example, I personally witnessed Complete Perfection monks on various occasions express and embody compassion and affinity with nonhuman beings: daily appreciation for the grace and carefree movements of fish and birds, awareness of the patterns of wind and water through local forests and valleys, and "activism" on the part of birds and dogs. With respect to the latter, some monks requested and secured the release of captured songbirds, owls, and monkeys, while others reprimanded young boys for abusing dogs.

A NORMATIVE DAOIST PERSPECTIVE

The preceding sections attempt to provide a fair, accurate, and realistic discussion of the place of vegetarianism and "animal advocacy" in Daoism, suggesting that the reasons for meat avoidance in the earlier religious tradition often don't conform to modern Western animal liberation philosophy. Daoist commitments to a vegetarian diet, more often than not, derive from anthropocentric, cosmocentric, or theocentric views, and are most frequently understood through a prism of personal benefit and communal requirements, whether ritual purity, immortality, soteriological import, or monastic conformity. While various dimensions of the Daoist tradition have the potential to inform a commitment to animal advocacy and animal liberation, including a distinctive religious ideal of concern for sentient beings and adherence to a vegetarian diet, few Daoists have expressed any such commitment.

In conclusion, I will attempt to provide a normative Daoist perspective on compassion across species and on vegetarianism as a spiritual commitment. Here I speak as a Daoist scholar-practitioner—as an adherent.

After some twelve years of commitment and practice, in 2006 I received ordination in the Huashan (Mount Hua) lineage of Complete Perfection Daoism. I am thus writing this section from the perspective of someone with formal lineage affiliation in the Daoist religious tradition. I hope that my words will inspire Daoists and non-Daoists to more fully embrace a commitment to the alleviation of suffering in the world, especially among sentient beings who are voiceless and helpless beneath the machinery of "technological progress" and "human consumption."

To begin, one does not need Daoist sources to plead for ecological commitments as expressions of compassion that reaches across species. Speaking frankly, to be human is to be humane. A lack of concern for suffering and dying reveals a loss of humanity. Many contemporary humans have been systematically conditioned to be ignorant about, insulated from, and anesthetized against caring for life. The point I wish to make is that perhaps people need to relearn what it means to be human before worrying about being Buddhists, Christians, Daoists, and so forth. Religious traditions can help us understand our shared humanity, but they also have potential for great division, deception, and delusion.

To this, I would add that for *anyone* who claims to have ecological commitments or environmental concerns, vegetarianism is a *minimal requirement*. At the very least, consumption of slaughtered animals should form a supplemental part of one's diet, and "meat" should only come from animals raised and slaughtered in humane ways. That is, "animal industries" ought be systematically undermined and eventually extinguished through a shift in consumption. The only justifiable exceptions to this largely vegetarian diet are people in situations of extreme need, people living in bioregional communities, or people whose medical condition requires animal products—if such a condition exists and can be verified. To bring about a larger ecological shift, people may have to remain strict vegetarians, even if this leads to premature death. I have taken such a vow. Beyond Daoism, in a modern

industrialized context, I suggest that "animal advocacy" is the fulfill-
ment of our humanity.[20]

"Daoist ideas" have too often been represented as mere intellectual
entertainment and distraction—exercises in futility aimed at *talking
about* change without actually *changing*: "One who speaks does not
know; one who knows does not speak" (*Daode jing*, chap. 56). The
latter sentence, which is followed by a set of *practice principles*, may
be amended to note that Daoists ought to be committed to application
and embodiment: "My words are easy to understand, easy to practice,
but no one understands or practices them" (*Daode jing*, chap. 70).
An emphasis on ideas extracted and disembodied from lived practice,
communities, and places, is a distortion of fundamental Daoist values.

The Complete Perfection order provides a clear Daoist response,
although a response that few wish to consider, let alone embrace.
Complete Perfection monastics live in Daoist sacred sites, usually in
wild places, and follow a renunciant way of life. They are celibate,
have very few material possessions, and maintain a vegetarian diet. In
some sense, this lifestyle is a "conservationist ethic," a commitment
to conserving external and internal landscapes: "Appear plain and
embrace simplicity; decrease selfishness and lessen desires" (*Daode
jing*, chap. 19). This way of life leads to specific benefits. Local wildlife is protected and respected, human reproduction is inhibited, and
"livestock" isn't sacrificed for human consumption. If one embraces
the principles and values expressed in these dimensions of Daoist
communal life, one will work to preserve, establish, and maintain
wildlife sanctuaries; one will find a way to live gently within the vast
landscape of existence. From a Daoist perspective, that landscape is
the Dao made manifest. A Daoist religious path involves "nourishing
life" (*yangsheng*).

Returning to some of the details mentioned above, I will advance
a more systematic argument for respect and compassion for sentient
beings. Daoist ideas of ritual purity can be extended to become all-
pervasive, existential commitments—commitments that derive from

personal observation, practice, and experience. Why should one only be "pure" in preparation for "ritual"? Is not all of life a "ritual process," a form of *communitas*, and as an expression of reverence for the sacred? It seems preferable to avoid the compartmentalization of life into "before," "during," and "after."

Daoist ritual purity requires the avoidance of animal slaughter and blood sacrifice. The Daoist stands before the universe as a sacred vessel filled with the numinous presence of the Dao; ritually informed Daoist vegetarianism extends Daoist views of cosmic harmony and "salvation" to include all sentient beings. In such a place of reverence and realization, one discovers that the altar is simultaneously temple platform, celestial locale, mountain peak, and internal center (see Schipper 1993). The altar is simultaneously in the world and in the self. We release animals from their former sacrificial role because no "sacrifice of other" is required.

Simultaneously, higher levels of Daoist training involve sublimation and rarification, self-cultivation and alchemical transformation, a shift from agitation to stillness, from turbidity to clarity. One also activates the Daoist subtle body, the energetic "body" within the body. This includes attentiveness to what one ingests and circulates. This Daoist view has clear implications for sentient beings through dietary intake: what one ingests is what one is. To consume the meat of slaughtered animals is to make suffering, injury, and violent death part of oneself. Meat eating is not the practice of priest or immortal; such is not the practice of "adepts *of* the Dao" or of realized beings.

Liberating oneself from a context of violence liberates those who inflict violence,[21] and those upon whom the violence is inflicted. Through a dietary shift away from animal products, one becomes less material and more rarified. Through a process of cosmicization, a state of transpersonal interconnection develops; one abides in the primordial undifferentiation of the Dao in which personal selfhood and selfish desires disappear, and beings are able to abide in their own natural places.

For Daoists with Buddhist-influenced, karma-based reincarnation models, models that are normative in many contemporary Chinese Daoist communities, there are yet more reasons to relieve suffering and support the nourishment of sentient beings. Vegetarianism/veganism is one of the simplest and easiest ways to reduce suffering and nurture all beings. Anyone who understands the realities of modern slaughterhouses ("meatpacking plants") and still has access to the core goodness of innate nature—the Dao made manifest in/as/through us—will accept the responsibility of vegetarianism. The consumption of meat enmeshes an individual in an interconnected system of suffering, exploitation, and murder—such are the perils of domination and domestication. A lack of direct killing does not lessen karmic involvement in slaughter for one who eats animal products. The personal consequences of such involvement may differ with each person, but the consequences for animals (human and nonhuman), for society, and for the world are quite clear.

One important consequence is suffering. This suffering is clearly audible, as is the inner call to relieve suffering. The choice of compassion for sentient beings, especially those who are unheard and unseen, has other important spiritual effects. One begins to free oneself from karma; one becomes part of a different community, lineage, and reality, a community in which reverence, sacred presence, and energetic aliveness are nourished and expressed. One's decision to rectify harmful patterns and cultivate beneficial patterns may also exert a transformative effect on one's family, community, and society. From a Daoist perspective, much of our life is determined by our ancestors. With the vision of reincarnation at hand, we would do well to expand our conception of who our ancestors are.

Daoists have reverence for Three Treasures, the sources of the Daoist religious tradition: the Dao, scriptures, and teachers. Each of these can help inform a Daoist way of life, including the challenges of living during a time of degeneration. As a Daoist, I am responsible for relieving suffering among sentient beings, especially those suffering and helpless under human hands: those in distant forests, rivers, and mountains; those experimented on for "human benefit"; those abused and neglected as domesticated animals; and those raised for consumption.

I endeavor to follow a Daoist way of life, a life based in attentiveness, reverence, and connection. Energetic sensitivity, observation, and deep listening reveal vast suffering. And yet, beneath this is the numinous presence of the Dao. We must cultivate the ability to recognize both suffering and the Dao in all beings. We may begin with a commitment to inquiry: What are we cultivating? What are we listening to? From a Daoist perspective, we may ask a perennial question: What does it mean to be fully human?

As inhabitants of community, place, and world, let us cultivate ways of nourishing life. Let us contemplate and embody fundamental Daoist values: attentiveness, clarity, stillness, conservation, noncontention, responsiveness, reverence, and simplicity.

PART TWO

ABRAHAMIC TRADITIONS

Jewish, Christian, and Islamic Traditions

8

Judaism

Global Warming, Animal Products,
and the Vegan Mandate

RICHARD H. SCHWARTZ

V eganism is a Jewish imperative because the production and
consumption of meat and other animal products violate
basic Jewish mandates: to preserve human health, treat animals with compassion, protect the environment, conserve natural
resources, help hungry people, and seek and pursue peace. Because
this is not part of the conventional thinking of most Jews, this article
explains this assertion, then addresses common objections.

PRESERVATION OF HEALTH

The preservation of one's health is arguably Judaism's most important commandment. The Talmud teaches that Jews should be more
particular about matters of health than matters of ritual. If it might
help save a life, one generally must (not may) violate the Sabbath, eat
nonkosher foods, and eat on Yom Kippur. (The only laws that cannot

be violated to preserve a life are those prohibiting murder, idolatry, and sexual immorality.)

Animal-centered diets have been irrefutably linked with heart disease, strokes, various types of cancer, and other diseases. Animal-based diets have been a major cause of recent skyrocketing medical costs, contributing substantially to local, state, and national budgetary problems.

COMPASSION FOR ANIMALS

Many Biblical laws command proper treatment of animals. For example, one may not yoke a strong and a weak animal nor muzzle an ox while he is threshing in the field. Moses and King David were chosen for leadership, and Rebecca was deemed suitable to be a wife for the patriarch Isaac, because they were kind to animals. Proverbs 12:10 teaches that "the righteous person considers the life of his or her animal." The Psalmist states that "the Lord is good to all, and His tender mercies are over all His works" (Ps. 145:9). Compassion for animals is even required in the Ten Commandments, in a verse that's recited every Shabbat morning as part of Kiddush, which indicates that animals, as well as people, must be permitted to rest on the Sabbath.

Contrary to these powerful Jewish teachings, most animals raised to produce food in the United States spend their entire lives under unnatural conditions in crowded spaces, where they are denied fresh air, exercise, and freedom of movement.

PROTECTION OF THE ENVIRONMENT

God said "It is very good" (Gen. 1:31) when the world was created, but today the world faces many environmental threats. Judaism teaches that Earth is the Lord's (Ps. 24:1), and that people are to be partners and coworkers with God in protecting the environment. Talmudic sages showed great concern for reducing pollution.

In conflict with Jewish environmental injunctions, animal-centered diets exacerbate extensive environmental threats, including global climate change. Global warming is much more than "an inconvenient truth." UN weapons inspector Hans Blix has said: "To me the question of the environment is more ominous than that of peace and war. . . . I'm more worried about global warming than I am of any major military conflict" (Norris 2003). Global warming is arguably the biggest social, political, economic, moral, and environmental issue facing our planet and its inhabitants. People are becoming increasingly aware of and concerned about global warming due to record temperatures, wildfires, an increase in the number and severity of storms, widespread droughts, rising sea levels, flooding, endangered species, spreading diseases, shrinking lakes, environmental refugees, and melting of glaciers, permafrost, and polar ice caps. We are overheating our planet with potentially catastrophic consequences. Of the warmest twenty-three years worldwide on record, twenty-two of them have occurred in the past twenty-seven years (Gore 2006, 72). We may be standing at a precipice. In 2008, several Midwestern states suffered massive flooding from a "500-year storm," and California saw a record number of wildfires after a long drought. California's governor stated that the fire season in his state used to last a few months, but now lasts all year long (Johnson 2008).

Almost all scientific and environmental organizations, journals, and magazines agree that global warming is real, serious, worsening, and caused by human activity. The evidence is overwhelming. In February 2007, the Intergovernmental Panel on Climate Change (IPCC) released its Fourth Assessment Report, which was researched and written by about 2,500 climate scientists over six years and vetted by over 130 governments (IPCC 2007). The report carefully delineates clear trends and potentially catastrophic consequences associated with climate change, warning of the possibility of irreversible damage, unless we make concerted efforts to counter global warming. The IPCC makes it plain that current and projected climate change is not simply "natural variation," but "very likely" (meaning *at least* ninety percent) the result of human activity. *Time* magazine (Walsh 2007) with agreement from the Brookings Institution (Easterbrook 2006), *National Geographic* (Hoffmann 2000), and other major publications, declared "case closed" on the human cause and reality of global warming, leaving only solutions to be debated.

Leading experts (including James Hansen of NASA and physicist Stephen Hawking) warn that global climate change may reach a "tipping point" and spiral out of control within a few years, with disastrous consequences, if current conditions continue (Hansen 2008). A seven-hundred page British government report authored by Lord Nicholas Stern, a former chief economist for the World Bank, projects losses of up to twenty percent of the world's gross domestic product by 2050 unless one percent of the current world domestic product is devoted to combating global climate change (Walker 2007). Other economic studies have projected even worse scenarios.

Further, an increase in the numbers of environmental refugees, along with greater anxiety over access to food, water, land, and housing, create increasingly unstable conditions, which give rise to anger, ethnic violence, terrorism, and war. The fallout from climate change may also impoverish and radicalize people leading to an increase in terrorism. A report commissioned by the U.S.-financed Center for Naval Analyses and written by eleven retired U.S. generals states: "On the simplest level, [climate change] has the potential to create sustained natural and humanitarian disasters on a scale far beyond those we see today" (Timmer 2007). This panel of generals, including retired General Anthony Zinni, former commander of U.S. forces in the Middle East, depicts global warming as "a threat multiplier for instability in some of the most volatile regions of the world," which could "seriously exacerbate already marginal living standards in many Asian, African, and Middle Eastern nations, causing widespread political instability and the likelihood of failed states."[1]

The planet and all life are threatened as perhaps never before, and major changes are needed to put our imperiled planet on a sustainable path—and soon. The latest Intergovernmental Panel on Climate Change report states: "Changes in lifestyles and consumption patterns that emphasize resource conservation can contribute to developing a low-carbon economy that is both equitable and sustainable" (Energy and Resources Institute 2008). The November 2006 book-length report from the UN Food and Agriculture Organization (FAO), "Livestock's Long Shadow" (FAO 2006), shows how personal "changes in lifestyles and consumption" can affect global warming. This report claims that animal-based agriculture causes approximately eighteen percent of greenhouse gas emissions (in CO_2 equivalent), contributing to global warming, an amount significantly greater than that caused by all forms of transportation on the planet combined (about thirteen-and-a-half percent). Senior author Henning Steinfeld, Ph.D., adds that meat consumption is "one of the most significant contributors to today's most serious environmental problems" (Knickerbocker 2007). Cars are still problematic, of course, but cows and other animals raised for human consumption are contributing significantly to global warming. What we eat is actually more important than what we drive, and the most important personal change we can make for the environment, as well as for our own health and the lives of animals, is to choose to be vegan.

According to the animal rights group FARM, each year the world feeds about fifty-six billion animals to fatten them for slaughter. Meanwhile, millions of people, disproportionately children, starve to death. It takes up to sixteen pounds of grain to produce a single pound of feedlot beef for human consumption (Robbins 1987). Over seventy percent of the grain produced in the United States (and about forty percent produced worldwide) is inefficiently and immorally diverted to feed farmed animals, to satisfy appetites for meat and money (GoVeg.com n.d.). The UN FAO study reports that the livestock industry, in total, uses and abuses roughly thirty percent of the planet's surface, thereby "entering into direct competition [with other activities] for scarce land, water and other natural resources" (FAO 2006). Further, overuse of land by livestock, leading to overuse of fuel and water, also degrades the land, erodes the topsoil, and pollutes water, contributing to additional environmental and health problems.

An animal-based diet also wastes energy. It requires seventy-eight calories of fossil fuels for each calorie of protein obtained from feedlot-produced beef, but only two calories of fossil fuels to produce a calorie of protein from soybeans. Frances Moore Lappé writes that grains and beans require only two to five percent as much fossil fuel as beef (Moore Lappé 1991, 74–75). The energy needed to produce a pound of grain-fed beef is equivalent to one gallon of gasoline (Durning 1986). Reducing energy consumption is not only a better choice in terms of fighting climate change; it's also a better choice in terms of being less dependent on foreign oil. Making all of the above points more serious, the consumption of animal products is projected to double in fifty years (FAO 2006). If this happens, it will be difficult, if not impossible, to reduce greenhouse emissions enough to avoid the most severe effects of global climate change. While growing concern over global warming is welcome, the many connections between the fast-spreading Standard American Diet (SAD) and global warming have generally been overlooked or marginalized. The production of meat contributes substantially to the emission of three major gases associated with global warming: carbon dioxide (CO_2), methane (CH_4), and nitrous oxide (N_2O), as well as other ecodestructive gases such as ammonia (NH_3), which contributes to acid rain, and hydrogen sulfide (H_2S), implicated in mass extinctions. *World Watch* editors conclude: "The human appetite for animal flesh is a driving force behind virtually every major category of environmental damage now threatening the human future—defor-estation, erosion, fresh water scarcity, air and water pollution, cli-mate change, biodiversity loss, social injustice, the destabilization of communities, and the spread of disease" (McKie and Davis 2008). Lee Hall, the legal director for Friends of Animals, is more succinct: "Behind virtually every great environmental complaint there's milk and meat" (Singer 2009).

Based on a verse in Deuteronomy, which prohibits the destruc-tion of fruit-bearing trees in time of warfare (Deut. 20:19–20), Talmu-dic sages prohibit the waste or unnecessary destruction of anything potentially beneficial to people. Rabbi Samson Raphael Hirsch (a leading nineteenth century Jewish leader and scholar) stated that this prohibition (*bal tashchit*) is the first and most general call of God. We are to "regard things as God's property and use them with a sense of responsibility for wise human purposes. Destroy nothing! Waste nothing!" (Hirsch 1962, sec. 397, 398). He also stated that the prohi-bition of *bal tashchit* includes using more things (or things of greater value) than necessary (Hirsch 1962, sec. 400). Contrary to *bal tash-chit*, animal-centered diets require up to twenty times as much land, fourteen times as much water, and ten times as much energy, and also require far more pesticides, fertilizer, and other resources, than vegan diets (Tell Youth Tell Truth 2007).

It is increasingly clear that eliminating—or at least sharply reduc-ing—the production and consumption of meat and other animal products is imperative if we are to reduce global warming and other grave environmental threats, and conserve natural resources. Vegan-ism preserves and protects our now endangered environment, and veganism is therefore a Jewish imperative.

SHARING WITH HUNGRY PEOPLE

Helping the hungry is fundamental to Judaism. The Talmud states: "Providing charity for poor and hungry people weighs as heavily as all the other commandments of the Torah combined" (Babylonian Talmud, *Baba Batra* 9a). The Torah requires farmers to leave the gleanings of the harvest and the corners of the fields for the poor (Lev. 19:9–10). On Yom Kippur, the holiest day of the Jewish year, Jews are told through the words of the Prophet Isaiah that fasting and prayers are not enough. They must work to end oppression and "share thy bread with the hungry" (Isa. 58:6–7).

Contrary to these basic Jewish teachings, animal-based diets involve the feeding of over seventy percent of U.S. grain, and forty percent of grain grown worldwide, to animals destined for slaughter (GoVeg.com, "Wasted Resources—Food"), while millions of people die every year from hunger and its effects. Recently there have been sharp increases in the price of many foods due to rising demand, droughts, and global warming, but the effects of feeding so much grain to animals are seldom considered.

SEEKING AND PURSUING PEACE

While not a pacifist religion, Judaism mandates a special obligation to work for peace. Jews are to "seek peace and pursue it" (Ps. 34:15). According to Talmudic sages, God's name is peace, peace encompasses all blessings (*Midrash: Leviticus Rabbah* 9:9), and the first words of the Messiah will be a message of peace (Isa. 52:7). While the Israelites did go forth to battle, they always yearned for the time when "nations shall beat their swords into plowshares . . . and not learn war any more" (Isa. 2:4).

Jewish sages noticed that the Hebrew words for bread (*lechem*) and war (*milchamah*) come from the same root. Based on this, the sages taught that one of the roots of war is a lack of food and other essentials. As indicated above, non-vegetarian diets involve the wasteful use of land, water, energy, and other agricultural commodities, resulting in widespread hunger and poverty, which frequently leads to instability and war. One might say that the slogans of the vegetarian movement and the peace movement can be the same: "Give *peas* a chance."

BIBLICAL TEACHINGS THAT POINT TO VEGETARIANISM

It would be reasonable to say "*dayenu*" (it would be enough) after reading even one of the above arguments, because each constitutes by itself a serious conflict between Jewish values and current practice. The above reasons should impel Jews to adopt a vegan, or at least a vegetarian, diet. In addition to the above serious problems associated with an animal based diet, scriptures also point to a vegan diet.

God's first dietary law was vegetarian/vegan: "And God said: 'Behold I have given you every herb yielding seed which is upon the face of the earth, and every tree, in which is the fruit of a tree yielding seed—to you it shall be for food'" (Gen. 1:29). Jewish classical biblical commentators noted that God's first intention was that people should be vegetarian, including Rashi, Maimonides, Nachmanides, and Abraham Ibn Ezra, and later scholars, such as Rabbi Samson Raphael Hirsch, Moses Cassuto, and Nechama Leibowitz. After providing this initial dietary regime, God saw everything that He had made and "behold, it was very good" (Gen. 1:31). According to Rabbi Abraham Isaac Hacohen Kook, first chief rabbi of pre-state Israel and one of the outstanding Jewish philosophers of the twentieth century, scriptural permission to eat meat (Gen. 9:3) was only a temporary concession to human weakness; a merciful God would not institute an everlasting law permitting the killing of animals for food.

The Torah connects the consumption of meat to uncontrolled lust (Deut. 12:20), while vegetarian foods are looked upon favorably:

> For the Lord thy God brings you into a good land, a land of brooks, of water, of fountains and depths, springing forth in valleys, and hills; a land of wheat and barley, of vines and fig trees, and pome-

granates; a land of olive-trees and honey; a land wherein you shall eat bread without scarceness; you shall not lack anything. . . . And you shall eat and be satisfied, and bless the Lord thy God for the good land which He hath given thee. (Deut. 8:7–10)

Many laws and restrictions (the laws of *kashrut*) concern the preparation and consumption of meat. Rabbi Kook believed that these regulations implied a scolding, and that they were an elaborate apparatus designed to keep alive a sense of reverence for life, with the aim of eventually leading people back to a vegetarian diet. This idea is echoed by Torah commentator Solomon Efrain Lunchitz, author of *k'lee Yakar*:

What was the necessity for the entire procedure of ritual slaughter? [It is for] the sake of self discipline. It is far more appropriate for man not to eat meat; only if he has a strong desire for meat does the Torah permit it, and even this only after the trouble and inconvenience necessary to satisfy his desire. Perhaps because of the bother and annoyance of the whole procedure, he will be restrained from such a strong and uncontrollable desire for meat. (Cited in Chill 1974, 400)

According to Isaac Arama, author of *Akedat Yitzhak*, God established another non-meat diet when the Israelites left Egypt: manna. Manna is described in the Torah as a vegetarian food, "like coriander seed" (Num. 1:7). This diet kept the Israelites in good health for forty years in the desert. However, when they cried out for flesh, which was reluctantly provided by God (in the form of quails), a great plague broke out and many people died. The place where this occurred was named "The Graves of Lust" (Num. 11:34), perhaps providing an early warning of the negative effects of meat consumption.

Rabbi Kook and Rabbi Joseph Albo believed that people would

again be vegetarians in the days of the Messiah. They base this on the prophecy of Isaiah:

> And the wolf shall dwell with the lamb . . .
> And the lion shall eat straw like the ox . . .
> And none shall hurt nor destroy in all My holy mountain. (Isa.
> 11:6–9)

WHY JEWS THINK THEY NEED NOT BE VEGETARIANS AND WHY THEY ARE WRONG

The above arguments strongly support the view that vegetarianism is the diet most consistent with Jewish values and God's wishes. Yet there are challenges to this assertion:

1) The Torah teaches that humans are granted dominion over animals (Gen. 1:26).

Response: Jewish tradition interprets "dominion" as guardianship, or responsible stewardship. We are called upon to work with God in improving the world. Dominion does not mean that people have the right to wantonly exploit animals, and it certainly does not permit us to breed animals and treat them as machines designed solely to meet human needs. Section 2 of "A Vision of Vegetarianism and Peace," a classic piece by Rav Kook states:

> There can be no doubt in the mind of any intelligent person that [the Divine empowerment of humanity to derive benefit from nature] does not mean the domination of a harsh ruler, who afflicts his people and servants merely to satisfy his whim and desire, according to the crookedness of his heart. It is unthinkable that the Divine Law would impose such a decree of servitude, sealed for all eternity, upon the world of God, Who is "good to all, and His mercy is upon all His works." (Ps. 145:9)

This view is reinforced by the fact that, immediately after God gave humankind dominion over animals (Gen. 1:26), God prescribed only vegan foods for humanity (Gen. 1:29).

2) The Torah teaches that only people are created in the Divine Image, meaning that God places far less value on animals.

Response: While the Torah states that only human beings are created "in the Divine Image" (Gen. 5:1), animals are also God's creatures, possessing sentience. The Talmud states that Jews are to be *rachmanim b'nei rachmanim* (compassionate children of compassionate ancestors) and that one who is not compassionate cannot truly be of the seed of Abraham, our father (Babylonian Talmud, *Bezah* 32b). It also states that Heaven grants compassion to those who are compassionate to others, and withholds compassion from those who do not (Babylonian Talmud, *Shabbat* 151b).

3) Vegetarians elevate animals to a level equal to or greater than that of people, which is inconsistent with Judaism.

Response: Concern for animals, and a refusal to treat animals cruelly, does not mean that vegans regard animals as equal to people. Whatever qualities animals have, humans are capable of imagination, rationality, empathy, compassion, and moral choice, and should therefore strive to end the unbelievably cruel conditions under which farm animals are currently raised. This is an issue of sensitivity, not an assertion of equality. In any event, there are many reasons for being vegan along with consideration for animals, including concerns about human health, ecological devastation, and the plight of hungry people.

4) Veganism places greater priority on animal rights than on the many problems related to human welfare.

Response: Vegan diets improve human health, help conserve food and other resources, and put less strain on endangered ecosystems. In view of the many threats related to today's livestock agriculture (such as deforestation and global climate change), working to promote veganism may be the most important action that one can take for humanity.

5) Putting veganism ahead of Jewish teachings creates a new religion with values contrary to Jewish teachings.

Response: Jewish vegetarians are not placing so-called vegan values above Torah principles, but are challenging the Jewish community to apply Judaism's splendid teachings at every level of daily life. As indicated, Jewish teachings require people to treat animals with compassion, guard health, share with hungry people, protect the environment, conserve resources, and seek peace. All are best realized by avoiding animal products.

6) Jews must eat meat on Shabbat and Yom Tov (Jewish holidays).

Response: Since the destruction of the Temple, according to the Talmud (Babylonian Talmud, *Pesachim* 109a), Jews are not required to eat meat to rejoice on sacred occasions. This view is reinforced in *Reshit Chochmah*, *Kerem Shlomo*, and in Rabbi Chizkiah Medini's *Sdei Chemed*, which cite many classical sources on the subject. Several Israeli chief rabbis, including Shlomo Goren (late Ashkenazic chief rabbi of Israel) and Shear Yashuv Cohen (Ashkenazic chief rabbi of Haifa), were/are strict vegetarians.

7) The Torah mandated that Jews eat *korban Pesach* and other *korbanot* (sacrifices).

Response: The great Jewish philosopher Maimonides believed that God permitted blood sacrifices as a concession to popular worship in Biblical times. It was felt that, had Moses not instituted sacrifices, his mission would have failed and Judaism might have disappeared. The Jewish philosopher Abarbanel reinforced Maimonides' position by citing a *midrash* (Rabbinic teaching) indicating that God tolerated sacrifices because the Israelites had become accustomed to sacrifices in

Egypt, but God commanded that these sacrifices be offered only in one central sanctuary in order to wean the Jews from idolatrous practices.

8) Historically, Jews have had problems with certain animal rights groups, which have opposed *shechita* (ritual slaughter).
Response: Jews should consider switching to veganism not because of the views of animal rights groups, whether they are hostile to Judaism or not, but because a vegan diet is most consistent with Jewish teachings. The Torah, not animal rights groups, is the basis for recognizing how far current animal treatment has strayed from fundamental Jewish values. As Rabbi Samson Raphael Hirsch (1962, chap. 60, no. 416) states: "Here you are faced with God's teaching, which obliges you not only to refrain from inflicting unnecessary pain on any animal, but to help and, when you can, to lessen the pain whenever you see an animal suffering, even through no fault of yours."

9) The restrictions of *shechita* (ritual slaughter) minimize pain to animals in the slaughtering process, and thus fulfill Jewish laws on proper treatment of animals.
Response: Focusing on ritual slaughter ignores cruel treatment of animals on "factory farms" for the many months prior to slaughter. Can we ignore the force-feeding of huge amounts of grain to ducks and geese to produce *foie gras*, the removal of calves from their mothers shortly after birth to produce veal (and dairy products), the killing of over 250 million male chicks annually immediately after hatching, the placing of hens in cages so small that the hens can't raise even one wing, and the many other horrors of modern factory farming?

10) If Jews don't eat meat, they will be deprived of the opportunity to fulfill many *mitzvot* (commandments).
Response: By not eating meat, Jews fulfill many *mitzvot*: showing compassion to animals, preserving health, conserving resources, helping to feed the hungry, and preserving Earth. By abstaining from meat,

Jews reduce the chance of accidentally violating several prohibitions of the Torah, such as mixing meat and milk, eating nonkosher animals, and eating forbidden fats or blood. It is important to remember that Torah laws sometimes regulate actions that God would prefer people avoid altogether. For example, God wishes people to live in peace, but he provides commandments relating to war, knowing that human beings will quarrel and seek victories. Similarly, Torah laws restrict taking female captives in wartime—a concession to human weakness. Indeed, the sages go to great lengths to deter people from taking advantage of such dispensations.

11) Judaism teaches that it's wrong not to take advantage of the pleasurable things that God has put on Earth. Since He put animals on Earth, and it's pleasurable to eat them, is it not wrong to refrain from eating meat?

Response: Can eating meat be pleasurable to a sensitive person when he or she knows that, as a result, health is negatively affected, grain is wasted, global warming is increased, the environment is damaged, and animals are cruelly treated? One can indulge in pleasure without reckless cruelty. There are many cases in Judaism where actions that people may consider pleasurable are forbidden or discouraged, such as the use of tobacco, drinking liquor to excess, having sexual relations out of wedlock, and hunting.

12) A movement by Jews toward vegetarianism would lead to less emphasis on *kashrut* (dietary laws), and would eventually bring people to disregard these laws.

Response: Quite the contrary. A vegan diet makes it easier and less expensive to observe the laws of *kashrut*. This has the potential to attract new adherents to kosher laws, and eventually to other important Jewish practices. As a vegan, one need not be concerned with mixing *milchigs* (dairy products) with *fleishigs* (meat products), waiting three or six hours after eating meat before eating dairy products, and storing four complete sets of dishes (two for regular use and two for Passover), complete with silverware, pots, pans, and so on, and many other requirements that affect non-vegans who observe *kashrut*.

13) If everyone were vegan, butchers, *shochtim* (slaughterers), and others dependent on the consumption of animal products for a living would be out of work.

Response: The same kind of question can be asked about other moral issues. What would happen to arms merchants if we had universal peace? What would happen to doctors and nurses if people took better care of themselves—stopped smoking, improved their diets? Immoral and inefficient practices should not be supported because some people earn a living in the process. In any event, labor can shift from the production of animal products to the production of nutritious vegan foods. In England during World War II, when there was a shortage of meat, butchers sold fruits and vegetables. Businesses can shift to selling tofu, miso, falafel, soy burgers, and vegetarian *cholent* (Sabbath hot dish). The shift toward veganism has been (and will likely continue to be) gradual, allowing time for this transition.

14) If everyone became vegan, animals would overrun the planet.

Response: This concern is based on an insufficient understanding of animal populations. For example, there are millions of turkeys around at Thanksgiving. This is not their choice, but is because farmers breed them for the dinner table. Dairy cows are artificially inseminated annually to cause them to produce milk. If we stop manipulating the reproductive abilities of animals in order to satisfy our cravings, their population will decrease, rather than an increase. We are not overrun by animals we *don't* eat, such as lions, elephants, and crocodiles.

15) Instead of advocating veganism, we should alleviate the evils of factory farming so that animals are treated better, less grain is wasted, and fewer chemicals are used that harm human health.

Response: The breeding of animals is "big business." The methods of modern factory farming are the most profitable. Improving conditions would certainly be a step in the right direction, but such changes are strongly resisted by the meat and dairy industries. Humane methods increase the cost of production. Why not abstain from eating animal products as a protest against present practices, while simultaneously working to bring improvements? Even under the best of conditions, why take the life of a creature of God, "whose tender mercies are over all His creatures" (Ps. 145:9), when eating meat is not necessary for proper nutrition?

16) One can work to improve conditions for animals without being a vegan.
Response: This is certainly true. Animal abuse is a widespread problem and there are many ways to improve conditions for animals. However, one should keep in mind that factory farming is the primary source of animal abuse in the United States. According to FARM: "The number of warm-blooded animals brutalized and slaughtered each year [for food] is approximately seventy times greater than the number of animals killed in laboratories, thirty times greater than the number killed by hunters and trappers, and 500 times greater than the number euthanized in pounds." Almost ten billion farm animals are killed annually in the United States alone to produce food. A typical meat eater is personally responsible for the slaughter of twenty-two warm-blooded animals per year, and 1,500 animals in the average omnivore's lifetime.

17) If vegan diets were healthy, doctors would recommend them.
Response: Unfortunately, while doctors are devoted to the well-being of patients, many lack information about food and health. Nutrition is not sufficiently taught at most medical schools. Also, most patients are resistant to dietary change. The accepted medical approach today is to prescribe medications first, and perhaps recommend a change of

diet as an afterthought. Dietary and health awareness are growing, but the financial power of the beef and dairy lobbies (and other groups who gain from the status quo) prevent rapid change.

18) I enjoy eating meat. Why should I give it up?
Response: Jews ought to be motivated by far more than pleasure: *mitzvot*, good deeds and acts of charity, sanctifying ourselves in the realm of the permissible, helping to feed the hungry, pursuing justice and peace, and so forth. Even if one is primarily motivated by considerations of pleasure and convenience, the negative health effects of animal-centered diets are important. It is more difficult to enjoy life without good health.

CONCLUSION

In view of important Jewish mandates to preserve human health, treat animals well, protect the environment, conserve resources, help feed hungry people, and pursue peace—and since animal-centered diets violate and contradict each of these responsibilities—committed Jews should sharply reduce or preferably eliminate their consumption of animal products. It seems particularly important that rabbis and other Jewish leaders recognize the importance of shifting to a vegan diet to avoid the unprecedented environmental catastrophe that is rapidly approaching. It is urgent that *tikkun olam*—the healing and repair of the world—becomes a central issue in synagogues and Jewish schools. Judaism has splendid teachings on environmental conservation and sustainability, and these teachings must be applied in response to current environmental threats. When we read daily reports of the effects of global climate change, such as record heat waves, severe storms, widespread droughts, and the melting of glaciers and polar icecaps, and when climate scientists warn that global climate change may spin out of control within a few years (with disastrous consequences) unless major changes are quickly implemented, it is essential that the

Jewish community fulfills its mandate to be a "light unto the nations," and lead efforts to address these severe threats. Veganism is a Jewish imperative, and for all of the above reasons, religious leaders must help inform Jews as to how animal-based diets and animal agriculture violate basic Jewish mandates.

A more extensive discussion of Jewish teachings on vegetarianism/veganism and how these teachings are violated by the production and consumption of animal products can be found in the author's book Judaism and Vegetarianism (2001), in his articles and podcasts at JewishVeg.com/Schwartz, and in A Sacred Duty: Applying Jewish Values to Help Heal the World (a one-hour documentary) at ASacredDuty.com.

9

Catholic Exemplars

Recent Popes, Medieval Saints, and Animal Liberation

JUDITH BARAD

INTRODUCTION

Philosophical writings by Thomas Aquinas on the nature of animals and the example set by Francis of Assisi continue to both enlighten and inspire contemporary Christians. These Catholic thinkers clearly illustrate the meaning of *catholic* as "universal" and "all-inclusive."

This chapter begins with an address from Pope John Paul II, followed by an examination the work of Aquinas exploring animal souls, which in turn provide an intellectual framework for understanding St. Francis's love for animals. Anecdotes from the life of St. Francis demonstrate the example that he set for modern animal rights activists. Finally, I explore why more people don't follow the lead of these important men from the Catholic tradition.

POPE JOHN PAUL II

In his 1990 address, Pope John Paul II proclaimed that "animals possess a soul and men must love and feel solidarity with" other animals.

He added that all animals are "fruit of the creative action of the Holy Spirit and merit respect," and that they are "as near to God as men are." The pope emphasized that "animals possess the divine spark of life—the living quality that is the soul" (Pacifici 1990). Pope John Paul II did not advance any new Christian ideas in this statement. His comments are rooted in the thirteenth century teachings of St. Thomas Aquinas (ca. 1225–1274), who acknowledged that animals possess a soul.[1]

AQUINAS ON ANIMAL SOULS

Aquinas begins by observing that some things are inert while others are capable of movement, perception, thought, and desire. We call the former "nonliving" and the latter "living." The source of "living" cannot, therefore, be physical. If it were, every material thing would be alive (Aquinas 1964, I.18). Aquinas reasons that a body is alive because of a nonmaterial cause. Without an immaterial substance, or soul, a body is "nonliving." Aquinas concludes that the presence of a soul distinguishes animate beings from inanimate things.

Some might argue that "living" is caused by a physical organ, such as the brain, heart, or lungs. But this alternative fails to consider that the brain, heart, and lungs are *each* a living organ. What makes each of these organs alive? According to Aquinas, only something essentially different from a bodily organ can make organs perform the activities, and bodies "living." This essentially different substance is the soul.

Aquinas outlines three types of souls for three distinct forms of life: plants, nonhuman animals, and human beings. Because plants are "living," Aquinas concludes that they must have souls. The vegetative soul causes a plant to absorb nutrition, grow by cell multiplication, and reproduce (Aquinas I.28.2). Animal souls not only cause individuals to absorb nutrition, grow, and reproduce, but also to have sensation, motion, consciousness, and self-direction. Since animals have a wider range of activities than plants, and can feel pain, Aquinas attributes a "sensitive soul" to animals (Aquinas I.75.3). Human life is yet again different, encompassing all the previously mentioned activities and inclinations, but distinguished from other life-forms by reason and free choice. The human soul, accordingly, is called the "rational soul."

No activity exists apart from substance. Try to imagine running without a body. Nor do color, pleasure, or weight exist without physical substance. In the same way, mental activities require physicality. The activities of perception, thought, and desire, which are unique to animate beings, also require the existence of soul, which unifies an entity. A soul unifies perceptions in a physical body. For example, because a cat has a soul, he or she connects the sound of a can opening with food.

According to Aquinas, humans and "higher" (warm blooded) nonhuman animals possess senses, desire (Aquinas 1951, Lectio V), memory, and imagination. Inferring emotions from the behavior of animals (Aquinas 1964, I–II.40.3), Aquinas acknowledges that they feel joy, sorrow, pain pleasure, fear, anger, and love. He also notes that animals respond emotionally to present events, and to things that they remember. In regard to future events, he writes that animals show hope: "If a dog sees a hare or a hawk spies a bird that is too far away it does not go after it, as though it had no hope of catching it. But if the prey be nearby it makes a try for it, as though it hoped to capture it" (Aquinas 1964, I–II.40.3). Aquinas argues that animals possess an "estimative sense," which provides continuity between nonhuman and human intelligence (Aquinas 1953, 25.2). By means of this sense, nonhuman animals are able to synthesize and organize images stored in their memories in order to act appropriately in a given situation. For example, a sheep will flee a wolf not because the wolf's color and shape are noxious, but because she perceives the wolf as dangerous to her well-being. When she flees the wolf, she is not merely responding to stimulus. Her judgment contains an awareness of a goal.

The Latin word for "soul," *anima*, is the root word in *animated*, which expresses that "which makes living things live." *Anima* also connotes breath. In his 1990 address, Pope John Paul II commented that animals came into being because of the "breath of God" (Pacifici 1990). The soul originates in God's "breath," offered equally to non-human and human animals. *Ruach*, a Hebrew term in the Old Testament, refers to wind, is associated with breath, and brings the power of life to any living organism (through God). *Nephesh*, a Hebrew term usually translated as "soul," is not only linked with breath, but with a range of emotions. In the Greek, Latin, and Hebrew, the term for "soul" is linked with breath, which is given to all living beings by the Creator.

SAINT FRANCIS

If we accept the argument posed by Aquinas, that the soul is the source of mental activities, then it makes sense to treat those with souls differently from inanimate matter.

St. Francis of Assisi (ca. 1182–1226) shared Aquinas's belief that animals have a soul, which means they have mental activities, and he treated them accordingly. He understood the link between the presence of mental activities in animals, and how we treat animals. Francis addressed animals as siblings, believing they would understand his words. His brotherly/sisterly address was based on his acute awareness that humans are also creatures of God. He felt no need to attempt to set himself above other created beings. "Like us, they derive the life of thought, love, and will from the Creator. Not to hurt our humble brethren is our first duty to them; but to stop there is a complete misapprehension of the intentions of Providence. We have a higher mission: God wishes that we should succor them whenever they require it" (AnimalChaplains.com n.d.).

Colorful stories from the life of St. Francis demonstrate his compassion and respect for nonhuman animals; such anecdotes exemplified Francis' heartfelt solidarity with other creatures. According to one story, Francis encountered a youth carrying turtledoves to market. "St. Francis, who ever had singular compassion for gentle creatures . . . looking upon those turtle-doves with compassionate eye, said to the youth: 'I pray thee give them to me, that birds so gentle . . . come not into the hands of cruel men who would slay them.'" After the young man gave the birds to Francis, he said to the turtledoves "sweetly: 'O my sisters, simple, innocent, chaste turtle-doves, why do you let yourselves be taken? Now I desire to save you from death and to make nests for you, so that ye may bring forth fruit and multiply'" (Ugolino 2007, 59). Francis made nests for the turtledoves, where they laid eggs. Eventually, they became as tame as "domestic fowls . . . and never did they depart until St. Francis with his blessing gave them leave to do so" (Ugolino 2007, 59).

Thomas of Celano, an early biographer of St. Francis, writes that when the saint "was staying at the town of Greccio, a little rabbit, that had been caught in a trap was brought alive to him." Francis was "moved to pity" and said: "'Brother rabbit, come to me. Why did you allow yourself to be deceived like this?' As soon as the rabbit was released, he or she "fled to the saint, and . . . lay quiet in his bosom as the safest place possible" (Celano 1200–c. 1260/1270). (Based on the rabbit's behavior, Aquinas would likely say that he or she was seeking the protection of St. Francis.) First Francis caressed the rabbit with "motherly affection," then released him or her to "return free to the woods." But each time the rabbit was placed on the ground, he or she returned "to the saint's bosom." Francis finally commanded the rabbit "to be carried by the brothers to the nearby woods" (Ugolino 2007, 59), freeing the rabbit both from oppression and captivity, much like animal rights activists.

Thomas of Celano records St. Francis's response to a man "who had two little lambs hanging bound over his shoulder. Hearing the lambs' bleating, Francis "was filled with pity, and coming close, he touched them and showed his compassion for them like a mother over her weeping child. And he said to the man: 'Why are you torturing my brother[/sister] lambs tied up and hanging like this?'" The man explained that he was taking them to market, where "'those who buy them will kill them and eat them.' 'God forbid,' replied the saint; 'this must not happen. Take the mantle I am wearing as their price and give the lambs to me'" (Ugolino 2007, 71). After rescuing the lambs, he was unsure what to do with them, so he returned them to the man, "commanding him not to sell them . . . nor to do them any harm, but to keep them, feed them. And take care of them conscientiously" (Celano 1200–c. 1260/1270).

Perhaps the most moving stories from the life of St. Francis are those that describe his response to helpless animals caught in the grip of human exploitation, indifference, and cruelty. In such stories we see Francis's love expressed in the protection that he offered these gentle, vulnerable beings. We also see the returned affections of non-human animals. Francis understood and acted on his responsibility to assist other creatures, and to shield them from harm. He satisfied their needs and liberated them, much the same as would contemporary animal rights activists.

Although Francis admired and frequently tended gentle, innocent animals, he also showed respect and care for more aggressive creatures (including humans). The most well-known of these incidents involves a wolf. The citizens of Agobio were tormented by a bloodthirsty wolf, who "not only devoured animals but also men and women" (Ugolino 2007, 54). Since all attempts to capture the wolf had failed, no one dared leave the city. When the townspeople wanted to kill the wolf, Francis intervened.

Walking along the road outside of town, Francis encountered the deadly wolf. Making the sign of the cross, he advanced, saying, "'Come here, brother wolf; I command you, in the name of Christ, neither to harm me nor anybody else.'" Francis was only armed with his love for God, and was aware of the presence of God in the wolf. Going over to the wolf, he greeted him as a brother and offered to make peace between the wolf and the people. The wolf "came, gentle as a lamb, and laid himself down at the feet of St. Francis" (Ugolino 2007, 55). (Using the analysis of Aquinas, we might surmise that the wolf used his estimative sense to judge that Francis meant no harm.)

Treating the wolf with respect and courtesy, St. Francis encouraged a pact of peace between the wolf and the villagers. Francis understood that the wolf only attacked townspeople and domestic animals because he was hungry, so Francis promised the wolf, on behalf of the citizens of Agobio, that the villagers would feed him regularly. He then secured the wolf's agreement that he would no longer prey on people or flocks. Agreeing "by movements of his body and tail and eyes, and by bowing his head, the wolf showed that he accepted that which St. Francis said" (Ugolino 2007, 56).

The wolf then followed Francis into the city, where the townspeople promised to feed him on a regular basis. The wolf, in turn, publicly confirmed his promise by giving St. Francis his right paw. From then on, the wolf "entered familiarly into the houses, going from door to door, neither doing injury . . . nor receiving any; and he was courteously nourished by the people; and, as he thus went through the town and through the houses, never did any dog bark after him" (Ugolino 2007, 58). Two years later, the wolf died of old age, and the people grieved greatly.

Some people find the anecdote of the wolf to be so unbelievable that they view this story as having no literal foundation. But those of us who, like Aquinas, are aware of animal intelligence, are also aware that animals, when treated with respect and love, are capable of responding much like the wolf in this story. We now have substantiated records of people listening to wolves and communicating with them; Jim and James Dutcher produced a documentary entitled *Living with Wolves*, which recounts their six-year interactions with a particular pack of wolves, recording their "deep relationship with the wolves." They note: "It was the kind of unshakable trust that wolves usually share only with their own pack, a bond that would last a lifetime" (see <www.livingwithwolves.org> and Ugolino 2007, 71).

Their documentary indicates that Francis's interaction with the wolf need not be viewed as symbolic.

CONTEMPORARY POPES AND CATHOLIC TRADITIONS

Francis was a model animal rights activist, one who never resorted to violence of any kind, but liberated animals and urged others to treat them with the respect generated by love. Perhaps St. Francis set an example for Pope Pius XII (elected in 1939), whose gardener brought him an injured bird. The pope named the bird Gretel, kept her in his apartment, and helped return the bird to health. The pope recognized that she was a social being with various desires that could not be met by humanity, and so he brought her several companions after she recovered. The birds were released from their cages while the pope ate, and the pope was aware of their pleasure when they perched on his shoulder, or on the table, where they enjoyed their own lunch— small dishes of seeds. Like St. Francis, Pope Pius XII rescued a bird from harm, saw to the bird's needs, and as with Francis, the birds responded by sharing company in trust.

Before Pope John Paul II spoke about animal souls, he visited Assisi, the birthplace of St. Francis. In his 1982 "Message on Reconciliation" (J. R. Hyland n.d.), he compared Francis's love for animals with anticipation of the Peaceable Kingdom, envisioned by the Prophet Isaiah, a world in which all God's creatures will live in peace. The pontiff also discussed Francis's "solicitous care, not only toward [people] but also toward animals and nature in general" (J. R. Hyland n.d.). He noted Francis's "faithful echo" of God's love (J. R. Hyland n.d.). As a result, Pope John Paul II stated that all Christians "are called to a similar attitude" (J. R. Hyland n.d.). With these words, John Paul II affirmed not only the ontological value of animals, but also our responsibility to treat other creatures as siblings—as similarly creatures of one creator.

Doubtless, St. Francis influenced Catholic teachings, which state:

Animals are God's creatures. He surrounds them with his providential care. By their mere existence they bless him and give him glory. Thus men owe them kindness. We should recall the gentleness with which saints like St. Francis of Assisi or St. Philip Neri treated animals. . . . It is contrary to human dignity to cause animals to suffer or die needlessly." (People for the Ethical Treatment of Animals n.d.)

It should now come as no surprise that, before becoming Pope Benedict XVI in 2002, Cardinal Ratzinger (when asked about the rights of animals) said:

At any rate, we can see that they are given into our care, that we cannot just do whatever we want with them. Animals, too, are God's creatures. . . . Certainly, a sort of industrial use of creatures, so that geese are fed in such a way as to produce as large a liver as possible, or hens live so packed together that they become just caricatures of birds, this degrading of living creatures to a commodity seems to me in fact to contradict the relationship of mutuality that comes across in the Bible. (People for the Ethical Treatment of Animals n.d.)

CONCLUSION

In our mechanized, technological society, we seem to need to feel special in relation to other creatures. While we are all special, unique individuals, we aren't "better than" other creatures, as our egos might indicate. Egotistical people ignore the needs and rights of others, maintaining a self-serving perspective, eager to gratify their own interests at the expense of others. This is not the Catholic way.

Egoism also manifests on a broader level through racism, sexism, homophobia, and religious bigotry. Egoism sees one's own group as superior to any other group. The supposed inferiority of another group is then used to justify differential treatment. In this way, egoism manifests as speciesism, which champions the view that nonhuman animals are inferior to human beings, and that we are therefore justified in exploiting nonhuman animals for our purposes, however paltry. This is not the Catholic way. The Catholic faith encourages believers to be spiritual rather than egotistical. Spirit, unlike ego, is not competitive.

Thomas Aquinas taught that animals are intelligent beings who possess a soul. St. Francis treated animals as siblings, adopting a humble, catholic (universal, all-inclusive) relationship with the many creatures of the earth. Spiritual people, like St. Francis, have a salutary humility lacking in egotistical people. If Christians adopt a spiritual viewpoint, following the example of medieval saints who influenced recent popes, the world will be a more loving and peaceful place for all living beings.

10

Christian Mysticism

Unity and Love for All

ANDREW FITZ-GIBBON

Little mouse! Little mouse! Little mouse, kindly one!
Little mouse! Little mouse!
Little mouse, beloved one!

—CARMINA GADELICA

A mystic is a person who is deeply aware of the powerful presence of the
divine Spirit: someone who seeks, above all, the knowledge and love of
God and who experiences to an extraordinary degree the profoundly per-
sonal encounter with the energy of the divine life. Mystics often perceive
the presence of God throughout the world of nature and in all that is alive,
leading to a transfiguration of the ordinary all around them.

—URSULA KING (2003, 3)

INTRODUCTION

As a religious phenomenon, mysticism is difficult to categorize. There
has never been a church of mystics; institutions run contrary to mysticism (though Quakers come close).

In Ernest Troeltsch's (1912/1992) sociological typology, mysticism is considered the "third" form of religion, and the least important historically. The church is the type of religion into which one is born, which provides rituals and life passages, and which provides communities with religious legitimacy. The sect is a form of religion one joins as an adult, characterized by disdain for the world and a radical commitment to specific aims. According to Troeltsch, mysticism is the form of religion chosen by one who is unhappy both with the compromises of the church and the radical nature of the sect. Both church and sect are irrelevant to the mystic, yet mystics can be found both in churches and in sects: "In the widest sense of the word, mysticism is simply the insistence upon a direct and inward and present religious experience" (Troeltsch 730).

William James shifts the discussion from a sociological to a psychological analysis in his classic, *The Varieties of Religious Experience* (1982). He agrees with Troeltsch that the essence of mysticism is experience, but notes that the importance of mysticism is in the "mystical state of consciousness."

Most mystics never align with mysticism, but are so labeled by others. What, then, characterizes the mystic? At its core, mysticism is characterized by direct spiritual experience, an understanding of the unity of all things, and a profound sense of love. In *Christian Mysticism* (1899, 335–48), W. R. Inge offers twenty-six classical definitions of mysticism, adding several more in *Mysticism in Religion* (1947, 25–26). Inge found remarkable consensus among scholars regarding mystics, with one exception: mystics divide over the value of ordinary consciousness and the visible world. Some mystics mistrust the material world; others recognize the sensible as symbolic of ultimate reality. Ursula King's contemporary definition, at the start of this chapter, summarizes this consensus, yet falls on the side of the sacramental (the sensible world as mediator of ultimate realities). This difference is crucial with respect to animal advocacy.

Historically, how have mystics thought about and treated nonhuman animals? The short answer is: mixed, but better than most. There is no systematic treatment of animal advocacy in the writings of the mystics. This is partly because animal rights/advocacy is a product of modernity; we cannot expect pre-modern mystics to address contemporary issues. Nonetheless, the mystical tradition provides hints and suggestions that offer valuable reflections on animal rights and animal advocacy. This chapter focuses on Christian mystics (though Asian mysticism is more similar than different) examining Oneness and the lives of mystics to explore what mysticism has to say with regard to animal advocacy.

MATERIAL WORLD AND MYSTICAL ONENESS

Mysticism has often been characterized as a renunciation of the sensual world in the hope of experiencing the transcendent. Ultimately, the material world is viewed among mystics as mere illusion—a shadow of the real; for many mystics there can be no friendship with the world. To dismiss nature as illusory might cause a mystic to dismiss nonhuman animals along with nature. If spirit alone is important, nature (including nonhuman animals) is at best irrelevant; at worst, it is something to be met with hostility.

Counter-intuitively, mystics have often proven to be exceptionally kind to nonhuman animals, caring for other animals as friends and companions (see narratives on desert mystics and animals below). Mystics generally feel compassionate love for all; their compassion reaches beyond the human community, and love seeks the best for the beloved. To seek the best precludes abuse and, for many mystics, prohibits eating flesh. Conversely, cultures focused on the material world have, at times, been exceptionally cruel (for example, consumerism, capitalism, and industrial cruelty in animal agriculture.) How might we account for this? Why would those dedicated to nonmaterial realities look *more* kindly on earthly creatures?

Mystics have generally been either pantheists or panentheists— the practical implications of both are much the same (see discussion in Soelle 2001, 103–8). Pantheism teaches that all that exists is God and God is all that exists. Panentheism says that God is in all things, immanently, yet God is also above all things, transcendently (Fox 1983, 88–92; 1991, 7–13). Mystics like Meister Eckhart (ca. 1260–ca. 1328) have been termed pantheist, though Eckhart's conception of the Godhead (unknowable, transcendent) suggests that he was more likely a panentheist, or at least in Soelle's (2001) words "a precursor of panentheism" (107).

Among traditions in the West, the early Celtic church was clearly panentheistic (influenced by pre-Christian paganism). James Mackey says of Celtic spirituality:

> This is a world of eternally immanent, incarnate spirit—spirit that transcends the whole universe of being toward the ultimate and eternal perfection of the universe, precisely because [spirit] is imminent in the whole. (Cited in Davies and O'Loughlin 1999, xv)

At least in the West, pantheism and panentheism share a common understanding of the unity of all—"the One" of Plotinus—and it is not always clear whether the One is to be understood in pantheistic or panentheistic terms:

> The power and nature of Soul encompass heaven and guide it according to its will. To all this vast expanse, as far as it extends, it gives itself, and every interval, both large and small, is filled with Soul. . . . Soul enlivens all things with its whole self and all Soul is present everywhere. . . . And vast and diversified though this universe is, it is [O]ne by the power of soul and a god because of soul. The sun is also a god, because ensouled, and the other stars, and if we ourselves partake of the Divine, this is the cause. (Plotinus 1991, 5.1.2)

> This universe is a single living being embracing all living beings within it, and possessing a single Soul that permeates all its parts to

the degree of their participation in it. Every part of this sensible universe is fully participant in its material aspect, and in respect of soul, in the degree to which it shares in the World Soul. (4.4.32)

The unity of all—all as divine (or infused by divinity)—is not easy for those schooled in dualisms (of fact/value, mind/body, and human/ nonhuman) to grasp. (Oneness even proves difficult grammatically.)

Historically, Oneness has been more prevalent in Asian religious traditions than in Abrahamic traditions; Western mystics who veered toward a sense of Oneness were often declared heretics. Yet the mystic's understanding of the divine encompassed in all that exists is intriguing for animal advocates (as for environmentalists). Oneness offers no duality between human and other forms of life. Because the divine dwells equally in nonhuman animals as in the human animal, all animals (as God bearers) must be treated with respect.

PRAXIS: ANIMAL NARRATIVES AND INCANTATIONS

While seeking ultimate reality often led many mystics to shun the company of other human beings, their search also tended to lead them toward the friendship of nonhuman animals. Myths of the lives of mystics often seem historically unlikely, but it is not necessary to claim these stories as such. These many animal narratives provide a strong religious tradition of care for nonhumans. It is beside the point whether St. Cuthbert's feet, on return from his night of prayer in the ice-cold sea, were literally dried by his sea otter friends. What matters is this accumulation of many stories about animals associated with mystics.

Helen Waddell (focusing on legends from the desert fathers and mothers of the fourth century, and Celtic traditions from the sixth and seventh centuries) translated many animal narratives from Latin into English (Waddell and Gibbings 1934/1995). Edward Sellner (1993) also compiled stories of Celtic mystics in which hermits, having chosen a life of solitude, encounter animals. Universally, relations between mystics and nonhuman animals are positive. A few instances from Waddell and Gibbings (1934/1995) make the point:

- A desert monk whose sole friend is an ox feeds a lion dates by hand (3–5).
- A horse anticipates and mourns Columba's death. Columba calls the horse "this lover of mine" (42–45).
- A lion is helped by abbot Gerasimus, then becomes the abbot's disciple. On the abbot's death the distraught lion lies on the old man's grave, and dies (23–26).
- A wolf shares a monk's bread, then becomes penitent after stealing bread in the monk's absence (6–7).
- Macarius heals the eyes of a hyena's whelp. The hyena brings a sheepskin to the saint, who refuses it: "As that which thou has brought to me comes of violence, I will not take it." (13) The hyena promises: "I will not kill a creature alive" but will only eat what is already dead. In the event that the hyena can find no food, the monk promises to share his bread (12–14).

And from Sellner (1993):

- A befriended fox carries Ciaran's Psalter, and Ciaran hides the fox under his cowl from hunting hounds (80–81).
- A stag visits Ciaran, allowing the monk to use his horns as a reading stand (82–83).
- In the story of Kevin, "a blackbird came from the woods to his hut" and hopped on Kevin's palm. "Kevin kept his hand so the blackbird would have a place to build her nest. He remained there until she had hatched her brood" (161).

In these stories, animals work alongside monks, and mystics show sympathy, kindness, and protection toward their animal friends.

Francis of Assisi is perhaps the mystic best known for his relationship with animals. Thomas of Celano (died ca.1260) wrote three volumes about Francis shortly after his death. Thomas says of Francis: "He was a man of great fervor, feeling much sweetness and piety even toward lesser, irrational creatures" (Armstrong and Brady 1982, 74). Francis talked regularly to animals and exhorted them to love God, and nonhuman animals "sensed the sweetness of his love" (75). Francis' care for nonhuman animal extended beyond mammals. He "had the same tender feeling toward fish. When he had the chance he threw back live fish that had been caught, and warned them not to be caught again" (75). "Even for worms he had a warm love. . . . Francis used to pick worms up from the road, and put them in a safe place, so that they would not be crushed" (90). Stories of Francis are stories of tenderness toward water birds, bees, pheasants, and a singing cricket whom Francis calls "my sister cricket!" (275).

Prayers and poems written by mystics also offer a glimpse into their relationship with animals. In the late nineteenth century, Alexander Carmichael traveled the highlands and islands of Scotland, listened to old Gaelic prayers, poems, incantations, and charms, and translated them into English. Though it's unlikely that these delightful runes go back to the early Celtic church, it is clear that they are part of a long and unbroken tradition of care for animals that is rooted in premodern Christianity. These poems reveal a world in which animals are greatly respected and loved, and are understood to have intrinsic value:

The charm placed of Brigit
About her neat [cows], about her kine,
About her horses, about her goats,
About her sheep, about her lambs;

Each day and each night,
In heat and in cold,

Each early and late,
Each darkness and light;

To keep them from marsh,
To keep them from rock,
To keep them from pit,
To keep them from bank. (Carmichael 1992, 339–40)

She milked some of her animals, and her approach to milking provides a stark contrast with factory farming and the contemporary dairy industry: "Give the milk, my treasure, / Give quietly, with steady flow, / Give the milk, my treasure, / With steady flow and calmly" (346).

CONCLUSION

It would be unfair to expect to find a full-blown discussion of animal rights among the works and stories of mystics from centuries long gone. Nonetheless, the mystical view of Oneness (that the divine *is in all*, and an ethic of compassionate love for all), and the tender stories of loving relationships between mystics and nonhuman animals (revealed in hagiographies, prayers, poems, and incantations) suggest a spiritual outlook and way of life deeply sympathetic to contemporary animal advocacy.

11

A Society of Friends (Quaker-Christian) View

Prophets and the Hidden Paradise

GRACIA FAY BOUWMAN ELLWOOD

T he foundation of Society of Friends (or Quaker) compassion for animals is the Divine Light, Love that is present throughout the universe, drawing all beings into unity. Its opposite, the force of alienation, blindness ("darkness"), and death, drives the massive cultural evils of exploitation, enslavement, and killing. In the tradition of Jesus and other Hebrew prophets, a Friend who advocates for animals becomes a voice and a means of liberation and unity.

GOD-WITH-US: THE INNER LIGHT

Members of the Society of Friends who defend animals welcome the burgeoning of animal concerns among Christians, whose basic motivation tends to be God's compassion for all creatures, and God's charge that we be good stewards of creation. While activist Friends have no quarrel with this motivation (which emphasizes God's transcendence), a Friend's starting point is the inner Light/Love, which places emphasis on divine immanence. Historically, proponents of these two motivations have been at odds, but there is no need for such antagonism. Both themes are integral to the Christian faith, and complement one another.

What Friends mean by the inner Light cannot be succinctly stated, partly because most Friends are more concerned with experience and action than with discursive thought or concrete definitions, and partly because the reality intended by the term cannot be encompassed in words. Light imagery began with the first generations of Friends (in seventeenth century England), particularly because of the religious, social, and political upheaval of that time. Many seekers were longing for illumination that carried conviction that could override warring human authorities. But the Light is not merely a figure of speech; spiritually aware persons have often perceived a timeless, mind-expanding radiance charged with love. The Light is both power and Presence.

THE OCEAN OF LIGHT AND LOVE

George Fox was among such spiritual seekers. His impassioned quest led him to abandon human authorities, and led to visions of a marvelous Light together with an unshakable conviction of being led by the divine Spirit. He writes: "I saw that there was an ocean of darkness and death, but an infinite ocean of light and love, which flowed over the ocean of darkness. And in that . . . I saw the infinite love of God" (Fox 1997, 19). To express this kind of experience, early Friends used not only the words *Light* and *Love* but also *Spirit*, *Christ*, *Teacher*, *Seed*, *Truth*, *Principle*, *Power*, *Life*, and *That of God*. Howard H. Brinton helpfully categorizes these terms as "personal" and "less personal" (Brinton 1965, 30); perhaps "impersonal" would be more appropriate. But some of these concepts are both. For example, *Seed* refers both to the divine potential within each person, and to Christ, the child of God and humanity. These words attempt to express the ineffable; they are means by which we, who are finite, try to describe what we know of the infinite.

Although the term *Light* is usually privileged by Friends, *Love* (emphasized in Fox's visionary account) is of equal importance. *Love* points to the divine as a magnetic power that draws together that which is separated: "As people come into subjection to the Spirit of God . . . they may . . . receive the Word of wisdom that opens all things, and come to know the hidden unity in the Eternal Being" (Fox 1997, 28). Another expression of this unifying power urges us to "mind that which is eternal, which gathers your hearts together up to the Lord, and lets you see that you are written in one another's hearts" (Fox 2008, Epistle 24).

As we are drawn to God, we find we are written in one another's hearts. We sense this when we "answer to That of God" (a favorite expression of Friends), which dwells in another person. Because we are aware of this link to God in each individual, we don't relate to others simply as independent beings. To the extent that we have given ourselves over to the Spirit, our words and actions include an element of light responding to Light, of love manifesting Love, of individual relating to the Infinite. This situation is not limited to the interaction of one spiritually awakened person to another, but of any awakened person to all other humans. To each and every individual is due reverence for the Light she or he bears. Even within the depraved, this Light is never extinct.

Because of this reverence for the inner Light/Love, Friends reject war and violence. Though we have the Light "in differing measures," depending on our degree of spiritual openness, the Light remains one; thus violence to another is violence to oneself and to God: "When you did it to one of the least of these My brothers [and sisters], you did it to Me" (Matthew 25:40). Jesus expresses this same principle of active nonviolence in a passage which Friends call the Peace Testimony: "Love your enemies and do them good" (Luke 6:35).

TESTING THE LIMITS

Traditionally, most Friends have understood the indwelling Light, which implicitly draws beings together and underlies the Friends' mandate for Peace, as strictly a human affair. In a world in which class, gender, race, sexuality, religion, and economic divisions foster violence, the principle of Light among all of humanity seemed radical enough. But some Friends' voices are now questioning this historic restriction to humanity. We are not the only sentient beings on this planet. Why have Friends been so certain that nonhuman animals are excluded from the community in which the Light, which is also Love, draws us together? If divine love is infinite, it is at work wherever a sentient being feels kinship with another.

No one can reasonably deny that nonhuman animals are strongly drawn to one another. Some, like barn owls and geese, mate for life. Most mothers must tend their young if they are to survive, and from cows to chickens, mothers show deep attachment and devotion to their young, as do fathers of many species, such as wolves and emperor penguins (Masson 1999). Among many who live in extended families, such as cows and sheep, one also finds sustained friendships. Some animals even bond across species and genus, such as the remarkable case of a giant tortoise and an orphaned baby hippo living in a preserve near the coast of Kenya after the tsunami of 2004 (Hatkoff *et al.* 2006). Humans have long demeaned such devotion by labeling it "instinct," rather than acknowledge any form of affection, caring, attachment, or love. But as we shall see, such reductionist language is no more to be trusted than the contemptuous terms slave owners used for the "lesser race," who were thought to be inferior in intelligence, and lacking normal human feelings.

THE HIDDEN PARADISE

An aspect of the implicit "unity in the Eternal Being," which I call "the hidden paradise," entails a state of harmony and beauty like that of Eden as depicted in Genesis. Invisible to most eyes, this hidden paradise permeates our world, despite pervasive alienation, violence, and pain. Fox experienced this hidden reality in another vision during the period of his spiritual breakthrough:

> Now was I come up in spirit through the flaming sword, into the paradise of God. All things were new; and all the creation gave unto me another smell than before, beyond what words can utter . . . [And] the creation was opened to me. . . . I was at a stand in my mind whether I should practice [herbal medicine] for the good of mankind, seeing the nature and virtues of things were so opened to me. (Fox 1997, 27)

Fox describes union with the renewed creation, manifest in a tele-pathic-intuitive perception of the essential nature of plants and other natural phenomena, a state in which "all things, visible and invisible, are seen by the divine Light of Christ" (Fox 1997, 29). This paradise is not a mere figure of speech describing an ephemeral mood; two or three years later, during a long and harsh interrogation by the magistrates in Derby (England), Fox asserted that he was in the paradise of God and in the state of Adam's innocence (Fox 1997, 51).

Other mystics and poets support Fox's account. For example, Fox's contemporary Thomas Traherne, a devout Anglican clergyman, describes a childhood in which he "seemed as one brought into the Estate of Innocence. . . . I saw all in the peace of Eden. . . . [A]ll time was Eternity. . . . The [grain was lustrous] and immortal. . . . The green trees . . . transported and ravished me . . . , they were such strange and wonderful things" (Traherne 1960, 109–10). Though he later learned "the Dirty Devices of the world" (110) and had to unlearn them, he never fully lost his awareness of the presence of hidden splendor: "The world is a mirror of infinite beauty, yet no man sees it. . . . It is the Paradise of God" (Traherne 1960, 15). Similarly, Wordsworth reflects on a "celestial light" that he experienced when he was a youth in "meadow, grove, and stream," but could no longer perceive in adulthood, a "sense sublime" of "a motion and a spirit" that dwells in nature and humanity (Wordsworth 1952, 260, 258).

Neither Traherne nor Wordsworth seemed to realize the harmony of Eden in their relations with animals, but poet William Cowper (1731–1800) did. In "The Task" he lovingly describes nature scenes, with occasional references to traces of paradise, and the "ray of heavenly light gilding all forms" (Cowper n.d., 100). He contrasts nature's harmony with the artificiality and corruption of the city; with prophetic fervor he excoriates the "detested sport" of hunting "which owes its pleasures to another's pain" (Cowper n.d., 47–48). He creates a mini-paradise for a few hares, whom he befriends, feeding them by hand and harboring them in his house from "the sanguinary yell of cruel man" and "the savage din of the swift pack" (Cowper n.d., 47). Although he believed that eating meat could be justified scripturally, it is likely that he chose vegetarianism, since he lived very simply, noting that we are only "carnivorous, through sin" (Cowper n.d., 113).

Recognition of the hidden paradise is also found in the work of Charles W. S. Williams (Anglican theologian and literary critic). In his poems and novels, and his studies of Dante and Wordsworth, Williams proposes that anyone who falls in love gains the temporary ability to perceive this same divine splendor in a human being, a splendor coexisting with the beloved's very real faults and sins. He views the in-love experience as an awakening, a challenge to the lover to learn to love *all* his or her neighbors in this same way, even after the light is no longer visible (Shideler 1962; Williams 2005).

FRIENDS AND THE DIET OF PARADISE

Animals are not explicitly mentioned in the context of Fox's vision, nor does he spell out the implications of the hidden paradise human/

animal relations. Although well versed in scripture, he apparently did not note that the diet of paradise in Genesis 1 and 2 is explicitly and exclusively a plant-based one. While Fox expressed compassion for a horse more than once (Fox, 1997, 376), and rejected hunting and hawking as frivolous pastimes, he never questioned the killing of animals for food. Furthermore, he denied that animals perceive by means of the divine Light: "What they know they know naturally. But all [persons] knowing one another in the Light . . . this differ[entiates] you from the beasts of the field" (Fox 2008, Epistle 149). He is not saying that the Light/Spirit is *not* present in animals, only that they don't have an unmediated knowledge of the world, which he expects Friends to have. However, later Friends, though aware of the Light, don't generally claim to experience this telepathic-intuitive knowledge.

Nonetheless, most Friends have adopted Fox's ambivalence regarding nonhuman animals, maintaining a theoretically benevolent outlook toward other species that is neither explored nor consistently lived. True, one finds occasional signs of deep compassion for nonhuman animals in Friends' journals. For example, when John Woolman (1720–1772) lived in England, he was so distressed over the cruel exploitation of horses for transport, in all weather, causing great suffering and sometimes death, that he refused to use stagecoaches for travel or mail (Woolman 1971, 183). He also showed compassion for chickens caged on the deck of the ship on which he sailed to England, some of whom became sick or died as a result of exposure. Woolman even discerned that God's love extended to sparrows, and "where the love of God is verily perfected . . . a tenderness toward all creatures . . . will be experienced," and we will not want to "lessen that sweetness of life in the animal creation which the great Creator intended for them" (Woolman 1971, 178–79). But in Woolman's case, as with most Friends, the institution of animal agriculture remains unchallenged.

However, Woolman's neighbor and a fellow Friend, farmer

Joshua Evans, not only showed sympathy for nonhuman animals, but understood the implications of this feeling for diet: "My mind was enlarged in love of God and to my brethren, my neighbors and fellow creatures throughout the world . . . [and] I considered that life was sweet in all living creatures, and taking it away became a very tender point" (cited in Brinton 1972, 90). He linked his concern for animal life to the biblical paradise story in Genesis. Before the Fall, "all the Lord's works were in harmony" (cited in Brinton 1972, 88). Not only did we begin in a shared paradise, but we are expected to return to this paradise. The new life in Christ is meant to restore that pre-Fall condition. A little later Evans writes: "I believe my dear Master has been pleased to try my faith and obedience by teaching me that I ought no longer to partake of anything that had life" (cited in Brinton 1972, 90). In referring to the Genesis creation story, in which a vegan diet is provided by God, Evans points out that paradise necessitates peaceful harmony with animals. Killing or otherwise exploiting sensitive fellow beings is incompatible with the Love that underlies this harmony. As a result, Evans (and perhaps several others in Woolman's circle), followed a vegetarian diet—even when pursuing a traveling ministry on foot in sometimes primitive conditions (Gilbert 2005, 1986). His religiously based commitment and discipline suggests that the unexamined benevolence of most Friends is unsatisfactory.

We also find a scattering of Friends in the nineteenth century who practiced the diet given by God. In Britain from 1902 until 2003 these Friends united in the Friends Vegetarian Society, spreading the word of peace via books, periodicals, and conferences. The Friends Vegetarian Society of North America, formed in 1982, likewise met in conferences and (until 1995) published an insightful quarterly journal titled *The Friendly Vegetarian*. In 2004, a group of California Friends established the monthly online journal *The Peaceable Table*, "for the mutual support, education, and inspiration of Quakers and other people of faith in the practice of love for our fellow animals and the observance of a nonviolent diet" (Ellwood 2008, home page).

ENGAGING THE OCEAN OF DARKNESS

But the paradise of Love and Light remains largely hidden. In this world, the ocean of darkness and death seems much more evident, and even spiritually awakened persons are not free of darkness. Throwing practical considerations to the wind and naively living as though all were paradise (as some newly awakened persons try to do) can create problems, and even put people in danger. Conversely, being acutely aware of the darkness, and acting to promote paradisal harmony, may cause the princes of darkness to feel threatened, and to respond with increased violence. *Therefore, it is necessary to live in both worlds at once—the world of Light and the world as it is.*

Because Friends stress the inner Light in all persons, including equality and social justice, Friends have tended to regard the ocean of darkness and death less in terms of personal sin than societal evils. The problem is not just wicked individuals, but wicked systems. Societal evil manifests in institutions when a dominant group systematically oppresses another class, shutting them out from many societal benefits, for the advantage of the dominant group. Nonhuman animals are not only oppressed, but cruelly exploited and systematically slaughtered for the perceived benefit of the dominant group.

With the collaboration of science and religion, institutions of societal evil attempt to hide their malignant nature by demeaning their victims, concealing the horrors of their actions with euphemisms, misleading images, and outright lies. Society's beneficiaries collaborate by ignoring evidence of evil. Until this pervading network of deception is broken, beneficiaries and many of those who carry out harmful acts cannot be considered fully responsible. Such semi-aware participants in society's evils are caught in original sin, but their poisonous outlook and actions, because they are not aware of their own cruelty, are not fully developed into actual or deliberate sin (Suchocki 1999, 16–19, 129–42). Some participants, however, may be quite deliberate in their evil acts, and all citizens must withdraw from their involvement, and return (Hebrew *t'shuvah*) to the Light, to God-with-Us.

Although Christians (and Christianity) have collaborated with many societal evils, they have inherited a tradition of prophetic challenge to evil from Judaism. "Prophetic" does not refer primarily to prediction of future events, but to making radical social-political critiques that tear away the mask of ignorance from societal evils. A rejection of slavery as experienced in Egypt is the bedrock of Judaism's Exodus. This narrative presents the god of Judaism as a god of justice and compassion, who identifies with victims of society's evils, and as a God who delivers the downtrodden through their own empowered and empowering actions. A number of prophets (beginning with Amos) carry forward this liberating tradition. They proclaim the word of God that (among other things) denounces oppression and demands a just and compassionate society. Some New Testament scholars have pointed out that under the exploitative rule of imperial Rome, Jesus' ministry of good news for the poor and despised, as reported in the synoptic gospels and as reflected in the epistle of James, reveals Jesus renewing this prophetic tradition.

Friends' conviction that all persons bear the Light makes them heirs to this prophetic tradition, though few Friends explicitly make this Biblical link. Reverence for the Light undercuts conventional social ranking and exploitative social systems; no one exists merely or primarily to benefit another. Friends' testimonials of simplicity and equality are guides in living out this central commitment to the god in every individual. Furthermore, our direct access to the Divine within means that this inner Spirit may call anyone to oppose a societal evil. Such a person will feel a "concern," and may be called to "speak truth to power," to take one's prophetic critique not only to the public but to those who control societal systems.

During the nineteenth century, individual Friends such as Anna

Sewell (author of *Black Beauty*) and her mother, Mary Wright Sewell, prophetically championed the cause of nonhuman animals. But there appears be no Friends' organization denouncing animal abuse until 1891, when the Friends Anti-Vivisection Association was founded in England, later expanding its focus to include other animal issues. In 1978, this group became Quaker Concern for Animals (QCA). The QCA maintains a website, publishes a newsletter twice yearly (both online and in hard copy), and networks worldwide with other faith-based groups on behalf of nonhuman animals. Most commonly, the QCA lobbies governments and other responsible bodies to bring change. Its present clerk, Marian Hussenbux, stresses the importance of enjoying the world's beauty, thus implicitly affirming the hidden paradise while working to save victims of the world's darkness (Hussenbux 2007).

Perhaps the most prominent Quaker challenging the abuse of animals was Ruth Winsten Harrison, who broke the silence surrounding factory farming in her influential 1964 book *Animal Machines* (with an introduction by Rachel Carson). As a result, some of the worst abuses of English agribusiness were outlawed.

FRIENDS AND ABOLITION

The long struggle against human slavery provides an apt historical example of Friends' prophetic opposition to cultural evil, and provides a model for present-day Friends working to free nonhuman animals.

Following scattered individual denunciations, the Friends' movement against slavery began officially in 1688 in Dublin, Pennsylvania, with a proposed minute (Friends' statement of belief) condemning human slavery (Henderich *et al.*, 1688). Friends passed the minute first to one and then another umbrella group, evading the issue until the minute was finally dismissed by the Pennsylvania Yearly Meeting. Shamefully, many Friends were complicit; they affirmed the inner

Light and equality, while simultaneously exploiting their human "property." However, other Friends remained concerned, and between 1675 and 1710 many Maryland Friends freed African-Americans whom they were exploiting as slaves. Other well-meaning Friends kept and even bought "slaves" to insure that they were humanely treated and received an education.

In 1727, with the support of many concerned Friends in North America, a minute censuring the slave trade was passed by the London (now Britain) Yearly Meeting (LYM), the British umbrella gathering of Friends. A generation later, in 1758, LYM condemned the slave trade again, and urged Friends everywhere to stay clear of "this unrighteous gain of oppression." The trade was condemned a third time in 1761, this time including a clause that disowned any Friend who accepted the institution of slavery. In 1772, under the continued influence of North American Friends—principally John Woolman— the LYM called for *all* slavery to be "utterly abolished." In the next two decades, slavery among Friends disappeared, partly due to economic conditions. The process of abolishing slavery had taken about one hundred years (Britain Yearly Meeting n.d.).

The love manifested in the labors of John Woolman, Joshua Evans, Anthony Benezet, and other compassionate and farsighted Friends was important to the eventual success of the abolitionist movement within the Society of Friends. Woolman was passionately and doggedly devoted to the cause, much given to prayer, and willing to follow divine love—whatever the cost in social comfort. During long journeys on foot in the 1750s and 1760s to speak to various Friends' meetings and individual slaveholders, he and his companions combined an unsparing prophetic critique of slavery with a sensitive concern for slaveholders. They spoke with gentle tact, and addressed formidable logistical problems (such as the danger of unemployment and starvation for liberated slaves). Woolman's ministry remains a cherished model of Light answering Light in Friend's history.

In the late 1700s, especially in Britain, Friends took action to end the entire slave system in the English-speaking world. This required them to invent new tools—boycotts and public petitions. In the 1780s, Friends formed the first antislavery society and soon joined Anglican and evangelical abolitionists to write newspaper essays, print and distribute informative flyers and booklets, promote boycotts of slave-produced sugar, gather signatures for a petition to Parliament, and lobby members of Parliament. They found a devoted ally in parliamentarian William Wilberforce, an eloquent statesman and man of prayer, who later cofounded the (Royal) Society for the Prevention of Cruelty to Animals. Their work culminated in an act of Parliament that abolished the slave trade in 1807. Slavery itself was abolished in English dominions in 1833.

Also in the late eighteenth century, and increasingly in the nineteenth, U.S. Friends turned to civil disobedience, particularly the Underground Railroad. Not only did they risk opprobrium, legal action, imprisonment, and assassination, their work was sometimes resisted by other Friends, who attacked them verbally and denied them the use of meetinghouses for strategy sessions. Notable heroes of this work were "stationmasters" Levi and Catherine Coffin of Newport, Indiana; Thomas Garrett of Wilmington, Delaware (who lost his hardware store to a five-thousand dollar fine); and prophet Lucretia Mott of Philadelphia. These Friends risked so much by unblinkingly facing down the horrors of enslavement in the Light of Love.

TOWARD ABOLITION OF ANIMAL SLAVERY TODAY

The shock value of the term slavery is important in awakening people of goodwill to the depths and extent of societal evils toward nonhuman animals from which they benefit. Its use will be protested by many who are ignorant of what factory farming entails, and the similarities between human and animal slavery. For such people, I provide a few examples:

- In both cases, abusers claim the right to own a living being.
- The bottom line of both systems is profit.
- The beneficiaries who consume the system's products don't wish to give them up (or their artificially low cost).
- Defenders of the systems use pejorative language to describe victims (animal terms, such as "dog" and "buck," were applied to African Americans with intent to degrade and justify abuse, whereas "dumb" and "stupid" are perhaps most commonly used with intent to degrade and justify the abuse of nonhuman animals).
- Abusers defend exploitation by claiming that their victims are better off than they would be if turned out.
- Victims are sold like objects at auctions, destroying families and friendships.
- Abusers deny or minimize the suffering of victims.
- Abusers employ branding, pens, collars, and shackles, and (when intimidation fails) physical battering or "execution."
- Victims undergo hellish transportation condition, and many die in transit.
- Not only the victims are damaged by slavery; the minds and souls of oppressors are hardened and dehumanized as well (Spiegel 1996).

These and other analogies strongly support the use of the language of slavery to discuss animal exploitation.

There are also notable differences. Most importantly, enslaved persons were potentially capable of speaking for and liberating themselves, whereas nonhuman animals cannot use human systems to bring about self-liberation. Furthermore, because of slavery's psychological and physical damage, and the disappearance of wilderness, few nonhuman animals who are freed from factory farms can ever be fully liberated. Most must remain under human care, though they can enjoy the company of their own, stable communities and friendships in spacious, natural, clean quarters. Instead of being forced to serve human interests, humans will serve the interests of those who were previously exploited.

CONCLUSION

Faith-based animal advocates may glean practical insights from the history of abolition among Friends. We must be prepared for resistance, perhaps hostility—even from members of our spiritual family—but we must respond with love. We must commit for the long haul. There will be a time for compromise, a time for civil disobedience, and a time for new visions that find new ways and means. Steadfastness, courage, and compassionate love for all beings are central to the spiritual journey. Anyone with a prophetic call to advocate for animals must keep turning to the Light that is Love, to God-with-Us, for courage and strength to take action against evil systems of destruction and death.

12

Christianity and Scapegoating

Understanding and Responding to Oppression

STEPHEN R. KAUFMAN

While violence seems to be as old as humanity, the last century witnessed the killing of humans and animals on an unprecedented scale. Increasingly, lethal weaponry and brutal methods of factory farming portend great risk for future human and animal beings. Some argue that violence is inevitable, and the wisest strategy is to be stronger than all possible adversaries. Others, blaming religion as the source of violence, have tried to show that rejection of irrational religious beliefs is the key to peace and well-being.

I argue that scapegoating has been a source of violence throughout human history, and that scapegoating underlies much of human cultures, including religion. If this view is valid, then eradicating religion will not eliminate violence and injustice, because nonreligious ideologies (such as nationalism) will replace religion to provide an excuse for scapegoating. Given that many progressives and social reformers have been inspired by religious convictions, perhaps religion can illuminate a path away from scapegoating and violence. I think that Christianity offers one such path.

RENÉ GIRARD AND ERNEST BECKER

In my view, René Girard (1972), Ernest Becker (1973), and their colleagues have offered profound insights into human violence and scapegoating.

One of Girard's central observations is that all cultures either engage in blood sacrifices or have myths that relate to past blood sacrifices. In order to explain this, he notes that humans are inherently mimetic; that is, humans unconsciously mimic other people. This "mimesis" is essential to our becoming human—children learn language, survival skills, and proper social behavior by mimicking others. Girard asserts that human *desires* are also mimetic. We are born with only rudimentary instinctive knowledge about which foods, sexual partners, and material objects are "desirable." We look to peers and general societal standards to determine which specific objects we should desire. Demonstrating mimesis, cultural ideals of sexual attractiveness for men and women have changed substantially over the past few centuries.

Mimesis raises a problem. If desires are mimetic, many people want the same things, and objects of collective desire inevitably become scarce. Indeed, what it means to "desire" something is to want something that is not readily available. As people compete for objects of desire, conflicts arise that can lead to hostilities, or even violence.

The insights of Ernest Becker (and colleagues) compliment those of Girard. Becker argued that fear of death is a principal human concern. Humans appear to share a survival instinct with other animals. This survival instinct manifests as fear in the presence of danger. Since we are aware of death's inevitability, and the fact that we could die at any time, we recognize that mortal danger is always present. Studies have shown that thinking about death causes anxiety (Pyszczynski,

Solomon, and Greenberg 2003), and ruminating on our own extinction can be terrifying.

Self-esteem is a salve against mortality fears; self-esteem gives people a sense that death is not the end of their existence. Those with high self-esteem tend to believe that they will be rewarded with everlasting life, or that their accomplishments will live on in the memory of future generations. Also, greater self-esteem tends to make people feel less vulnerable to dangers that might terminate their lives at any moment. In general, we gain self-esteem by performing well in activities that our culture tells us are important. Such activities include raising children, participating in and passing down religious and other cultural traditions, or making a "lasting" contribution to our culture. If we do these tasks well in relation to other people, we have a sense of being "good" people, people who are worthy of being remembered or being rewarded with everlasting life. In these ways, we gain a sense of "death transcendence," which helps reduce mortality fears.

Applying Girard's thoughts to Becker's, mimesis dictates what one must accomplish to be "good" and in order to gain self-esteem, and this is necessary because we are not born knowing what to accomplish in order for the community to deem us "good." Goodness could mean excellence in sports, proficiency at making money, or being a leader among those who share and offer charity.

Since we judge our worth in comparison to others, self-esteem is a limited entity and not everyone can be "good." Competition for objects of desire, including whatever it takes to be regarded as "good," leads to rivalries and, eventually, hostilities. As mimetic creatures, people respond with hostility to another person's hostility, and harsh feelings can readily escalate to disrupt relationships, divide families, and sever communal ties. As social creatures, we find such divisions unsettling, and social disruption can have lethal consequences in communities where people depend on each other for survival. If we can't maintain communal cohesiveness, people become more vulnerable to the vicissitudes of life, including crop failures, loss of jobs, illnesses, or invasions from neighboring tribes or nations.

When hostilities escalate and threaten communal bonds, what Girard called a "sacrificial crisis" arises. Sacrificial crises can also arise as a consequence of mysterious natural events that people don't understand, such as plagues, droughts, and earthquakes. In such instances, people start to blame each other, and communal bonds dissolve.

Girard asserts that communities respond to sacrificial crises by blaming one or more scapegoats. Generally, peripheral members of the community (who are unable to defend themselves) are accused of ill-defined, impossible-to-defend charges, such as "casting spells" or, to use more contemporary examples, "having communist sympathies," "opposing family values," and "not loving your country." Just as desires are mimetic, so are accusations, and communal accord grows. The community then banishes or kills the scapegoat(s). Typically, communal members justify such violence by claiming that their god(s) endorse punishing the perceived evildoer. The camaraderie that accompanies the communal "punishment," or destruction of the scapegoat, helps regenerate communal cohesiveness.

When sacrificial crises are related to natural events, they are generally short-lived: plagues run their course, droughts abate, and earthquakes are momentary. Consequently, the banishment or death of the scapegoat confirms the scapegoat's guilt because the crisis soon passes.

Girard maintains that myths and rituals evolved to reenact the original sacrificial crisis and its resolution through sacrificial violence (scapegoating). Meanwhile, cultures have developed taboos against whatever they believe has contributed to past sacrificial crises. These taboos consist of rules or laws, such as who can marry whom, and which caste or group rules over another.

If people believe that taboos maintain peace and order, and prevent sacrificial crises, they'll defend taboos with a degree of fervor and ruthlessness that often strikes outsiders as irrational, even savage. Passions often override reason as people vigorously defend taboos that they believe prevent chaos and terror. Likewise, most people readily believe accusations against scapegoats if they also believe that killing or banishing the scapegoats will resolve a sacrificial crisis.

With the rise of humanism, we are less inclined to scapegoat humans, but animals have often been substitute victims. Indeed, animal sacrifices in the Hebrew scriptures (Lev. 1–8) appear to have largely served as alternatives to human sacrifices that were then commonplace, even among ancient Hebrews (2 Kings 3:27; Judg. 11:30–40; Jer. 32:35; Mic. 6:7).

Not surprisingly, people often fail to recognize animals as contemporary scapegoat victims. Many people blame predator animals for declining prey populations (even when human activities are primarily responsible); deer for car/deer collisions; and farmed animals for spreading diseases that arise as a consequence of stressful, intensive "factory farming." Instead of empathy, people often feel contempt for animals habitually abused by people, such as pigs, chickens, and turkeys, blaming these animals for the abuses they receive.

Scapegoating involves attributing excess guilt to a specific victim. Victims are not necessarily totally innocent (though animal victims generally are), but they are not as guilty as scapegoaters believe. Herein lies the injustice of scapegoating. Victims are punished out of proportion to their guilt, often suffering for the sins of scapegoaters themselves. For example, we might rightly condemn thievery, but the larger community is often responsible for the unjust distribution of resources that leaves some people in desperate straits, which contributes to theft.

When it comes to the human quest for self-esteem, animals are frequent victims. Those who might feel a sense of inadequacy (financially or physically, for example) might gain a sense of competence, power, and control by killing or otherwise tormenting nonhuman animals. Further, eating farmed animals has symbolic meaning, in addition to being a means of sustenance (Fiddes 1991). For many people, consuming animals offers a sense that one is superior both to animals and to the natural world.

With human hopes, fears, and other powerful emotions blinding us to the scandal of scapegoating violence, the prospects for transcending scapegoating might seem grim. However, many religious leaders have sought to end this injustice, and toward this end I find the Judeo-Christian tradition particularly insightful and inspiring.

HEBREW SCRIPTURES

Hebrew scriptures describe peaceful coexistence among all creatures as ideal. At its inception, the world was vegan and harmonious (Gen. 1:29–30), and Isaiah prophesied a similar peaceful world at the end of time (11:6–9). Nevertheless, Hebrew scriptures are replete with violence, some evidently done with God's approval, such as animal sacrifices prescribed in Leviticus, and the ancient Hebrews' brutal conquest of the Promised Land described in Joshua (and elsewhere).

While earlier prophets and the initial stories about the Hebrews describe God as principally concerned with the Hebrew people, later prophets depict God as more universally loving, compassionate, and opposed to the scapegoating inherent in sacrificial violence (in which humans project their own weaknesses and sins onto a sacrificial victims) (Lev. 16:21). Several prophets objected to animal sacrifices (Jer. 7:22–23; Amos 5:22–24; Hosea 6:6; Isa. 1:11–13); Micah declared, "What does the Lord require of you but to do justice, and to love kindness, and to walk humbly with your God?" (6:6–8)

Why, then, did the Levitical law given to Moses involve animal sacrifice? Perhaps sacrifices were "necessary" because early Hebrews, like all ancient people, could not imagine worshipping a God who did not require sacrifices. Animal sacrifices, in this view, were a substitute for human sacrifices that were then prevalent. In this way animal sacrifices, while regrettable, constituted an (arguably) unavoidable step toward eliminating *all* sacrificial violence.

The Songs of the Suffering Servant in Isaiah offers insights into the scapegoating process, and show a path out of sacrificial violence. The text describes the servant as friendless and ugly, and scapegoats are typically just such peripheral members of the community. The servant was innocent (Isa. 63:9), but Isaiah relates: "We esteemed him stricken, smitten by God, and afflicted. But he was wounded for our transgressions, he was bruised for our iniquities" (Isa. 53:4–5). Isaiah reveals a universal pattern—the scapegoat has been blamed for the community's sins, and the community has attributed their scapegoating violence to their god(s). Because of mimetic, communal accord regarding the scapegoat's guilt, religious texts often hide the victim's innocence, but this remarkable text explicitly recognizes that "he was wounded for our transgressions."

The Songs of the Suffering Servant boldly indict the community for scapegoating an innocent person. Once people recognize their own guilt, they will see that scapegoating is grounded in lies about the victim's guilt. Consequently, scapegoating will lose its ability to resolve sacrificial crises. Once the general populace acknowledges the victim's innocence (or comparative innocence), then blaming and punishing these victims will not offer a sense of security based on the belief that the evil in their midst has been eradicated. The community will then have little choice but to find alternatives to scapegoating.

Even when people start to recognize scapegoating as scandalous, its attractions remain. It is tempting to relieve anxieties and reunite the community by blaming a scapegoat for a community crisis. If we are to refrain from the injustice that is inherent in scapegoating, we must first recognize our propensity to scapegoat, and then resolve to avoid victimizing innocent individuals. We must seek to hear the voice of victims, listening to their claims of innocence, and recognize those, like the suffering servant, who "had done no violence, and there was no deceit in his mouth" (Isa. 35:9).

THE NEW TESTAMENT

Jesus ministered to peripheral members of society—typical victims of scapegoating. He stood with and assisted those who were marginalized and vulnerable to scapegoating, such as widows, children, the infirm (John 5:2–14; 9:1–7), lepers (Mark 1:40–45), a woman with perpetual bleeding (Luke 8:43–48) (who was "unclean" according to Jewish law), an adulteress (John 8), and those deemed "possessed" (Mark 1:23–25). His concern evidently extended to nonhuman animals, and he drove from the temple the animals slated for sacrifice, as well as those selling these innocent victims (John 2:15).

When Jesus was killed, the mobs that had previously hailed his entry into Jerusalem cried, "Crucify him!" This reversal illustrates the mimetic nature of sentiment among crowds. Caiaphas, among those encouraging the condemnation of Jesus, articulated the logic of scapegoating: "You know nothing at all; you do not understand that it is better for you to have one man die for the people than have the whole nation destroyed" (John 11:49–50). Roman authorities feared an uprising, particularly during the Passover season, when the theme of liberation from Egypt threatened to inspire rebellious sentiments among Jews. Similarly, Jewish authorities feared that a rebellion could invite a catastrophic Roman response to insurrection. Therefore, Caiaphas expressed the utilitarian logic of scapegoating— the sacrifice of one or a few individuals in the hope of protecting the larger populace from disaster. Jesus was crucified for a crime, yet the Gospels place him at "the right hand of God" after resurrection (Mark 16:19), indicating that Jesus was innocent. Indeed, the Gospels emphasize Jesus' innocence (Matt. 27:3–5; Mark 14:55–57; Luke 23:4, 23:40–43, 23:47). The understanding of the victim's innocence, and the consequent guilt of the mob, are perhaps why "all the multitudes who assembled to see the sight, when they saw what had taken place, returned home beating their breasts" (Luke 23:48). People have always recognized scapegoating as unjust; the challenge has been to identify scapegoating when it is taking place.

A view of the Bible informed by a "Girardian" outlook suggests that Jesus' death was necessary to expose and condemn scapegoating. Had he violently resisted arrest, or disputed the accusations (potentially exposing him to charges of perjury), there might have been grounds for believing that he deserved harsh punishment. Instead, the falsity of charges against him became apparent when witnesses contradicted one other (Mark 14:55–57). Only through willingness to be a victim could Jesus reveal the lies that underlie scapegoating. Jesus stated: "For this I was born, and for this I have come into the world, to bear witness to the truth" (John 18:37).

I think the Apostle Paul understood that Christians are called to emulate Jesus, and Girard has called such emulation "good mimesis." Paul's letters frequently encouraged *pisteos Christou*, which can be translated as either "faith in Christ" or "faith of Christ." Paul used the same words to describe Abraham's faith when Abraham nearly sacrificed Isaac. It makes more sense to admire the faith of Abraham, than have faith *in* Abraham (as if Abraham were a god). When Paul clearly wished to communicate "faith *in* Christ," he used the Greek word *en*. Therefore, it appears that Paul encouraged us to adopt the "faith of Christ," which includes a conviction that God sides with those who are weak and vulnerable, and that God rejects the scandal of scapegoating.

Hebrew Scriptures contain many passages describing animal sacrifices, evidently with God's endorsement. Scholars differ on the reasons for these sacrifices (I discuss this in my book *Guided by the Faith of Christ*). I think it is reasonable, in light of Jesus' general ministry, to conclude that he rejected scapegoating completely, which includes sacrificial violence.

Along with encouraging Christians to have the "faith of Christ," Paul encouraged followers to have the *mind* of Christ (1 Cor. 2:16; Phil. 2:5), which transforms people into "new creations" (2 Cor. 5:17). Christianity teaches followers to adopt the "faith of Christ" by abiding in Jesus and in God. Jesus said: "I am in my Father, and you in me, and I in you" (John 14:20), and "If you keep my commandments, you will abide in my love, just as I have kept my Father's commandments and abide in his love" (John 15:10).

Jesus believed that he had a divine mission to serve and defend those who were weak and vulnerable. Even as Jesus was dying on the cross, he said: "It is finished" (John 19:30). In this statement Jesus indicated that he had found his life meaningful and valuable. If we adopt the "faith of Christ," we can similarly gain self-esteem through faith that God loves us and from a conviction that any works of service for God's creation, however humble, are valuable. This faith, then, can give our lives direction and meaning, despite our limitations, despite our transgressions and frailties, despite the travails that often accompany human existence, and despite the impermanence of life. Christian faith can provide a path toward self-esteem that does not involve harming or belittling others. Less anxious about our mortality and more confident in God's love and concern, we need not be tempted to scapegoat.

CONCLUSION

The Bible does not appear to categorically condemn all forms of animal exploitation, evidently because some people have had no choice but to use animals for labor or food in our imperfect world. However, those who *can* avoid harming animals should do so. The Hebrew Scriptures condemn cruelty to animals (Deut. 25:4). Indeed, the author of Proverbs wrote: "A righteous man has regard for the life of his beast" (12:10), and the psalmist declared: "The Lord is good to all, and his compassion is over all that he has made" (145:9).

Once we recognize animals as victims of scapegoating, it follows readily that the Bible's condemnation of scapegoating demands faithful Jews and Christians to change their behavior and stop victimizing nonhuman animals.

13

Islam

Muhammad, Sacred Writings, and Animal Liberation

LISA KEMMERER

It is not their eyes that are blind, but their hearts. (Qur'an 22:46)

INTRODUCTION

From the compassion of Muhammad to the inclusion of animal rights in *shari'a*, Islam has much to offer a world that seems increasingly indifferent to the lives of chickens, cattle, turkeys, and pigs. Islamic sacred writings and famous Muslim exemplars provide a rich array of teachings and traditions that beckon Muslims to rethink human/ nonhuman relations, including their purchases at the supermarket.

THE PROPHET MUHAMMAD

Compassion is central to the life and teachings of Muhammad, who is reported to have said: "He who is devoid of kindness is devoid of good" (Friedlander 1977, 65). What we know of Muhammad's life reveals that he lived with compassion, and showed care both for human and nonhuman animals (Haq 2003, 147).

Hadith ("tradition"), the most authoritative Muslim texts after the

Qur'an, hold a collection of texts that preserve the life and words of Muhammad as remembered by his followers. Hadith demonstrate that Muhammad "loved animals and displayed great kindness to them, and encouraged other Muslims to do likewise" (Nasr 2003, 97). The Prophet frequently reminded "his companions to take the interests of nonhuman animals into consideration" (Foltz 2005, 19). *Hadith qudsi* states: "The heart of man is the throne of God" (Stoddart 1985, 19, 81); it is through the *heart* that Allah touches the human soul (Stoddart 1985, 46–51).

The Prophet taught his followers that kindness to nonhuman animals was a requirement of Allah. Once, when wiping the mouth of a horse with his own personal cloth, his followers asked what he was doing. The Prophet admitted that Allah had reprimanded him for having neglected the horse (Masri 2007, 36). Later, on seeing a man treating a camel roughly, the Prophet reminded the man: "[I]t behooves you to treat the animals gently" (*Sahih Muslim* 4:2593 in Masri 2007, 35). The prophet was "kind and loves kindness," and therefore encouraged camel riders to allow their camels to stop as needed, and to travel by night, when it was cooler and easier for the laboring camels to travel (*Muwatta* 54:15:38).

Hadith demonstrate that the Prophet tried to mitigate nonhuman animal suffering at the hands of human beings (Haq 2003, 147). He considered the killing of nonhuman animals without justification "as one of the major sins" (Masri 2007, 46). He denounced the use of wild animal skins, condemned target practice on living creatures, forbade inciting animal fights for human entertainment (Masri 2007, 46), and deplored "blood sports"—killing for "mere sport" (Masri 2007, 36). According to one of his prominent contemporaries, Jabir bin Abdullah, the prophet did not allow branding or hitting a nonhuman animal in the face (*Sahih Bukhari: Guided* 67:449), and on seeing a mother bird's distress at losing her clutch, Muhammad forbid his followers from taking a bird's eggs (*Sahih Bukhari* referenced in Hind).

When the prophet was asked if there was a heavenly reward for good deeds done to nonhuman animals, the prophet duly noted that the way in which we choose to live, how we treat nonhuman animals, matters (Haq 2003, 150). He also told his followers that acts of kindness and charity to nonhumans will be rewarded by Allah, and recalled both a woman condemned for cruelty to a cat, and a man blessed for saving a dog's life (Masri 2007, 46). Muhammad is recorded as having said that any Muslim "who plants a tree or sows seeds" that are eaten by a hungry human or bird—or any other living being—is regarded as having offered "a charitable gift" (*Sahih Bukhari: Guided* 3:39:513). Another saying from the prophet notes that a good deed done for a nonhuman animal "is as good as doing good to a human being; while an act of cruelty to a beast is as bad as an act of cruelty to a human being" (*Mishkat* 8:178). One of the sayings of the prophet in the *Mishkat* (a secondary source of Hadith) states: "If anyone wrongfully kills [even] a sparrow . . . he will face God's interrogation" (Haq 2003, 149).

Muhammad taught his followers that nonhuman animals matter in their own right. The Qur'an and stories of the life of the Prophet both indicate that nonhuman animals are members of their own communities—individuals in their own right—due proper care and respect: "Any act of cruelty toward animals is strongly forbidden" (Siddiq 2003, 455). The Prophet encouraged kindness and compassion, and taught his followers that how we treat nonhuman animals—how we invest our time and money—is noted by Allah and will be a matter of considerable importance on the day of judgment.

LOVE AND COMPASSION

Love is fundamental to Sufi traditions (the mystical branch of Islam); "love is kindness" (Grisell 1983, 33). The prolific mystic Ibn 'Arabi (born in Spain in 1165) traveled much of the Islamic world, and wrote of his love for all creatures, noting that love is the core of his faith—love *is* his faith:

My heart has opened unto every form: it is a pasture for gazelles, a cloister for Christian monks, a temple for idols, the Ka'ba of the pilgrim, the tables of the Torah and the book of the Qur'an. I practice the religion of Love. (Stoddart 1985, 51)

The late Turkish Sufi master Said Nursi is "heralded by his followers as a model animal-lover." He "opposed any killing of animals, even flies" (Foltz 2005, 94–95).

Islamic stories of religious adepts reveal that those who are close to God are also close to nonhuman animals, and share compassionate, companionable, and peaceful relations with them. Many stories of Islamic saints recall holy people helping other creatures in need. Ebrahim al-Khauwas (ninth century, Iraq), who was famous for long journeys through the desert, is reported to have paused by some water under a tree, where he noticed a great lion limping in his direction. The lion approached, then rolled over at the ascetic's feet. One gigantic paw was "swollen and gangrenous"; he lanced, drained, and bandaged the paw (Attar 1990, 273). The lion rose and went his way, but returned, "bringing his cub," showing appreciation and trust to the man who had relieved his suffering (Attar 1990, 273).

The famous Persian (Iranian) poet Jalal al-Din Rumi (1207–1273) tells of a man who kept but did not feed a dog. When the dog starved to death, the man wailed loudly, calling attention to his loss. When questioned by his neighbor, he admitted that he was too stingy to feed the dog, and the "neighbor, on hearing this, rebuked him for his hypocrisy" (Rumi 2007, 228). To claim to be a Muslim while starving a dog, Rumi notes, might cause even "the infidels [to] strike thee down with their very looks when they hear the reading of the Koran" (Rumi 2007, 228).

Few acts of devotion carry the moral and spiritual weight of compassion; no matter how far one might have fallen from the straight path outlined by the Qur'an, Hadith teach that a Muslim with a compassionate heart is likely to be spared (Schuon 1979, 9). This is supported by a well-known Muslim story recounting a Muslim who "was damned because she allowed her cat to die of hunger," while a prostitute "was saved because she gave a drink of water to a dog" (Schuon 1979, 9). This same theme is repeated in the story of a compassionate Sufi saint, Sofyan al-Thauri (eighth century, Iraq), who came upon a bird trapped in a cage, "fluttering and making a pitiful sound." He bought and freed the bird (Attar 1990, 132). After the death of the saint, a "voice issued from the tomb": "God has forgiven Sofyan" on account of "the compassion he showed to His creatures" (Attar 1990, 132).

Nonhuman animals provide "a means by which God allows Muslims to earn his pleasure through their compassionate acts" (Foltz 2005, 80), and for those who are Muslims, "the overriding ethos enjoined upon humans is one of compassionate consideration" (Foltz 2005, 27). "Prevention of physical cruelty is not enough"—much more is required (Masri 2007, 48): Muslims must not only avoid harming nonhuman animals, but assist them when they are in need, and look not only to the physical needs of other creatures, but to their emotional needs—"Mental cruelty" is equally forbidden (Masri 2007, 48). Allah created the universe with a "breath of compassion" (Bakhtiar 1987, 16–17), and "Islamic teachings have gone to great lengths to instill a sense of love, respect and compassion for animals" (Masri 2007, 45).

VICE-REGENCY

Islam shares the Judeo-Christian belief in a benevolent, all-powerful creator who placed people "in dominion on the earth" (Qur'an 7:10). But Allah is righteous and compassionate, and has created Earth for "just purposes" (Denny 1987, 8). Therefore, we are appointed as Allah's caretakers—we are to tend rather than exploit, to assist rather than dominate—and our very salvation is dependent on personal submission as Allah's vice-regents. Vice-regency does not entitle humans to exploit and harm the rest of creation. The Qur'an teaches that Earth, and all that exists therein, has been designed and created for the benefit of all—not just for humanity (Ozdemir 2003, 23). As vice-regents, Muslims are expected to make choices that benefit creation as a whole; we are to avoid decisions that merely satisfy human whims and self-interests (Dutton 2003, 329). As appointed vice-regents, humans will be held accountable. If we are cruel or indifferent to pigs or cats, we will need to answer to a just and compassionate creator on Judgment Day.

Allah has put people in charge of tending and protecting creation. In serving Allah as vice-regents, humans are expected to look to the needs and desires of nonhuman animals. While humans share the creatureliness of all animals, we have been given the responsibility of looking after the rest of creation on behalf of the Creator.

ZAKAT

The Prophet noted that those who give food from the heart "will enter paradise with peace" (Friedlander 1977, 72). *Zakat*, giving to those in need, "is considered an act performed for God" (Cragg and Speight 1988, 45); almsgiving is not limited to human beings. Indeed, those who limit their attentive hand to human beings also limit their heavenly rewards. Planting a tree or cultivating land that provides "food for a bird, animal, or man" is charity, and satisfies the requirement of *zakat* (Friedlander 1977, 100). The mystical poet, Rumi, understood religious life as reaching *through the experienced world* to Allah, through compassion and benevolent assistance to those in need—whoever "those" might be. Rumi writes:

> Doing kindness is the game and quarry of good men,
> A good man seeks in the world only pains to cure.
> Wherever there is a pain there goes the remedy,
> Wherever there is poverty there goes relief. (Rumi 2007, 86)

Those who provide food for nonhumans have "given a charitable gift" that will yield great rewards from above (Haq 2003, 145). Eighth century mystic, Ma'ruf al-Karkhi (Iraq), was known both for generosity and devoutness. Yet when he shared his bread with a hungry dog, his uncle asked if he was "not ashamed to eat bread with a dog." Ma'ruf replied: "It is out of shame that I am giving bread to the poor" (Attar 1990, 164).

ISLAMIC LAW AND NONHUMAN ANIMAL RIGHTS

Allah provided nonhuman animals with legal rights against humanity, as found in the Qur'an and supported both by Hadith and by various bodies of written law based on the Qur'an, called shari'a. Shari'a explicitly outlines that which humans *owe* nonhumans. Shari'a instruction and guidance on animal rights and human obligations "are so comprehensive that we need not go elsewhere for any guidance" (Masri, 2007, xi). Contemporary Egyptian cleric Yusuf al-Qaradawi comments: "It is a distinctive characteristic of the shari'a that all animals have legal rights which must be enforced by the state" (Foltz 2005, 88).

Shari'a provides nonhuman animals with legal rights because every living being is "owed its due" (Nasr 2003, 97). Most fundamentally, Islamic law forbids cruelty. Numerous Hadith denounce "hunting or killing for sport or amusement," as well as goading animals to fight with one another, or killing for "vanity," such as for ivory, fur, or feathers ("Selected" n.d.). Shari'a also forbids human-induced animal fights orchestrated for human entertainment, such as dog or cock fights (Llewellyn 2003, 194). Additionally, Islamic law forbids people from keeping wild animals as pets. Wild animals "should be allowed to live their lives unmolested. . . . Birds should be allowed to fly free" and should not be "kept in cages" (Foltz 2005, 33).

A shari'a jurist of the thirteenth century wrote a legal treatise titled *Rules for Judgment in the Cases of Living Beings*, in which he recounts human obligations to domesticated animals. He reminds farmers that they are required to provide for retired working animals exactly as they provide for younger beasts, and that those who tend or exploit nonhuman animals keep them in ways that are safe and comfortable. (For example, they may not be kept with other creatures who might cause them harm, and their quarters should be cleaned regularly [Foltz 2005, 34].)

DIET AND HUNTING

There have always been devout Muslims who abstained from eating meat for spiritual reasons, some with the understanding that humans were "created by Allah to be vegan" (Foltz 2005, 111). Many Sufis, for example, advocate "harmlessness as a principle of faith," and are therefore likely to abstain from nonhuman animal products (Said and Funk 2003, 174). Abd al-Karim al-Qushayri (twelfth century) tells of Ibrahim ibn Adham's awakening when he was out hunting:

> Four times he heard a voice crying, "Awake!" but he steadfastly ignored it. At the fourth cry he spied a deer and prepared to give chase. However, the deer turned around and spoke to him, "You can not hunt me; I have been sent to hunt you. Was it for this that you were created, and is this what you have been commanded?" At this last revelation Ibrahim . . . gave a great cry and made sincere repentance. ("Hazrat" n.d.)

Rumi used hunting metaphors in a negative light, reminding those of faith that selfish ways are spiritually self-destructive. He understood that a flesh habit is harmful to nonhuman animals—even emotionally harmful. He tells the story of a handful of travelers who lost their way and were without food, and were ultimately faced with the choice of whether or not to kill an elephant to satisfy their hunger. A sage told the hungry travelers that there was a plump young elephant in the area, but added that if they were to kill and eat this elephant, that youth's "parents would in all probability" hunt them down and avenge the killing of their. Nonetheless, on sighting the young elephant, the travelers could think only of their hunger. They killed the young pachyderm, and all but one traveler ate of the little beast: "But no sooner were they fast asleep than a huge elephant made his appearance and proceeded to smell the breath of each one of the sleepers in turn. Those whom he perceived to have eaten of the young elephant's flesh he slew without mercy," and so only one traveler remained (Rumi 2007, 111). Rumi's story reminds readers that it is better to be hungry and merciful than selfish and mercilessly well-fed—and condemned.

The medieval Sufi poet Farid al-din 'Attar tells of the gentle eighth century saint and mystic Rabi'a, who ventured into the mountains for a day, and was "soon surrounded by a flock of deer and mountain goats, ibexes, and wild asses." When two contemporaries approached, the nonhuman animals fled, causing them to feel "dismayed." One of the men, Hasan of Basra (Iraq), asked Rabi'a: "Why did they run away from me and associate so tamely with you?" Rabi'a minces neither words nor flesh, asking: "What have you eaten today?" Hasan, who minces both, avoids the question. Rabi'a knows that he has been feeding on bits of nonhuman animal bodies, and asks a second direct question: "Why then should they not flee from you?" (Attar 1990, 44–45).

Followers of the late Sri Lankan Sufi teacher M. R. Bawa Muhaiyaddeen (twentieth century) are all vegetarians. This is not surprising, given that Muhaiyaddeen encouraged those who would eat flesh to kill the nonhuman animal themselves, while looking into the animal's eyes, watching the last spark of life fade. He believed that a good heart cannot stand to see the cost of consuming flesh—life giving way to death. If people killed in this way, Muhaiyaddeen concluded, there would be few eating flesh (Hamid 1998, 246). Muslims who continue to eat flesh when killing with their own hands will either have no other choice, or no conscience.

Muhaiyaddeen puts the matter more gently: "We must be aware of everything we do. All young animals have love and compassion. And if we remember that every creation was young once, we will never kill another life. We will not harm or attack any living creature" (Muhaiyaddeen 1985, 28). Muhaiyaddeen also emphasizes the importance of diet with regard to justice and judgment:

> All your life you have been drinking the blood and eating the flesh of animals without realizing what you have been doing. You love flesh and enjoy murder. If you had any conscience or any sense of justice, if you were born as a true human being, you would think about this. God is looking at me and you. Tomorrow his truth and justice will inquire into this. You must realize this. (Muhaiyaddeen 1985, 26)

Dr. Rehana Hamid, a devout Sufi and vegetarian, grew up in New York City under the careful watch of a Jewish mother and Muslim father. She currently worships at the Bawa Muhaiyaddeen mosque. As a Muslim, Hamid believes that compassion and empathy prevent her from participating in any way in unnecessary slaughter, including the consumption of flesh (Hamid 1998, 259).

Muslims draw "close to God by inculcating God's qualities of compassion and mercy, thus a true Muslim is one who honors, sustains, and protects the lives of creatures of God and does not kill them for her own food" (Foltz 2005, 111). In short, the compassionate, spiritual choice is to eat without slaughter—even *halal* slaughter. To avoid causing slaughter, we must not buy products from companies that use cow's nursing milk, or hen's reproductive eggs, because these companies treat the animals that they exploit cruelly, and send them to slaughter when they are but adolescents.

HALAL AND THE VEGAN IMPERATIVE

Halal requirements remind Muslims that all life is sacred, and that we have no right to take life without the permission of the Creator

(Masri 2007, 145–46). *Halal*, or "permissible" flesh, is taken from the body of a nonhuman animal that has been kept, tended, killed, and prepared according to clearly established Islamic principles, which require compassion. Muslims must be certain that any flesh—and dairy or egg products—which they choose to consume meet these requirements. According to the Islamic Food and Nutrition Council, *any* foods about which *any* question exists regarding whether or not it is *halal* "should be avoided" (Foltz 2005, 116–17).

Most fundamentally, *halal* flesh must come from a nonhuman animal who has been killed humanely (Llewellyn 2003, 233). Undercover footage invariably demonstrates that "humane" does not apply to assembly-line, slaughterhouse deaths, which are now common around the world. Additionally, *halal* products can only come from farmed animals who have been kept in quarters where they don't harm one another. Factory farmers, rather than provide adequate room and separate trouble-causers, simply dock tails and sear off beaks to prevent the harms caused by the aggression that stems from overcrowding. Factory farmed flesh, dairy, and eggs, sold in supermarkets through the world, are therefore forbidden:

> The basic moral question is—how right is it to deny these creatures of God their natural instincts so that we may eat the end product? For Muslims these questions pose the additional question of a fundamental moral pertinence—would our Holy Prophet Muhammad have approved of the modern methods of intensive farming systems if he were alive today? His overwhelming concern for animal rights and their general welfare would certainly have condemned (*La 'ana*) those who practice such methods, in the same way as he condemned similar other cruelties in his day. He would have declared that there is no grace or blessing (*Barakah*)—neither in the consumption of such food nor in the profits from such trades. These are not just hypothetical questions. The cruel and inhumane methods of intensive farming are being practised in most Islamic countries

these days, even in countries where indigence is no excuse. (Masri 2007, 44)

Many devout Muslims would refuse to eat flesh *on religious grounds* if they knew the horrors entailed in contemporary factory farming (Berry 1998, 245–46). By extension, Muslims in industrialized nations would also refuse milk and eggs (and any product containing milk or eggs) if they understood the suffering (and ecological degradation) inherent in *all* mainstream animal industries. Islamic theologian Al-Hafiz Basheer Ahmad Masri (a twentieth century Indian-born Muslim, educated in Cairo) prayed for the day when "average, simple and God-fearing Muslim consumers" are informed of "the gruesome details" of nonhuman animal industries in Islamic countries (Masri 2007, 45). He was sure that informed Muslims would "become vegetarians rather than eat such sacrilegious meat" (Masri 2007, 45).

Some contemporary Muslims already have gone vegan or cut back on the consumption of animal products, noting that "*halal*" meat facilities regularly buy flesh "from farms that do not treat animals in accordance with Islamic rules. . . . In other words, even 'halal meat' is not really halal and Muslims should refrain from eating it" (Foltz 2005, 119). Contemporary Muslim scholar, Tariq Ramadan, agrees: "Islamic teachings on respect for animal life are clear," and the way that nonhuman animals are treated in contemporary food industries "is unacceptable" (Foltz 2005, 118).

Furthermore, according to the Qur'an, Muslims are to only eat foods that are *Halal and Tayyib*:

Tayyib means wholesome, pure, nutritious and safe. Traditionally, Muslims in North America have emphasized the Halal over the Tayyib when it comes to meat consumption. . . .

For instance, great emphasis is placed on ensuring that animals slaughtered for consumption are [killed] in the Islamic manner. . . .

However, little to no attention is given to whether or not the animal itself is healthy, free of disease, hormones, antibiotics, and chemicals at the time of slaughter. Also, what kind of food [the animal] consumes is not taken into consideration. ("Halal V/s" n.d.)

Overall, contemporary animal products are neither as safe nor as nutritious as other food options. Animal products are not particularly healthy, and according to Islamic food requirements, "unless proven to be safe," items sold for consumption "should be kept out of the halal food chain" ("Halal—Into" n.d.).

In short, Muslims gain both physical and spiritual benefits when they commit to a vegan diet (Foltz 2005, 116). Contemporary Muslims have a host of faith-based reasons to choose a vegan lifestyle, many of which are mentioned in this anthology: human health, environment, animal suffering, and commitment to any one of the world's major religions—all of which hold compassion as a fundamental ethical requirement.

Many Muslims live in nations that lack adequate food supplies, and a vegan diet also helps address world hunger. Our tendency to use land to raise farmed animals is downright wasteful and inefficient (Masri 2007, 64–65). Such waste contributes to chronic hunger "for 20 percent of the world's human population, a disproportionate number of whom are Muslims. . . . [Yet] more than half of all land under cultivation is given over to crops destined for livestock consumption" (Foltz 2005, 120):

The reality of meat production today is that it entails severe environmental degradation and inefficiently diverts food resources that could be used to nourish hungry humans instead of doomed livestock—even apart from the fact that it condemns millions of innocent creatures to a life-time of unimaginable torture. Most Muslims, like people everywhere, support this immoral system out of ignorance. Once the facts are more widely known, it will be difficult for sincere Muslims to justify modern meat production methods on the basis of Islamic legal principles. (Foltz 2005, 126–27)

What strikes me as most remarkable is the fact that "this absurd extravagance and waste is being perpetuated in spite of modern scientific evidence that the human body can—and should—derive all its nourishment from a fibrous diet exclusive of meat and other animal products" (Masri 2007, 68). In short, "for the vast majority of Muslims the eating of meat is not only unnecessary but is also directly responsible for causing grave ecological and social harm, as well as being less healthful" than a vegan diet (Foltz 2004, 11).

Choosing a diet that unnecessarily harms other sentient beings and causes premature death is neither consistent with a life modeled on that of Muhammad, nor a life of submission and service to a creator who remains invested in—and is the rightful owner of—each created individual, whether that individual is a small spotted pig, a handsome red hen, a shimmering turkey, or a shy black cow.

CONCLUSION

To spare the lives of sentient individuals—to choose a vegan lifestyle, or at least cut back on the consumption of animal products—Muslims need only submit to the will of Allah (Muttaqi n.d., 2). Humans have been given vice-regency by a compassionate creator, and we are expected to be both merciful and kind as we tend and protect creation on behalf of the Creator, as exemplified by Muhammad. As vice-regents, we have no rights over other creatures. Instead, nonhuman animals are protected from human cruelty, indifference, and greed by Islamic law, and a vegan diet is therefore incumbent on any Muslim who is informed with regard to the realities of factory farming.

14

Al-Hafiz B. A. Masri

Muslim, Scholar, Activist—Rebel with a Just Cause

NADEEM HAQUE

I n a game park in the middle of Africa in the 1950s, three aggra-
vated Masai tribesmen were arguing with the principal of a
local school. Apparently, the school overlapped with Masai
tribal grounds; if they wanted to stay on those lands, the principal would have to physically defeat the tribesmen. The principal
was willing to take on the Masai—three against one—on behalf of
the students. The savannah became a gladiatorial arena for a full-
contact stick-fighting contest. Somehow the principal defeated his
challengers. The tribesman ran away, claiming that the principal
was a magician—so skillful in battle that they were not able to land
a single blow.

The principal was Al-Hafiz B. A. Masri (1914–1992). By any standards, Masri was an outstanding man. The sense of justice that motivated him to take on three Masai tribesmen was part of a core attitude
that shaped Masri's life, and drew him to the interchange between
human beliefs and animal welfare/rights. This chapter explains how

Masri came to be the first twentieth century thinker to demonstrate that Islam has both the theoretical and practical power to protect nonhuman animals.

INDIA: THE LAND OF MASRI'S BIRTH

Masri was born to a saintly father and a strict mother in Punjab, India, in 1914. His father, the learned Shaikh Abdul-Rahman, was born to an upper caste (*Kshatriya*) Hindu family. Changing religions, especially from Hinduism to Islam, was considered worse than someone being infected with a highly contagious disease. Nonetheless, Abdul-Rahman embraced Islam at the age of eighteen, and was promptly excommunicated from his family, receiving none of the property that a Hindu son would normally have inherited. In fact, his father threatened to kill him with a sword if he did not revert back to Hinduism. Abdul-Rahman replied: "My body may belong to you, but my soul belongs to God!"

In time, Abdul-Rahman became both scholarly and spiritual, traveling to Egypt to study Islam at the world's oldest center of learning (Al-Azhar University). On return to India, he was given the honorific surname Misri (the name for Egypt). (His son, Basheer Ahmad, eventually changed his father's surname from Misri to Masri for easier pronunciation.) On return to India, Abdul-Rahman married and started a family, and named his first son Masri. To fulfill a promise, he set about teaching Masri the Qur'an, and five years later, at age thirteen, Masri had memorized the entire text, earning him the title Al-Hafiz—one who has memorized the whole Qur'an verbatim.

Masri married a Muslim named Salima in 1935, and started a family, but because of his opposition to the Qadiani Movement (followers of Mirza Ghulam Qadiani), they immigrated from India to East Africa (in 1941) with a price on Masri's head. Before Masri could get away, a henchman tried to assassinate him; in the process, one of his colleagues was killed and another injured. Masri landed a blow to the assailant's head with a cudgel, but the culprit ran away, leaving a trail of blood that led the police to his door. The murderer was tried and executed (Masri 1988).

POLITICS IN EAST AFRICA

In East Africa, Masri's sense of justice led him in a variety of directions. He became vice-president of the Uganda SPCA (Society for the Prevention of Cruelty to Animals), and secretary of the Tanganyika SPCA. (Tanganyika, was an East African territory between the Indian Ocean and the largest of the African great lakes, and eventually became part of Tanzania.) Africa was teeming with wildlife at the time, and Masri gained tremendous practical knowledge of the local flora and fauna. He had a unique way of working with African wildlife, and it served him well. Once, when Masri and two friends were out hunting for food, they came across three male lions. Rather than succumb to fear, Masri took a huge step forward and roared like a lion. He wanted the lions to believe that he was defending *his* territory, that *they* were encroaching on his area. It worked, and the lions went their way.

Masri moved to Uganda from Tanganyika in 1952, and like the Argentine Marxist revolutionary Che Guevara sought socioeconomic emancipation from colonialism. With Milton Obote (who eventually became Prime Minister and then President of Uganda) Masri co-founded the Uganda People's Congress, which the two men hoped to build into an enlightened political party. The British, who were ruling East Africa at the time, pursued Obote, intent on blocking his efforts to create an independent Uganda. Masri protected Obote in his home, but ultimately the two men broke ties and went their separate ways. Masri headed for England with his family, where he became prominent both in the Muslim world and in the animal welfare/rights movement of the mid to late twentieth century.

ANIMAL WELFARE/RIGHTS IN ENGLAND, EGYPT, AND BEYOND

In England, Masri studied journalism, and between 1963 and 1967 he served as the joint editor of the prestigious *Islamic Review*, published by the Shah Jahan Mosque, built in Woking in 1889. (*The Review* carried articles from the world's pre-eminent Islamic thinkers/scholars, such as Muhammad Marmaduke Pickthall, Syed Qutb, and Malik Bin Nabi.) In 1964, Masri was the first Sunni imam (worship leader) to be appointed at the Shah Jahan Mosque, and three years later, Masri wrote and delivered a speech to 500 delegates from Western nations at the International Association for Religious Freedom, in London. In his talk, "Islam: The Precursor of Intellectual Age," Masri noted that Islam calls the faithful to rethink their conception of and relationship with the Creator, who forms a triangular relationship between rationality, justice, and peace, gifting humanity with a message of peace and justice that prophets have expounded for thousands of years, culminating in the voice of Prophet Muhammad. Masri, imam of Europe's main mosque, made a name for himself as a thinker and a lecturer.

As time passed, Masri's reputation grew, and sometimes his *khutbas* (sermons) were broadcast by British television. In one of his most well-received talks, a presentation that reached hundreds of thousands of British viewers, Masri corrected common misconceptions about Islam. Now at the forefront of Islamic affairs, Masri met such famous Muslims as Malcolm X (at the London School of Economics) and Muhammad Ali (the recently titled boxing champion, at the Shah Jahan Mosque). Some of Britain's most famous personalities sought Masri to learn more about Islam, such as Lord Hugh Dowding, commander-in chief of the Royal Air Force, who was responsible for winning the "Battle of Britain" during World War II. Dowding became one of Masri's closest friends. The two men shared a common concern for animal welfare; in later years, Masri's contact with the Dowding family put him in touch with various animal welfare organizations and animal activists.

By 1967, Masri's three children—Taher, Mubarak, and Tahera (my mother)—had long since reached adulthood, and Masri resigned as imam of the Shah Jahan Mosque to undertake a three-year, forty-five nation car-and-caravan tour with his supportive wife Salima. Masri and Salima traveled through Western and Eastern (Communist) Europe, North Africa, Turkey, Iran, and Pakistan. They stayed in Egypt for a year, where Masri studied Arabic at Al-Azhar University. It was during this period, as a traveler in foreign Islamic nations, that Masri was confronted with animal cruelties that he could not ignore, and which he recognized as contrary to Islamic teachings. One of these pivotal moments was at Al-Azhar, when he heard one of the leading lecturers curse pigs. According to the Qur'an, Muslims are not supposed to eat swine flesh because the Qur'an states that such "meat" is harmful and unhealthy. Masri begged to differ, and politely referenced Hadith, noting that there was nothing wrong with pigs—that pigs are not intrinsically evil. Scavenging pigs, Masri explained, help to maintain ecosystems, and they have an important role, for which they were designed by the Creator.

ANIMAL WELFARE AND ISLAM

In the 1980s, Masri began to ponder animal welfare and Islamic teachings with great zeal. He was in "early retirement," but people remembered his knowledge of Islam, and his eloquence in English, and continued to invite him to talk on various subjects relating to Islam. Consequently, when the International Association Against Painful Experiments on Animals (IAAPEA) wanted a definitive

Islamic view on the subject, they contacted Masri. Masri's first paper on animal welfare and Islam was presented in 1984 at the IAAPEA conference on animals and religions (later published in the anthology: *Animal Sacrifices: Religious Perspectives on the Use of Animals in Science* (Masri 1986)). In this paper, Masri posed the following fundamental questions:

> Can human beings rightly claim to be the apex of value in the world?
>
> If such a view is religiously justified, what moral implications does this carry for other life forms, particularly with regard to non-human animals (Masri 1986, 171)?

To answer these questions, Masri quoted extensively from the Qur'an and Hadith. He discussed the importance of the preservation of species, noting that other animals are owed their legitimate share of the planet, and noting that the Qur'an states that God created animals to live in communities like our own. He also demonstrated that the position of humans who choose to do evil is "lower" than that of any other animal:

> In the words of [William] Hazlitt: "Man is the only animal struck with the difference between what things are, and what they ought to be." Animals don't possess this freedom of choice. That's why the Qur'an characterizes those humans who fall short of this endowment as the "lowest of the low" (Regan 1986, 177).

Masri noted that Islamic "laws strongly deprecate all direct or indirect acts of cruelty to animals" (Masri 1986, 185). He lists six acts that are common in animal experimentation (as well as in other forms of contemporary animal exploitation), which are forbidden under Islamic law:

> subjecting animals to pain,
> killing animals for luxuries,
> enclosing animals in cages,

breeding animals in confined and unhygienic conditions, and using traps that cause lingering death. (Masri 1986, 185)

He concludes:

> The basic and most important point to understand about using animals in science is that the same moral, ethical, and legal codes should apply to the treatment of animals as are applied to humans. (Masri 1986, 192)

Masri then recounts Hadith quoting Prophet Muhammad, stating: "Anyone who kills even a sparrow or anything smaller than that, without proper justification, will be held accountable to God" (Masri 1986, 192).

Based on his work for IAAPEA, Compassion in World Farming (CIWF) commissioned Masri to write a book, which resulted in his short work, *Islamic Concern for Animals*. This book became the first chapter of his later work, *Animals in Islam*, which presents his definitive position on animal welfare and Islam. At the very outset, he writes:

> Quite a few of my friends have been surprised to learn that I have chosen "Animals" as a subject to write on from the Islamic point of view. . . . The way I look at it, however, is that life on this earth is so inextricably intertwined as a homogenous unit that it cannot be disentangled for the melioration of one species at the expense of another. (Masri 1989, vii)

In *Animals in Islam*, Masri discusses, with great analytical depth—for the first time in the modern era—key issues with regard to animal welfare/rights and Islam. This definitive work focuses on basic Islamic principles, derived from the Qur'an, such as animals as members of communities like our own, and also discusses key Hadith

(Masri 1989, 4–5). Through these sacred writings Masri examines factory farming, and the consumption of flesh. He also discusses animal sacrifice, demonstrating that this practice has nothing to do with appeasing God, and that Islam does not permit such superstitious, ritualistic practices (Masri 1989, 114–116). He speaks out against such waste and meaningless ritualism, especially the waste from the mass slaughter of animals for the Hajj (Masri 1989, 119). He suggests that wealthier pilgrims offer cash to the poor, rather than kill innumerable animals (Masri 1989, 116).

DIET AND ISLAM

Masri accepted meat consumption under certain conditions. In Chapter 6 of *Animals in Islam*, "The Islamic Method of Slaughter (*Dhabh*)," Masri explores *halal* meat using Hadith and the Qur'an, noting that it's almost impossible to be certain that flesh bought in local markets is *halal*. Nonetheless, he concludes that flesh might be considered *halal* in non-Muslim countries so long as no name other than the name of God has been invoked during the time of slaughter. (In truth, of course, it is impossible to know what has been uttered over an animal during slaughter.) He adds that one who chooses to consume flesh should invoke the name of God just before eating meat (Masri 1989, 131–140).

Masri argues in *Animals in Islam* that pilgrims from Western countries ought to slaughter animals for food by proxy, allowing meat distribution among the poor in distant nations. (This suggestion was acknowledged favorably by the Saudi Arabian government [Masri 1989, 124].) While Masri accepted the eating of flesh, he also accepted—even encouraged—other options, such as a vegetarian diet (and by extension, in contemporary times, a vegan diet):

> The spirit of sacrifice lies in offering the animal as charity to the indigent IN THE NAME OF GOD AND NOT TO GOD. . . . It needs to be repeated here, especially for the benefit of general Muslims,

that Islam neither recommends nor forbids the eating of meat (Masri 1989, 157).

This leaves the dietary choice of vegan, vegetarian, and omnivore to individual Muslims according to place and time, provided one maintains a healthful diet. This responsibility requires Muslims to apply other Islamic ideas to our dietary choice—such as the requirement for compassion—and that Muslims know how animals are treated on factory farms, and in slaughterhouses, and not remain blissfully ignorant.

By way of curbing ignorance, *Animals in Islam* discusses pre-slaughter stunning, and Masri concludes that Qur'anic principles only permit captive-bolt stunning. Electric stunning, gas stunning, and mechanical stunners fail to pass the crucial Islamic requirement for blood flow. Furthermore, Masri notes that captive-bolt stunners (applied just before the ritual slaughter method) cause the least pain, and are therefore a considerable improvement over "ritual slaughter" (in which the jugular vein is cut without stunning) (Masri 1989, 157–196). In addition, Masri emphasizes that Muslims who eat flesh must *know* how the animals whom they consume are killed. After assessing nutritional factors, the anatomy of humans, the economics of food, protein levels, and a comparative analysis of various major world religions, Masri concludes:

> Our moral responsibility toward the rest of the species demands that we employ all our scientific knowledge to acquire as much of our nutrients as possible from sources other than the flesh of those animals whom God has created and who are at our mercy. (Masri 1989, 46)

Masri also created a video, *Creatures of God*, stemming from his most fundamental and critical understandings of Islam. Cruelties inflicted on cattle exploited for their milk and hens exploited for their eggs, from a Qur'anic viewpoint, cannot be justified—and the

vegan diet is therefore more meritorious in the eyes of the Creator.
Masri emphasized that the ideal Islamic diet—most consistent with
the Qur'an—avoids factory farmed flesh. Were he alive today, he
would surely have extended his comments to protect hens and cows
enslaved in the egg and dairy industries. The cruelties of factory
farming have greatly increased animal suffering since Masri's time,
yet even then, he was deeply concerned for the welfare of farmed
animals.

That said, I think Masri would *not* have required contemporary
Muslims to adopt a vegan diet *if* farmed animals were treated compassionately, and he would definitely require Muslims to purchase
foods from farms devoid of animal cruelty—but such farms simply don't supply today's supermarkets. Consequently, Masri would
doubtless have emphasized the ideal nature of a vegan diet, given
contemporary factory farming methods. Masri's ideas on vegetarianism, and by extension veganism, would include the following
factors:

The Creator who designed this dynamic universe has infinite knowledge and wisdom. The Creator allowed humans the choice of whether
or not to eat certain animals, but requires that we minimize psychological and physiological suffering in our choice of foods.

If one can obtain the proper diet without causing suffering, then
one ought to do so. It is currently possible for many of us to choose
a balanced diet, but this diet is still not possible for many people
around the world.

Because animal products are permitted in the Qur'an, it is difficult
to convince Muslims to reconsider their dietary choices.

A healthful vegetarian/vegan diet places Muslims on a higher
spiritual plane because such a diet reduces pain and suffering, and
engenders compassion. Furthermore, such a diet is healthier for
our bodies and our environment, and allows more people to have
access to essential food and water. Choosing a vegetarian/vegan diet

is in perfect consonance with Qur'anic teachings and the Creator's expectations.

In his writings, Masri stressed the sacred duty of Muslims to make sustainable choices—choices that eliminate or at least minimize eco-system damage, strive for compassion, and maintain nature's dynamic balance (*mizan*). He would therefore have suggested, no doubt, a vegan/vegatarian diet—or at least a diet with reduced consumption of all animal products.

LAST DAYS AND LEGACY

Over time, Masri's ideas evolved from a human sociopolitical focus to a broader perspective, in which he recognized that all life is intercon-nected, and that nonhuman animals must be treated with respect and compassion. Masri espoused a vibrant, non-relativistic ecumenism, requiring believers to rise above doctrinal irrationality, ritualism, and parochialism, to embrace a universal worldview:

> My humble and sincere advice to those who are trying to seek spiri-tual guidance through literalism of their scriptures is to pay more regard to the spirit of the messages. . . . The Qur'an calls upon us over and over again to rack our brains and use our common-sense in grasping the quintessence of the Divine messages (Masri 1991).

Masri remained an advisor to the World Society for the Protection of Animals, and maintained connections with the World Wildlife Fund, until his death in 1992. He told me, a few months prior to his death, that he believed he would be remembered most for his work in the area of animal welfare/rights and Islam. Indeed, Masri's ideas continue to spark interest in the area of animals in Islam. For example, in 2005 Masri's "bold statements on animal cruelty and the required Muslim response have been used by PETA . . . in a campaign against cruelty to animals occurring in Australia, where sheep are being exported to Muslim countries" (Haque 2007, 550). One of God's fundamental messages for humanity, according to the Qur'an, is that we are to be compassionate and just. Masri's influence is likely to continue as humanity seeks religious support for sustainable, compassionate lifestyle choices.

Fearless when standing up for the rights of others, whether schoolchildren in Africa, Indians or Africans under colonial rule, or factory farmed animals in England, Masri's devotion to a singular God, coupled with his determination to take action on behalf of justice, inspired his fascinating and rewarding life. His simple tombstone in Woking, England, is emblazoned with Prophet Muhammad's maxim: "Whoever is kind to the Creatures of God, is kind to himself" (Amin 1965, 200).

PART THREE

ANCIENT INDIGENOUS RELIGIOUS TRADITIONS AND MODERN WICCA

15

Indigenous Peoples

Kinship and Killing

LISA KEMMERER

INTRODUCTION

The sharp division Westerners find between humans and other species does not tend to exist in indigenous belief systems. Instead, indigenous peoples view animals as kin, and humans and nonhumans are similar in critical ways, perhaps sharing language, culture, or an afterlife. It is also common for indigenous peoples to view humans and other creatures as "interpenetrable," eradicating the notion of distinct and separate species. The indigenous understanding of the relationship between humans and nonhuman animals affects how humans interact with nonhumans, and these deep-rooted beliefs, commonly shared across indigenous traditions, raise questions about contemporary hunting in indigenous communities.

RELATIONSHIPS

Indigenous peoples often assume that humans and other mammals, as well as fish, birds, and reptiles, share similar, basic qualities, and that a social and spiritual relationship exists between all creatures (Gill 1982, 121). Indigenous peoples tend to recognize similar thoughts and feelings across species. For example, the Koyukon (interior Alaska) understand that otters and suckerfish, weasels and ferrets "have a variety of emotions, different personal traits, talk to each other, and understand human language and behavior (Kinsley 1995, 38). In the Koyukon understanding, nonhuman animals even "have religious natures" (Kinsley 1995, 38). For the Waswanipi people of the Canadian subarctic, all creatures are "bound together" not only through common mythic origins, but also by "kindred 'human' qualities" such as their capacity for consciousness, and "their inherent and unquestioned 'social' worth" (Suzuki and Knudtson 1993, 68). In the Waswanipi view, all creatures "act intelligently and have wills and idiosyncrasies"; they "understand and are understood" by human beings (Suzuki and Knudston 1993, 68; italics removed).

The Chewong of Malaysia do not have a word for "human" that holds our species separate from all other animals; their language demonstrates that they recognize themselves to be just one animal among many. The Chewong also foster relativity of perception, which leads them to natural empathy for other creatures (Suzuki and Knudtson 1993, 109). They acknowledge that each species has a particular worldview—their own perception of reality; each conscious being has its own "eyes." There is an orangutan way of perceiving the world, a sun bear way of viewing life, a cobra way of knowing, a tufted duck way of seeing, a cave swift way of thinking, a water snail way of understanding, and a Javan rhinoceros way of comprehending reality (the latter of which we are in danger of losing forever, since there are only about sixty Javan rhinoceroses remaining in the wild). The Chewong have no "correct" way of perceiving reality; in order to understand gibbons or carp, one must endeavor to see the world through their eyes. Such an attempt lends compassion and grants "enormous freedom for each species to pursue its own peculiar strategy for survival" (Suzuki and Knudtson 1993, 110–11).

Like other indigenous peoples, some Sub-Saharan Africans find "themselves to be in a neighborly relationship with . . . earth, trees, animals and spirits" (Opoku 2006, 351). They communicate with other species, and understand turacos, elephants, and skinks to be "just like ourselves" (Opoku 2006, 351). People in this culture are not likely to envision themselves as separate and distinct; they are more likely to understand human beings "in relation with the world around them" (Opoku 2006, 353). Humans are not understood to be separate and complete in their own right in most indigenous African communities: "One of the cardinal beliefs in the traditional religious heritage of Africa is the interconnectedness of all that exists, and African people who continue [this] tradition believe themselves to be interconnected with, and interdependent on, all that exists" (Opoku 2006, 353).

INTERPENETRABILITY

Indigenous cultures often include a unique vision of species-relations best described as "interpenetrability" (Valladolid and Apffel-Marglin 2001, 658). An antelope is a human is a gopher; all are persons. Non-human animals take on human form, and humans take nonhuman forms. White Buffalo Woman is both human and buffalo (Erdoes and Ortiz 1984, 48). Haida myth (British Columbia, Canada) explains how a young woman who loved to swim gradually morphed to become the first beaver (Erdoes and Ortiz 1984, 392). A Mistassini Cree story remembers a hunter who took a caribou for a wife and then found that the caribou appeared to him "as humans who have a society" just like a human society (Kinsley 1995, 17). A Cherokee myth describes a man who moves in with bears, learning to live as they live and growing thick body hair—though he continues to walk upright. When hunters kill his closest bear friend, he returns to his human community and his wife, but soon dies because he "still had a bear's nature and could not live like a man" (Brown 1979, 22).

Yup'ik myths (northwestern Alaska) tell of nonhumans who "lifted up their beaks or muzzles, transforming themselves" into human beings (Feinup-Riordan 2001, 545). Sometimes their myths tell of nonhuman animals who join Yup'ik communities; other times they report humans who have gone to live with nonhumans. A boy who lived among geese flew away with the goose-people during autumn migration; a female goose came to live with people for a short time, staying out late in the spring and returning home with mud smeared on her face from eating grasses in the marshlands (Feinup-Riordan 2001, 545).

Snakes have a prominent place in myths in general, especially in myths of species transformation. One Sioux myth explains how three out of four brothers turn into rattlesnakes (Erdoes and Ortiz 1984, 405–7), while another recalls a band of warriors who turn into snakes, but remain friendly to their people (Spence 1985, 274). In a Tewa story (North American), fish-people fail in their prayer vigil, which causes a flood, after which a woman turns into a snake. Her friends carefully deliver her to the snake community, saying: "You are now a young lady snake, and with the help of the Great Spirit you will live among your own kind." To the snakes in the colony her friends add: "I have brought you a sister; take her into your arms" (Erdoes and Ortiz 1984, 416).

ETHICS

Myths contain and foster a people's understanding of their place in the world. Because nonhuman animals and humans are kin, because species are viewed as fluid, many indigenous communities feel an ethical and spiritual responsibility for other species—other members of their extended family (Noske 1997, 185; Kinsley 1995, 33). As a consequence of the reverence that indigenous peoples tend to feel toward the natural world, indigenous ethical codes teach respect for nature (VanStone 1974, 122). The peoples of the Great Plains of North America upheld values such as "truthful speech, generosity, kindness, and bravery," which "translate concretely into relationships with the beings whom humans meet in their everyday life—the animals, plants" and all of nature (Harrod 1987, 91). Community ethical obligations, such as respectful communication, carry across species. For example, indigenous peoples in western Canada still speak of nonhuman animals "with the same respect [they] have for humans," insisting that the forests must be protected because nonhuman animals "have a right to those forests, too" (Suzuki and Knudtson 1993, xxxv).

Indigenous peoples in India generally accept that "there is no distinction between the sacred and the profane or even between nature and humans" (Prabhu 2001, 58). The Bhima Saoras of central and southeast India accept Bengal tigers, jambu fruit doves, and the slender loris as part of their extended community, included within the framework of basic civilities and ethical obligations. Therefore, before the Bhima Saoras clear a new patch of ground, they offer a prayer to acknowledge that they are "robbing" the wild creatures of their homes and endangering their lives. In that same prayer, the Bhima Saoras ask "creatures big and small" to "go away with their children," so that people might cultivate the land without causing harm to the many creatures that live nearby (Prabhu 2001, 57).

The Bhima Saoras feel a deep affinity with other creatures, and find bats and whirring insects to be individuals and communities worthy of ethical and spiritual consideration. They view themselves as but one species among many, all of whom depend on the land for survival. They understand that clearing land for cultivation is an encroachment on the lives of other creatures, and they politely ask nonhumans to take their "children" and go elsewhere. Their inclusive understanding restricts the amount of land they are willing to take for crops, even though many of their own children die of starvation each year. Consequently, their inclusive vision prevents the devastating ecological affects of population growth among the Bhima Saoras (Prabhu 2001, 57).

Consistent with other indigenous peoples, the Nicobarese (Nicobar Islands, east of mainland India) view all life as part of one sacred community, a community that shares language and similar interests. They talk to plants while they gather the plant's leaves, begging to be forgiven for taking from the plant, and explaining why they have done so. "For the Nicobarese, there is animate life even in plants and trees," and they must maintain respectful relations with these green and growing beings (Prabhu 2001, 57–58). Their conversations with plants reveal humility—a recognition that they don't own other living entities—and that they cause harm when they sustain themselves by taking leaves. Their words are directed to the plants, but their conversation is an ongoing dialogue with their surroundings that is fundamentally spiritual in nature.

The Nahua (near Mexico City) also communicate with their surroundings, whether banana trees or toads, and they consider all who dwell in the *Cemanahuac* to be kin, standing within the human ethical sphere (Silva 2001, 319). The *Cemanahuac* is "that which surrounds us"—everything—and the Nahua understand that every aspect of one's natural surroundings is "important for the existence of any one being" (Silva 2001, 303, 319). Like the Nicobarese, the Nahua ask permission before taking from the trees. They see power in nature, and the Nahua believe that the forest can bring harm to those who overexploit, or who lack reverence. Indigenous peoples tend to understand more readily than modern people that "nature has its limits, can be exhausted, and is invaluable" (Silva 2001, 319). And the Nahua also expect other creatures to take from human beings. For example, the Nahua don't seek to eliminate "competitive" species, but accept other critters to eat part of the produce they plant (Silva 2001, 319–20). For the Nahua, sharing with individuals from other species is common sense. Why would any reasonable human wish to thrive while hoping that others starve?

Indigenous myths tend to encourage people to allow each creature habitat, and encouraging each individual and species to flourish.

Stories in the *Popol Vuh* (Mayan), for example, expresse the Creator's intent for ungulates and birds: "You the deer: sleep along the rivers, in the canyons. Be here in the meadows, in the thickets, in the forests, multiply yourselves. . . .You precious birds: your nests, your houses are in the trees, in the bushes. Multiply there, scatter there, in the branches of trees, the branches of bushes" (Montejo 2001, 183). Animals are *intended* to live in their natural homes, to multiply and prosper. "The fact that the Creator and Shaper provided each animal with [her or his] own habitat means that each has the right to a place and the right to live without being exterminated" (Montejo 2001, 183). In the *Popol Vuh*, nonhumans—and the plants and land itself—don't belong to people; "rather, people belong to the earth" (Henare 2001, 202). The Mayan *Popol Vuh* obligates humans to show "understanding, respect, and compassion" for all of the natural world (Montejo 2001, 183).

The Andean Quechua word *ayllu* refers to an ethical community containing both humans and nonhumans. "It is not only that everything is alive, but that everything is a person with whom one converses and shares, equally" (Valladolid and Apffel-Marglin 2001, 655):

> In this worldview humans are the equals of the maize, the llama, the mountains, the stars, rocks, lakes, the departed who are also alive, and so on. All are nature; humans do not feel alienated from her, nor superior to her. Humans are not distant from nature, they are part of nature. Humans feel that all are their *ayllu*, a Quechua word that in its broadest sense refers to the family that extends beyond just the human relatives. The rocks, the rivers, the sun, the moon, the plants, the animals are all members of the *ayllu*. All those that are found in the territory where they live in community are their *ayllu*. (Valladolid and Apffel-Marglin 2001, 656)

All that Andean peasants see in the world around them has its own life *in community with humans*, as part of the *ayllu*. From the smallest beetle to their majestic mountain protector, Apu Huanshan—all are one community, and "all are important" (Valladolid and Apffel-Marglin 2001, 657–58).

Consequently, Andean peasant cultivation is a ritual infused with love not only for plants and animals, "but also for the whole landscape that accompanies them in the nurturance of their fields, or '*chacras*,' which they consider to be members of their family, or *ayllu*" (Valladolid and Apffel-Marglin 2001, 651–52). And like the Nahua, Andean peasants expect to share what they cultivate. These experienced agriculturalists plant "a furrow for the hail, another one for the frost, another for insects, because they feel that, as members of the *ayllu*, these also [must] eat, and they do not worry when the frost lightly burns the leaves of their crops. They say, 'The frost has come to take its portion'" (Valladolid and Apffel-Marglin 2001, 657). When the snow comes late in spring and destroys leafy vegetables, when the mole digs under and hurts the roots of the growing greens, Andean peasants recognize that other community members have come to the table. Such a worldview leaves little room for anger, disappointment, or blame, and provides no incentive to control or dominate nature.

With regard to the natural world, for indigenous peoples, the "essential focus [is] relationship, [and] the guiding sentiment [is] respect" (Cajete 2001, 626).

THE PEACEABLE COMMUNITY

For indigenous peoples, who view sea lions and wildebeests as kin, killing "creatures who possess consciousness and life" for survival can be spiritually problematic, creating a "moral dilemma" (Harrod 1987, 45). For example, the Inuit hunter must, at some level, "confront considerable psychological pain in the process of slaying [nonhumans] that he believes are endowed with the vitality, sentience, and sacredness inherent in his own human kin" (Suzuki and Knudtson 1993, 104). Hunters live close to the animals they kill, know their habits, watch them go about their daily lives, and come close enough to kill them, most often without the benefit of modern technology. Many myths reveal a troubled conscience among indigenous peoples who kill nonhuman animals—kin—to feed themselves, and their families (Serpell 1992, 29).

Given the requirement for respect between humans and the rest of nature, there is a healthy measure of fear that accompanies any killing. An Inuit hunter comments on hunting in light of his understanding of the nature and power of nonhuman animals:

> The greatest peril of life lies in the fact that human food consists entirely of souls. All the creatures that we have to kill and eat, all those that we have to strike down and destroy to make clothes for ourselves, have souls, like we have, souls that do not perish with the body, and which must therefore be propitiated lest they should revenge themselves on us for taking away their bodies. (Suzuki and Knudtson 1993, 104)

Many creation stories (from most religious traditions) speak of a time when there was no bloodshed (Harrod 1987, 44). For example, a Hopi myth recalls: "In the old days many Hopis lived at Oraibi, with birds and animals living as equals among them" (Brown 1979, 14). The Cheyenne of the Great Plains remember the original creation, where "people and animals lived in peace. None, neither people nor [nonhuman] animals, ate flesh" (Erdoes and Ortiz 1984, 390). A Navajo myth (southwestern United States) recalls a time when there was plenty of food for everyone. In this peaceful community all living beings "spoke the same language, and they all had the teeth, claws, feet, and wings of insects" (Rosenberg 1994, 499). These long-ago creatures could remove their wings; they lived in caves, and "ate only what food they could gather and eat raw, such as nuts, seeds, roots, and berries"—they were vegan (Rosenberg 1994, 499).

While myths recall a time of peace, these ancient yet living stories also explain why or how "the interrelatedness of the creation is disturbed"—why and how killing began (Harrod 1987, 44). A Cherokee myth remembers a time when "humans and animals freely communicated" as one community (Bierlein 1994, 115); then humans began killing other animals for fur and food. "It was easy to do at this time, as the animals were completely unprepared to be hunted and they walked up to human beings, trusting them. Then the animals became angry" (Bierlein 1994, 115). The bears met in council and decided on open warfare (Spence 1985, 249). Then the deer met in council, then fish and reptiles, birds and insects. They were angry with the humans and responded by inflicting humans with diseases and bad dreams (Bierlein 1994, 115). From an original world of peace, humans started a life of predation, which brought discord and misery.

Cheyenne (Great Plains) myths record a long-ago world that was created as an interrelated whole, where all beings shared kinship: minnows, blue herons, and people "lived together as friends" (Harrod 1987, 49). As time passed, being large and powerful, buffalo came to feel superior, and thought that buffalo-people might kill and eat human-people. Humans reminded buffalo that all creatures were created equally, and that one should not eat the other. But the humans went on to say that, if one creature *did* reign supreme, it ought to be humans. At an impasse, they decided to have a contest—a race—to determine who would be the dominant species. Interestingly, humans admitted that they were slower before the race was underway, so birds were pitted against buffalo on behalf of humans—an admittance of human inferiority even before the contest began.

When the day of the great race arrives, Slim Buffalo Woman is pitted against Hummingbird, Meadowlark, Hawk, and Magpie—four against one, and not one human standing at the starting line. At the end of the race, only one bird remains, Magpie, who defeats Slim Buffalo Woman by a hair, and so "people became more powerful than the buffalo and all the other animals"—even the birds, who raced on behalf of physically challenged humans (Erdoes and Ortiz 1984, 390–

92). After the great race, buffalo were frightened of human beings, and humans began to eat flesh—the original community of beings had been broken (Harrod 1987, 50).

The indigenous myths demonstrate that indigenous peoples have long understood that predation is not the best way to interact with kin. The Peaceful Community of earlier times is remembered fondly in these indigenous myths, and is portrayed as preferable.

HUNTING AND FISHING IN CONTEMPORARY TIMES

Indigenous religious beliefs and practices tend to limit and guide what humans may do to other creatures, to slow lorises and gophers, caribou and herring.

Victoria Tauli-Corpuz, who grew up among the Igorot in a small community in the northern Philippines, remembers an important indigenous concept that means something like "'exercise caution,' 'don't do it,' or 'have limits'," which guides human relations with "other human beings, other creations (animal, plant, microorganisms), the spirit world, and nature in general." Tauli-Corpuz recalls another closely related concept that restricts what humans may do to other creatures, which means "taboo, forbidden, holy, or sacred." For Igorot people, these two words are "fundamental principles which underpin the traditional religion of the Igorots and by which every Igorot should live" (Tauli-Corpuz 2001, 281). They must use restraint and stay within the bounds of ethics and maintain respectful relations when dealing with the natural world.

Indigenous hunting and fishing were once rooted in necessity, and were undertaken respectfully, with a measure of fear, because killing one's powerful kin is a risky way to put food on the table. Hunting and fishing without necessity run contrary to sacred indigenous teachings and practices; such killing is dangerous, taboo, and contrary to ancient lifeways. An Iroquois myth records how a man in his time of need and desperation was saved by animals because they "remembered his kindness to them in former days, how he had never slain an animal unless he really needed it for food or clothing, how he had loved and protected the trees and the flowers" (Spence 259). A Waswanipi Cree hunter (Canadian Subarctic), commenting that technology now allows people to kill beyond what is necessary, cautions against doing so, noting that "killing them for fun or self-aggrandizement" demonstrates "the ultimate disdain" for other creatures (Suzuki and Knudtson1993, 106, italics removed).

Koyukon and Yup'ik people (Alaska) consider nonhuman animals to be both sacred and powerful, and human survival is believed to be dependent on harmonious relations between humans and nonhumans. In the sacred lore of the Koyukon, Raven created a world infused with spiritual powers, and constant reverence is therefore required to avoid misfortune brought on by insulted spirits (Nelson 1983, 240). Humans are at the mercy of other animals. One Koyukon noted: "Each animal knows way more than you do. . . . [T]he old people . . . told us never to bother anything unless we really needed it" (Nelson 1983, 225).

Just as Koyukon communities have no ruler, they do not envision an almighty ruler of the universe. Koyukon and Yup'ik people associate with other animals *as spiritual powers* (VanStone 1974, 65), and nonhumans are understood to be very powerful indeed. "Nature is not governed by God, nature *is* God" (Nelson 1983, n.p.). A hunter who abuses those on whom he depends for food is likely to find himself and his family without sustenance.

CONTEMPORARY APPLICATION OF INDIGENOUS LIFEWAYS

Hunting and fishing—consuming nonhuman animal products of any kind—is now optional for most indigenous peoples, especially in Western nations. For the vast majority of indigenous peoples, hunting and fishing are no longer necessary for survival. *No one can "kill respectfully" when survival does not require one to kill.*

Some indigenous peoples maintain historic traditions in contemporary times by denouncing unnecessary killing and environmentally destructive practices. Three examples of such indigenous practices in Washington State demonstrate that the historic environmental ethic, based on harmony, kinship, and killing only when necessary, is alive and well:

> In January of 2000, four indigenous groups in western Washington accepted three hundred pounds of deer and elk flesh from those nonhuman animals who had been inadvertently killed on roadways. Because they prefer to eat flesh, and because they knew they could not justify hunting when there was already plenty of food to eat, they gave up their legal right to hunt in exchange for subsisting on roadkill, thereby saving the lives of many nonhumans (Kelley 2000).

Barbara Aripa, a Colville elder in eastern Washington, "has taken it upon herself to preserve her people's way of life. She fought successfully to ban clear-cutting and herbicide spraying in the reservation's forests" (Associated Press 1999, C5). Aripa is currently fighting against plans for a gold mine that could leak cyanide into surrounding wilderness. She is working to protect the sacred lands on which she lives; she also teaches traditional beliefs and practices that don't entail killing, such as how to make shawls and dresses (Associated Press).

Elders of the Makah tribe in western Washington, a tribe that traditionally hunted whales for survival, have spoken out against a renewed hunt because killing whales is no longer necessary. Isabelle Ides (age ninety-six), Harry Claplonhoo (seventy-eight), Margaret Irving (eighty), Ruth Claplanhoo (ninety-four), Viola Johnson (eighty-eight), Alberta N. Thompson (seventy-two), and Lena McGee (ninety-two) denounced plans to renew a now unnecessary whale hunt. Alberta Thompson noted that such a hunt would be viewed differently "if the whale meat were truly needed . . . as in the times of the ancestors. . . . But that is no longer true today" (Dunagan 1998, n.p.). Environmental organizations provided space in the *Peninsula Daily News* for Makah elders to speak their minds:

> We are elders of the Makah Indian Nation (Ko-Ditch-ee-ot) which means People of the Cape. We oppose this Whale hunt our tribe is going to do.
>
> . . . The Whale hunt issue has never been brought to the people to inform them and there is no spiritual training going on. We believe they, the Council, will just shoot the Whale, and we think the word "subsistence" is the wrong thing to say when our people haven't used or had Whale meat/blubber since the early 1900's.
>
> For these reasons we believe the hunt is only for the money. They can't say "Traditional, Spiritual and for Subsistence" in the same breath when no training is going on, just talk.
>
> Whale watching is an alternative we support. (Ides *et al.* 2000, n.p.)

These contemporary examples demonstrate the resilience and vitality of indigenous teachings that require human beings to respect nature, including nonhuman animals. Many indigenous peoples continue to maintain their traditional lifeways and their traditional ethics (which only permit killing for survival), offering an example of the consistent application and maintenance of ancient traditions and lifeways in contemporary times.

CONCLUSION

Indigenous traditions tend to exemplify a spiritual vision that includes all of nature, a worldview of universal respect and interdependence. Indigenous peoples generally understand that humans and other animals are similar in critical ways, and they envision the species of an individual as fluid. For many indigenous peoples, all that is natural in their surroundings is considered to be part of their community, including nonhuman animals. Communities of other creatures, and other creatures themselves, are envisioned as similar to human communities and individuals in all significant respects. Indigenous ethics teach people to respect nature, including nonhumans, who are believed to be spiritually powerful.

Many indigenous myths teach of a pre-existent state of peace in which humans and nonhumans lived without bloodshed. Indigenous myths explain how this peace was lost, and invariably portray this previous, vegan existence as preferable. Myths also reveal that killing a powerful individual who is considered to be one's own kin, is an undesirable—even dangerous—enterprise. Hunting and fishing are only permissible when necessary for survival.

Ancient indigenous worldviews challenge contemporary indigenous peoples to rethink hunting and fishing in today's world. Many indigenous peoples, especially those living in Western countries, no longer need to hunt or fish to survive. Consequently, some contemporary indigenous peoples are speaking out against hunting and fishing, and are making choices that demonstrate an ongoing commitment to ancient lifeways of respect for nonhumans—a respect that only permits killing out of necessity.

16

Mother Earth and All Her Children

LINDA G. FISHER

S ince I was a young child I've had an affinity for painting, draw- ing, and animals. Now a professional artist and animal activist, I still make animals the primary subjects of my paintings. But there's more to my work than love for all animals. Amid my large col- orful paintings and hundreds of animal photographs is a small black- and-white photograph—carefully placed in a shrine-like niche. This picture is the focus of my studio. Why, people ask me, is the Native American Duwamish Indian, Chief Seattle, the focus and inspiration for most of my work?

FISHING WITH MY FATHER

My sensitivity to the suffering and deaths of other animals has been with me since my earliest days. I remember when I was eight years old we went camping and my father decided to introduce his three young children to the joys of fishing. To ensure that my brother, my sister, and I would not be disappointed, he took us to a man-made lake that was frequently supplied with live fish. We paid a fee, for which we were guaranteed a catch.

I was excited because I thought that fishing was synonymous with swimming, playing, and having fun in the water. Being a child, I giggled joyfully and jumped up and down when they handed me my fishing pole. After what seemed an awful lot of preparation, I slowly dropped the line into the lake, ready to wait patiently. To my surprise, I very quickly felt a tug on my fishing pole, and the reel began to spin. My excitement and joy vanished as the line swayed back and forth with the fish's flight. I held on as tight as I could, but was frightened, and quickly called for help. My father came running, yelling "Pull him in! Turn the reel!"

The tighter I held the pole, and the more I tugged, the more the fish resisted, desperate to escape. As if the fishing line were a transmitter traveling through the pole, I could feel the fish's fear and terror, and they became my fear and terror. The fish panicked; I panicked. He or she thrashed back and forth; I screamed. I felt horrible and I wanted to be rid of the pole, the line, *and* the fish.

I dropped the pole and ran away crying. I was crying for the fish, and also crying because I felt embarrassed for running away. I wanted to be like others. I wanted to enjoy fishing, but I hated it. I was confused and I didn't understand why the fish's pain and fear bothered me—only me—and not anyone else. There was only one thing I knew for sure: The fish was frightened, desperate, and fighting for his or her life. I never fished again.

LEARNING ABOUT SNAKES AND HUMANS

My paternal, white grandfather was a large, easy-going man, who in his younger days was neither patient nor docile. Having many more years behind him by the time his grandchildren came along, he'd grown a bit more tolerant and loving.

When I was nine or ten, my grandfather came to live with us while our parents were traveling on business. We lived in the country, and he helped us with our chores and showed us how to make things. We three children came upon a snake one day, and called our grandfather with great excitement so that he would come and see our discovery. But for reasons I will never understand, he decided to show us how a snake can still wiggle if you cut him or her into sections. We watched an innocent snake be cut into pieces, slice by slice, bit by bit, and yes, his body parts wiggled just like my grandfather said they would. Why did I need to see that? Was the snake's life worth nothing?

I do not understand cruelty and indifference, whether directed toward people or other creatures. I didn't know what to think when my grandfather destroyed a snake for no justifiable reason. I just remember thinking it was wrong to cut up a snake. Was my grandfather an unreasonable and cruel man? No. Not any more than anyone else. Lots of people cut up snakes for no reason.

MOTHER EARTH AND NATIVE TRADITIONS

Chief Seattle (c. 1780–1866) was considered one of the greatest Indian orators. A man of great wisdom, he was honored and respected not only by his own people but also by many non-Indians. He spoke about Indian ways, traditions, and spirituality, which translated into a simple plea to respect Mother Earth and Her animals.

The Indians of yesterday were true conservationists. They understood the inherent dangers of overtaxing Earth and Her creatures, so much so in fact that no species would ever be hunted to scarcity or extinction, not even for religious purposes. Indians relied on Earth to tell them about their lives and spiritual practices. They understood the changes of life, the cycle of seasons, and the tendencies of evolution. They took their direction from nature. They killed only to stay alive.

There was a time in history when Native Americans were considered heathens because they regarded the land as Mother, believing that spirit was not just in animals, but also in rocks and trees. Historical records indicate that as early as the 1700s, the white man's pollution and dirty ways offended Indian people. But as centuries passed and Westerners became more aware of their polluted rivers and air, the Indian concept of conservation, of protecting the environment, was respected by some non-Indian people. Native American philosophy, once thought heathen and barbaric, has become politically correct.

When I hear about natives slaughtering whales in the twenty-first century, about killing eagles for the sake of ceremony, or killing any animal for the sake of vanity and "tradition," I wonder what has happened. What has changed? In contemporary times, when people have traded in guns for cameras, why has traditional Indian philosophy become unfashionable and politically *incorrect*—don't kill unless you *must*? Where will Indian culture draw the line for maintaining bloody traditions in a modern, ecologically minded society?

At one time, the Mayans sacrificed young maidens each season to keep their gods happy, casting them into deep pits. Some peoples of the rainforests in New Guinea and New Zealand practiced cannibalism for spiritual and religious purposes until recently. When Europeans invaded those territories, these religious practices were outlawed. So what of a cannibal's right to retain tradition? Should they renew these ancient practices, too?

A century ago, a ceremonial drum was taken from a native tribe, and eventually ended up in a prestigious, non-Indian museum, where it was safely protected in a climate-controlled environment—until recently. The tribe fought a vigorous legal battle to retrieve their drum, which had been taken by the American government, and won. The tribe regained custody of their sacred possession. On hearing the news, I felt a sense of vindication for my people. The tribal chief indicated that the drum would be used once again for ceremonial and spiritual purposes. On reflection, I realized that this drum—protected and carefully guarded for over a hundred years—was instrumental in educating millions of people about the beauty of an ancient culture.

Back with its rightful owner, the drum will offer a sense of spiritual awakening, but what about our children's children? How many more decades of pounding can an ancient drum withstand? How long will it survive before it disintegrates and is lost forever?

WHITE WAYS, NATIVE WAYS: ANIMAL EXPLOITATION

The traditional Hollywood perception of a Native American diet and lifestyle is not representative of ancient Native Americans. The Americas were a rich and fertile land, providing plentiful berries, vegetables, nuts, beans, squash, roots, fruits, corn, and wild rice. Most tribal people survived comfortably eating meat sparingly, while thriving on the cornucopia of the land. When it was necessary for an animal's life to be taken for food, all remaining parts of the animal were used for other necessities. Nothing was discarded or wasted. For example, clothing was made from hides and fur, and tools were made from bone. It wasn't until the Europeans introduced the commercial fur trade that buffalo were pushed nearly to extinction.

The modern day meat industry is filled with unimaginable horror and suffering. After watching a load of chickens (en route to a poultry processing plant) fall from a truck, I wrote this poem, *Poultry Processing Plant*:

> I couldn't take it any longer.
> I had to turn around and go back—
> I had to speak out for chickens that had fallen off the truck,
> onto the Highway
> while I watched oncoming cars take what was left of their
> fragile and tormented lives.
>
> I approached the office entrance.
> The stench was strong though I had not yet entered.
> When the door opened, I was overcome with the smell of horror.

It looked like any other office,
Except for the overpowering, putrid odor.

 "How can you work here?" I said
To a woman in a dress and high heels.

I had accomplished my task and I left,
but I felt no relief.
I felt contaminated.
The pain, suffering, and death were still on my skin and my clothes,
and high up in my nostrils.
When I got home, I took a shower,
but the smell would not leave.

I talked to the victims:
I am sorry, chickens, for your painful and sad existence.
No one can hear your cries, your suffering;
no one can see your fear.

I am sorry that I tried to wash away
the only "voice" you have.
I embrace it as a reminder never to abandon you,
    to, passionately speak for you
until you are free.

FINDING THE INDIAN PATH

Is our desire to retain outmoded traditions not sometimes selfish and unwise—even destructive? Ironically, is this not the same grasping mentality that white men had when they took Indian land? Reflecting on the recent renewal of the whale hunt by northwestern tribes, and the reclaiming of an ancient drum, I can't help but see an analogy—is the whale not like the drum? Perhaps if we preserve the whale rather than the hunt, and preserve the ancient drum—while making a new drum—our children's children will be able to appreciate and witness a part of the splendor of their peoples' history.

Less than a hundred years ago American Indians were still being driven from their lands and forced onto reservations. They not only lost their lands, they lost their language, their religion, and their identity. As I watch the news and read the headlines, following the battle that my relatives are fighting to maintain native traditions, I understand their struggle. Centuries of injustice, deeply embedded in their lives, are painful sores that do not seem to be willing to heal. We are constantly reminded. Ongoing battles for the protection of tribal lands, and tribal rights, are a continuing source of concern for Indian peoples. The injustices that were perpetrated against the native people constitute an American holocaust. Hopefully, American immigrants have learned from this cruelty and indifference, from the blood that their ancestors shed, and the lives that their ancestors destroyed. Maybe modern native peoples can learn something from this, too.

In this new millennium, it appears that the white man and the Indian are on the same course at last . . . but it's not a good course. Both pursue self-interest without hearing the messages of Earth and the animals.

Being part Ojibway and Cherokee, I attend powwows and other Native American functions, where I proudly wear my inherited Ojibway beaded jewelry. But as I become lost in the hypnotic and joyful sounds of drumming, I feel uneasy when I realize that I am surrounded by leather clothing, feather headdresses, and trinkets made of bear claws, cougar teeth, turtle shells, and whale bones—all in the name of a proud Indian culture now part of the modern commercial trade. I feel torn and saddened by what I see. Most of us—including the American Indian—no longer need to hunt to survive, yet we still kill.

We continue to associate the Indian (even today's Indians) with wearing and using animal hides, furs, and feathers. But I assure you, in spite of my vegan diet and my avoidance of hides and fur, my Indianness is alive and quite evident. And the same is true for my mother, who is both an elder of our Ojibway tribe and a vegetarian. Interestingly, it's not our dark hair, dark eyes, and Indian features that speak for who we are, but something much deeper, something not visually apparent: our commitment to the teachings of our ancestors.

Ironically, the modern animal rights philosophy resonates with native prophecy. Many centuries ago, an Ojibway prophet predicted that the Indian people would have to change their ways to survive. He called it the Seven Fire Prophecy. It seems that we are now on the seventh prediction, a time during which those who once denied their heritage will return to embrace their Indianness. An ancient Ojibway prayer titled "To Walk in Our Sacred Way" speaks to us in this time of need:

> Grandfather,
> Look at our brokenness.
> We know that in all Creation
> Only the human family
> Has strayed from the Sacred Way.
> We know that we are the ones
> Who are divided
> And we are the ones
> Who must come back together
> To walk in the Sacred Way.
>
> Grandfather,
> Sacred One,
> Teach us love, compassion, and honor
> That we may heal the Earth
> And heal each other.

As I sit in front of my easel before a stark, white canvas, waiting to bring a variety of colorful animals to life in my studio, I gaze into

Chief Seattle's eyes and wonder what wisdom he might share today. In light of our destruction of Earth and nonhuman animals, I believe my Indian ancestors would say that history is not the present. If we asked them about our "right to hunt," granted by the immigrants who have taken over this land, I believe they would tell us not to harm our cousins because we do not need to kill to live. I believe they would tell us to regard Mother Earth's plea—it is a time to protect and preserve, not destroy and kill.

17

Wiccan Spirituality and Animal Advocacy

Perfect Love and Perfect Trust

DIANNE SYLVAN

Wicca is a religion of Earth and stars, wind and rain, of ivy growing in spirals and people dancing in spirals. It is a religion of field and forest and creatures that dwell therein. It is also a religion of responsibility and compassion with only one true dogma, the Wiccan Rede: "And it harm none, do what you will." Interpretations of this guideline vary because Wicca is also a religion of the individual. Within a fairly loose set of practices and ideas, the individual is responsible for his or her ongoing spiritual evolution and relationship with the sacred. The challenge, and the beauty, is that in the Wiccan worldview, "sacred" encompasses everything.

Wicca is the religion I have practiced for the last fourteen years. It is one of many neopagan religions, or paths, that have resurfaced from a nearly forgotten pre-Christian past, or—like Wicca itself— these neopagan religions are a modern synthesis of ancient ideas and mythology. My religious beliefs have done many things for me as I have matured. Wicca has helped me to reclaim the sanctity of my body, to see the holiness of the environment and of every living thing, to give voice to the part of me that knew God as both feminine and masculine, and to embrace the ethical imperative of animal advocacy.

Wicca was brought into the public eye in 1954 by an Englishman named Gerald Gardner (Hutton 1999, 206), and although debate continues as to whether he invented the religion or simply popularized something that already existed, few would argue that Gardner, his students, and a subsequent generation (that brought the religion to America) are responsible for its emergence as one of the most rapidly growing spiritualities in the Western world (Robinson 2001).

New religions appear when established religions no longer serve practitioners, or suit the world in which they live, or when religious institutions are unable to evolve as society evolves. In this era of environmental devastation, relentless animal slaughter, and wars that threaten our civilizations—all in the name of the gods of greed and fear—a shift to spiritual paths that revere the natural world and regard all life as sacred is not only timely but absolutely necessary. Sometimes this change comes from within established religions, and other times, entirely new religious ways provide alternatives.

We have, as a society, turned Mother Earth into a factory farmed dairy cow: hooking her up to cruel machines that pump her dry, taking away her children to torment and slaughter, and chopping up and selling off anything that's left after she has given all her bounty to our consumer lusts. In this, we have committed the ultimate sacrilege, and only a total paradigm shift will enable us to pay penance and restore balance. It is this paradigm shift, from a hatred and fear of the feminine (and Earth), to a reverence for life—whether footed, furred, leafed, or finned—that Wicca and other neopagan religions seek to awaken in each person who takes up the path of Goddess and God.

However, when Earth and the natural world—including nonhuman animals—are viewed in this new light, the rationale for exploitation suddenly evaporates. What is held sacred must not be degraded.

What is held sacred must not be bought and sold, must not be treated as soulless and mindless. If Earth is sacred, then so are plants and animals that grow, and live, and die on her skin, and as such must be treated with the same reverence. Corporate America, and a great many politicians, would lose influence and power (and above all, profit) with such a transformation, and so we are bombarded by media images of the "perfect" materialistic life, with only occasional lip service given to the consequences of our relentless desire to own and have more, more, more.

Wiccans (and most neopagans) revere Earth as a manifestation of the divine. Wiccans commonly refer to Earth as an aspect of the Great Mother; we worship both the masculine and feminine deity as two halves of a dynamic, organic whole. We consider the cycle of the seasons to be a holy metaphor for the cycle of creation and destruction, and also for the cycle of our own individual lives. Some people use this metaphor as a means to justify taking life for food, and many neopagans eat meat (and hunt); they claim that the relationship between predator and prey is natural and sacred, and consider themselves to be natural predators. Many neopagan groups revere hunter gods of the woods and find hunting and killing animals to be a religious experience. But in my experience, once people are presented with the facts about how animals are treated on factory farms before their bodies and body parts arrive in the supermarket, about how animal death industries pollute and destroy the sacred environment— merely to place nonritual hamburger on its Styrofoam plate—it is no longer possible to spiritually justify supporting such industries. With this information in hand, a great many neopagans turn to a vegan or vegetarian diet, or at least move decisively away from factory farmed animal products (including milk, eggs, and flesh).

There's nothing natural or spiritual about a chicken confined to a crate with four of her sisters, unable to walk, peck, or scratch, forced to lay eggs for human consumption. There's nothing holy about a "dairy" cow hanging by her hind leg waiting to have her throat slit, with the screaming echo of her terrified herd-mates all around. Milk is the product of one of the most egregious violations of nature: the manipulation of the maternal instinct of cows, who are fed full of hormones and forcibly impregnated (over and over), only to have their babies taken away at birth, for the sake of the dairy industry.

The animal industries are a rape of nature, the rape of the Mother Goddess. There's no reverence in dumping tons of animal waste and industrial byproducts from factory farms into rivers, Mother Earth's blood vessels. It is not a coincidence that most of the cruelest torments are inflicted on factory farmed females—hens, cows, turkeys, and sows. Historically, the Divine Feminine has been denigrated, relegated to subservient roles, and finally denied existence in Judeo-Christian religions. Neopagan religions are bringing Her back from this patriarchal shadow.

Neopagans protect freedoms and individuality. We have no pope, no ruling class, and therefore no single set of absolute laws that govern all. Certain practices and concepts are taught to most initiates, but the interpretation and enactment of those concepts remains a personal matter. Therefore, it's impossible to say "all Wiccans do this," or "all Wiccans believe that." To attempt to speak for the community as a whole is inaccurate as well as dishonest. I can, however, say that a large number of Wiccans practice some form of advocacy—many are involved in social causes such as heightened GLBT rights, environmental protection, and/or the cause of animal rights. Those who become involved in one form of activism often find themselves championing many other causes, because Wiccans view the entire universe as an intricately connected and interdependent whole. They take to heart the popular activist mantra: "No one is free while others are oppressed."

Wicca is an extremely eclectic religion, embracing mythology and religious symbolism from all over the world. One of many Asian aspects of the Goddess, Green Tara, perfectly embodies the concept of *ahimsa*. I have adopted the Eastern ideal of *ahimsa*, a Sanskrit term that's translated directly as "noninjury" ("*Ahimsa*" 2008), but which contains a connotation of "dynamic harmlessness." Tara is often depicted resting upon a lotus flower with Her right leg extended, a symbol of readiness to stand up and take action when compassion and mercy are needed. She is gentle, but can be fierce in the service of love. Tara's image often adorns the altars of neopagans, who practice Yoga and meditate, or who (like me) find *ahimsa* and the Wiccan Rede inextricably linked.

"Rede" means "counsel, advice," not "law" ("Rede" n.d.). As with most everything else in Wicca, rede is left to the individual to interpret, but it's my feeling and experience that the two halves of the phrase—"harm none" and "do what you will"—indicate a need to seek balance between the harm every human being does simply by consuming and interacting with other beings, and the tremendous gift of free will. Rede does not encourage passivity, simply allowing events to occur around us; the rede carries an overtone of "dynamic harmlessness" like *ahimsa*. The rede encourages us to take action, like Green Tara—to stand up and make a difference, even a slight one, for Earth and Her children.

Nature, the outward form of deity, is our greatest teacher. Most Wiccans seek to connect with four natural elements: earth, air, fire, and water. This connection is not simply intellectual or symbolic, it is a visceral, body-and-soul relationship of fingers in the soil and bare feet on the grass. We practice our seasonal and lunar rituals not simply to recall a distant, pagan past, but to reconnect firmly in the present, with a world that surrounds and supports us. We not only revere nature, but are part of nature. We don't see ourselves as apart or above, or as having been given dominion over plant and animal kingdoms; we see ourselves in relation with all beings, who are fellow travelers, each one on their own individual path with their own individual purposes.

From nature we learn that every person, every animal, every plant has a part to play and should be allowed to fulfill their role in life with equal freedom. How can anyone believe that intelligent, playful creatures like pigs are *rightly* tormented and sentenced to a lingering death in factory farms? Nature has given each species tools to survive and thrive in the natural world. Nature is far too wise to waste millions of years of evolution on a being whose only purpose is to stand knee deep in manure, to be systematically dismembered in their youth. If that were the only purpose of a pig, a pig would not need legs, a curly tail, or a brain—yet pigs are as intelligent as dogs (Duchene 2006).

It is impossible to work for the preservation of the natural world and fail to see the link between earth and animal liberation. Wiccans tend to be critical thinkers who have changed their religious affiliation after questioning the religion of their childhood; this tendency toward questioning and examination leads many Wiccans to question established societal norms, even those that are most deeply rooted. Once we have uncovered the truths buried under the propaganda of "happy cows and chickens," we can no longer turn a blind eye to such a blatant assault on that which we hold sacred: Earth, our Goddess and our God. For most neopagans, recycling cans isn't enough— in the name of our deities, based on our conscience, more action is required.

Wicca's holistic worldview emphasizes the value of each individual's contribution to the world. We are each equally vital in the unfolding of creation, we are each a cell in the body of Gaia, the Earth Mother. Personal empowerment and responsibility are vital to our worldview. In the absence of large institutions such as churches, Wiccan individuality encourages each of us to make a difference—first on a personal scale, then on a local level, and then extending out into the global community of which we are each an integral part. We answer to our deities and to our consciences; we don't answer to a guru, minister, or faceless bureaucracy.

Not only can one person make a difference; one person *must* make a difference. Therefore, we work both in the spiritual and the phys-

ical realms. We sign petitions and join protests; we take in homeless animals and cook vegan meals. We practice rituals, magic, and
methods of spiritual ecstasy like dance, drumming, and meditative
trances, in order to create positive change in the material world. We
chant, dance, light candles, and make petitions to deities, praying for
a kinder, more compassionate world, where the ideal of *ahimsa* and
the guidance of the Wiccan Rede can lead us, one person at a time,
into rivers of blessed humanity, into the light of compassion. We seek
to do our part to save this planet, Gaia, the Mother of All, and rest in
the knowledge that we have extended a hand of friendship to our fellow creatures, for we are all Her children, in joy and suffering, in life
and death, in perfect love and perfect trust.

Change is the only eternal truth. We understand that change
begins with the individual. Only by changing each strand in the great
web of life, one by one, hand over hand, can we reweave the pattern
of the world. We understand that each part affects the whole, and that
responsibility for our personal lives must eventually intersect with the
lives of others, including both nonhuman and human animals. The
universe is a vast interconnected web of cause and effect; changing
the weave of a single strand can have repercussions that alter the very
fabric of the world. Knowing that, the question is not "Can one person make a difference?" but "What difference do I intend to make?"

A Vegan Pagan's Prayer (Sylvan 2008)

Lord of the forest and field, Lady of the starlit night,
I acknowledge the truth that for me to live, something must die.
I give thanks for the gift of free will,
And I acknowledge the responsibility that comes with freedom of
    choice.
I choose to abstain from the cycle of unnecessary suffering.
I pledge to be an agent of healing, not a bystander to slaughter.
I say to the animals:

You do not have to suffer and die for me.
I say to the workers:
You do not have to kill for me.
I say to the corporate death machine:
You will no longer profit from my blindness.
I say to the Earth and all that is holy,
Though we are taught to feast upon war,
I choose to lay down the sword
And take up peace instead.
I ally myself with Nature, not as her master, but as her child.
I will not claim dominion over that which is wiser than I.
Lord of the forest and field, Lady of the starlit night,
May compassion fulfill and transform me,
May I give as You give, may I love as You love,
And may my choices bring grace to my life
As You bring grace to the world.
Blessed be.

18

Wicca, Ecofeminism, and Animal Advocacy

The Earth Path Less Traveled

FIREWEED

"If we *all* sit on the road, they can't arrest us *all*! If we *all* sit on the road . . . !" The sound of these words chanted in unison, over and over by hundreds of protestors, still echoes clearly in my mind. As it turns out, everyone who sat on the road that day was arrested.

The year was 1993. The place was British Columbia, Canada, where concerned people from around the world gathered to try to save the ancient old growth forests of Clayoquot Sound. Over the course of that summer, some eight hundred women, men, and children were arrested for conscientious objection to corporate-driven "power-over" and government-sanctioned ecosystem destruction. We formed what eventually became known as the largest civil disobedience action in Canadian history.

Protestors who streamed through our campaign's Peace Camp came from many walks of life, cultural backgrounds, and religious persuasions. We were united by the common goal of protecting *bio-diversity*—a commitment not only to the trees that are in essence the lungs of our planet, but to the lives of bears, wolves, salmon, marbled murrelets, and countless other creatures that exist interdependently in this pristine old-growth habitat.[1] Fifteen years later, some of the last fully intact temperate rain forests remain at risk.

While reporters focused on capturing images of protestors pleading passionately for an end to "the war against nature/the war against wildlife," a less well publicized form of animal advocacy was championed discreetly behind the scenes. Volunteer cooks fueled the dissidence of thousands of demonstrators, all summer long, with animal-product-free meals.

International media took note that "ecofeminism"—the merger of feminist consciousness and environmentalism—was instrumental in the Clayoquot campaign. Some of us, inspired by ecofeminism, ground our activist politics in a worldview that unites personal with political and spiritual. When confronted on the front lines by angry loggers wearing t-shirts with slogans like "Wipe Your Ass with a Spotted Owl" and "Bugger a Tree Hugger," our courage was bolstered by the solidarity we also shared as Witches.

Great diversity exists within neopagan and other Western Earth-based traditions that identify as contemporary witchcraft, but recognition that *all* of creation is contained within the holy body of a great cosmic Mother lies at the heart of what many Witches of European descent refer to today as the Craft, Wicca, or the Old Religion. In sharing my own personal reflections in this chapter, I speak "out of" a Wiccan tradition, but not for all Wiccans, or for all Wiccan traditions.[2]

Most of the women and men I've known who identify as Witches, or Wiccans (not everyone uses these terms interchangeably as I do), equate honoring the Divine Feminine principle with respecting "the natural world."[3] (Yet how the concept of "respect" is interpreted and enacted differs considerably, with significant consequence for animals, as we shall see.)

Any choice I make to sacrifice my own freedom, comfort, and safety for Earth and Her creatures is both personal and religious, rooted in spiritual understandings carried by Wiccan incantations such as this:

By the Earth that is Her body,
By the Air that is Her sweet breath,
By the Fire of Her bright spirit,
And by the Waters of Her living womb.[4]

My ancestry is primarily Celtic, with traces of Mi'kmaq (from the east coast of Canada). Ecofeminist consciousness encourages women and men to look to their cultures of origin for Earth-based spiritual sustenance. Going back far enough, many of us can lay claim to a heritage rooted in the Earth Mother, a heritage that provides ancient wisdom that can be adapted to contemporary life.

Women in particular, disillusioned with patriarchal constructs of mainstream religions that uphold human dominion over Earth, have found a home in the Craft, sharing company with others who revere the Great Goddess in Her many manifestations across time and space. Some ecofeminists reject feminization of the primal life force, because they fear that equating women and nature in a patriarchal culture will only further their mutual subjugation. But for those of us who find a profound sense of empowerment in this relationship, *She is alive in us, as we are alive in Her*.

Wiccan rituals honor the life, death, rebirth, and cycles of renewal inherent in nature's seasons, as well as external and internal processes and phases that are integral to our individual and collective lives. There's no heaven or hell in my worldview, nor any karmic wheel from which to transcend the material plane of earth and flesh. We are part of nature, neither higher nor lower than any other part. In my ecofeminist, earth-based religious tradition, the sacred is as present in the here and now as it is in the past or future. Wicca's animistic cosmology holds physical and mystical realms to be inseparably embedded in one another. There's no "spiritual dimension" more holy than day-to-day reality:

> Ecofeminism is a movement with an implicit and sometimes explicit spiritual base. Yet to use the term "spirituality" is itself almost misleading, for the earth-based spirituality that influences ecofeminism has nothing to do with systems of thought which divide "spirit" from matter. (Starhawk 1989, 174)

Not all ecofeminists describe themselves as religious, let alone Wiccan, or even vegetarian. Not all Wiccans are ecofeminist, either, but ecofeminism promotes an ethos of care and compassion that inspires many Witches. Those who find themselves at odds with a world that has been ravaged by the violence of war, greed, and other injustices are often moved to work as ecofeminist peacekeepers and healers, actively engaged in restoring the sacred balance. In all our diversity, ecofeminists agree that the domination of women and the domination of nature are fundamentally connected. We challenge the false dualities that are inherent in the patriarchal mind-set, which values spirit over matter, masculine over feminine, competition over cooperation, reason over emotion, economic prosperity over environmental protection. Offering a comprehensive critique of domination, ecofeminism views sexism, racism, classism, speciesism, and other forms of inequality as interconnected oppressions, which are best addressed collectively rather than individually.[5]

The Craft is an anarchic path favoring freedom of choice and personal responsibility over dogma. Within this context, Witches live by the following "rede" (or guideline), a basic tenet of our religion: "And it harm none, do as ye will."[6]

The Wiccan Rede is generally embraced pragmatically, as an ideal to which we aspire rather than as an attainable goal under every circumstance. In contrast, the reduction of harm is more often considered a Witch's obligation (leaving room for interpretation). Some of us, who recognize the sacred as immanent in nature (the body of the Mother of All), see our own bodies, our own lives, and the lives of other beings as equally worthy of consideration and liberation. For example, our commitment to reducing harm extends beyond habitat protection (which is aimed at protecting species), to encompass individual lives, including the lives of nonhuman animals.

Since the act of eating is equated, at its most fundamental level, with self-survival, it is only natural that dietary preferences be regarded as personal—even private. However, there are few habits that impact the world as much as do our daily patterns of consumption, which makes the politics of food *everybody's* business.[7]

Although many vegetarian women and men gravitate to the Craft expecting to find solidarity, in my experience dietary reform as a method of animal advocacy lacks significant support in the broad-based Wiccan community. Ongoing allegiance to the consumption of animal products is generally seen as a "right of choice" among Wiccans. Regarding a ceremonial pig roast, Marion Bowman (2000) notes that "food . . . rather than thealogy/theology might be seen as one of the few issues that presents a real challenge to the importance many pagans place on tolerance" (n.p.). (Thealogy is a discourse that reflects on the meaning of Goddess and Her relationship to myriad life forms.) Consequently, most meat-eating Wiccans (and others) seem reluctant to address the thealogy/theology behind the killing and consuming of animals, and ethical vegan or vegetarian Witches know that they may be exposed to animal corpses at Wiccan gatherings, and that an exploited animal's lack of choice and untimely death may be marginalized or ignored at such gatherings.

In the Wiccan community, as in mainstream society, consciousness raising about related oppressions—such as those of women and animals—is made all the more difficult by complex emotions surrounding these issues, as well as differing attitudes toward animals. Prior to the trial of convicted serial killer Robert Pickton, for example, People for the Ethical Treatment of Animals introduced an ad campaign in

Vancouver, Canada, drawing a grisly parallel between the slaughter of the pig farmer's human and nonhuman victims.[8] While PETA is right—there is a link that needs to be addressed—their ad demonstrated an extraordinary lack of sensitivity to the grieving families of missing and murdered women, and harmed ecofeminist efforts to bring animal issues to the fore in the regional women's community.

While Wiccans vary in their sensitivity to the needs and sufferings of nonhuman animals, there is some commonality to be found. Worshipped as both creator and destroyer in ancient and modern cultures alike, "the Goddess" has been associated with animals of all kinds. While the ritual slaughter of animals in religious rites remains legal in limited contexts in Western cultures, most adherents to the Wiccan Rede are vehemently opposed to animal sacrifice.[9] Aversion to incorporating animal *flesh* into Wiccan rituals for anything *other than food* is certainly the norm, but there the commonality ends. For ecofeminist Witches who are ethical vegetarians/vegans, this ambiguous delineation between animals killed for food and animals killed for any other purpose conflicts with an Earth-honoring spiritual practice based on immanence, interconnectedness, and harm reduction.

This difference of outlook, however, does not necessarily reflect a difference in core Wiccan beliefs. Starhawk writes: "Compassion is our ability to feel with another, to value other lives as we value our own, to see ourselves as answerable and accountable to those who are different from us" (Starhawk 1989, 180). Starhawk is not a vegetarian or a vegan, but her commitment to compassion calls for a diet free of animal products. Nonetheless, in *The Earth Path* (2004), she claims that others may thrive comfortably on a vegan diet, but because our bodies are all different, some women may feel that they need to eat meat: "Meat is higher in what Chinese medicine calls *ch'i*, or vital life force, and those of us who are working with subtle energies in the way Witches do seem to crave it" (115). Feminist author and self-described Green Witch, Susun Weed, is another defender of the consumption of animal body parts and byproducts. This well-known herbalist is an honorary board member of the Weston A. Price Foundation, and has actively discouraged students from adhering to strictly plant-based nutrition.[10]

Witches who do not hold a meat-eater mind-set question those who claim that animal-based protein is necessary for optimum health, particularly in areas of the world where so many health problems are directly connected with an animal-based diet, and where a variety of nutritious plant-based sources are easily accessible. Many vegetarian/vegan ecofeminists recognize the notion that meat is superior "energetically" or nutritionally as a product of patriarchal reasoning. Numerous feminists have exposed the connection between meat eating and masculine self-identity and privilege, and have linked this ancient connection with sexism, racism, and other forms of violence.[11] Because vegetarian foods have been feminized, they continue to be stereotypically and erroneously regarded as weak and incomplete: "Men are typically given a disproportionate share of meat, and men who do not eat meat are often viewed as effeminate" (Kheel 2004, n.p.). In the *Sexual Politics of Meat*, Carol Adams points out the long-standing, cross-cultural association of meat with masculine privilege, virility, and aggression, as well as with sexual potency (Adams 2004, 165–73).

Along these same lines, my associate, Anthony Marr, a Canadian animal activist of Chinese descent, is helping curb the illicit trade in tiger bone, a trade that contributes to the decimation of this endangered species. Marr deliberately employs his ethnicity to voice opposition to cultural traditions—superstitions—that are deadly to animals (Crockford 1997).[12] Most notably, the belief that sympathetic magic can transfer the *ch'i* of once-living creatures to human recipients, including men hoping to increase their virility through the consumption of another animal's body parts.

Rejecting the patriarchal notion that meat is "king," vegetarian and vegan ecofeminist Witches emphasize our relationship to other animals as "kin." We carry the memory of persecution levied against both women and animals, through the "Burning Times" right up to the present day, and we say, "Enough is enough!"[13] Just as feminists advocate for a woman's right to exercise control over her own body, we challenge patriarchal control over the bodies of nonhuman animals, which reduces these individuals to "flesh."

As Marti Kheel emphasizes, animal advocacy exists in spite of patriarchal forms of dominance and control that receive widespread government and industry support (Kheel 2004, n.p.). My experiences as an animal activist confirm this assertion. I have been the recipient of strong conservative backlash. Animal body parts have been left in my yard and the sound of gunshots has been left on my answering machine. For ecofeminists who regard eating meat as both an expression of a patriarchal worldview and one of its central supports, adopting a vegan/vegetarian diet is a nonviolent act of resistance.

In my commitment to animal advocacy as an ecofeminist Witch, I reserve the right not to participate in Wiccan ceremonies or "feminist-conscious" gatherings where the lifeless bodies of animals are served as meals. When I encourage meeting organizers to provide vegetarian food for all, it is not my intention to offend or alienate women who choose to eat animals. Ecofeminists understand that dietary choices are culturally and socially complex. Because the personal *is* political, I advocate for ecofeminist principles that challenge dietary norms. I deliberately and respectfully disrupt the status quo by opting not to participate in the marginalization (or rendering invisible) of animal lives.

It seems ironic in the context of an animistic cosmology, but many Witches consider thanking an animal's spirit adequate "respect" in exchange for consuming his or her body. Sally Abbot suggests that perhaps prayers uttered to the dead are primarily intended for ears that can still hear (Abbot 1990, 35–40). "Abstraction," writes activist pattrice jones, "is the antithesis of ecofeminism, which is all about embeddedness, embodiment, and embrace" (jones 2004, 142). Starhawk is concerned that "one aspect of our nature-based religion that too often gets neglected is our actual relationship with nature" (2004, 4–5). To be a Witch, she reminds us, "we can't simply honor nature's cycles in the *abstract* . . . a real relationship with nature is vital" (2004, 4–5).[14]

Those who are determined to eat other animals might establish a more authentic relationship by taking personal, *direct* responsibility for the slaughter of those whom they choose to consume. There is no denying the violence and trauma involved in taking the life of another, or that death does not necessarily come easily for those who would prefer to live. Killing is the opposite of "embeddedness and embrace"—it is the ultimate, intentional separation between self and other. Meat eating condones and reinforces domination and exploitation.[15]

Healing the wounds of patriarchy requires a radical shift in perspective. On the Earth path less traveled, vegan and vegetarian ecofeminists are committed to "unlearning" *power-over*, which objectifies "the other." To deepen respect literally means to *look again*, to *re-spect*. We are choosing neither to look away from animal suffering, nor to resist the *power-with* of compassion. It is an appropriate choice in Wicca to look again, and with new vision, to see beyond our own reflection in the eyes of those looking back.

Appendix

Factory Farming and Fishing[1]

LISA KEMMERER

EGG AND DAIRY INDUSTRIES

There are many more vegetarians than vegans; many people become vegetarians, and only later some vegetarians become vegans. Unfortunately, vegetarians generally do not understand that an increase in the consumption of dairy products and eggs causes yet more suffering for farmed animals. Because of this lack of understanding, I am adding an appendix that focuses on the suffering and death that are inherent in the consumption of dairy and eggs.

Increasingly, people reject red meat and turn to eating chickens or fish. Unfortunately, this choice often reflects a personal concern for one's own health without regard for the lives of others. Other conscientious consumers buy "free range," "cruelty free," and "organic" animal products without realizing that they are doing little to nothing to help farmed animals.

To understand the moral and spiritual importance of this topic, it is important to view undercover footage that shows what happens behind the scenes, when those who deal with animals think that no one else is watching. Undercover footage can be found on many websites.[2]

ANIMAL AGRICULTURE

Hens lay eggs and cows produce milk as part of their basic biological functioning—not because they're well cared for or happy. Even the most miserable female human carries eggs, conceives when artificially inseminated, and lactates after birth—even if she is raped. The same is true for females of other species. Hens and cattle who are exploited for eggs, veal, and dairy products are the most cruelly treated of all farmed animals. I hope that on learning more about dairy and eggs, readers will not opt for a vegetarian diet, but will rather choose to *cut down consumption of all animal products*—or better yet, adopt a vegan diet.

"DAIRY" CATTLE

As with human females, cows produce milk only after they give birth—not because they're happy. Cows, like all mammals, lactate only after giving birth. In order to create the dairy industry—yogurt, cheese, milk, and cream—cows are artificially impregnated once a year.

Cows who are exploited in the dairy industry carry their young for ten months; their calves are taken away shortly after birth. Cows—like most mothers—try desperately to protect and keep their offspring, but they cannot protect their newborns against the animal agriculture industry.

What happens to calves who have been stolen from their mothers on dairy farms? Veal exists because we consume dairy products. The veal industry was created to take advantage of an abundant supply of unwanted calves (mostly males) born to cows enslaved on dairy farms.

Calves who are born of cows exploited for dairy products are either killed shortly after birth and sold as "bob" veal (for low-quality meals such as frozen TV dinners), or they are chained by the neck in a two feet wide by five feet long wooden crate, where they're unable to turn, stretch, or lie down comfortably. While we consume their milk, these calves are fed a milk-substitute that is deficient in iron and fiber, designed to create an anemic, light-colored flesh that is prized by the veal industry and veal consumers. Calves who are exploited for veal are usually slaughtered at just four months of age.

Life is no better for their mothers. Genetic manipulation and dietary controls cause extraordinary and unnatural milk output. With their calves chained in crates, their mothers have milking machines attached to their teats both morning and evening. Cows are so exhausted by the repeated process of pregnancy, birth, excessive production of milk, and then pregnancy once again, that after four or five years their milk production drops and they are considered "spent" in the dairy industry. Dairy cows are then shipped to slaughter. Most dairy cows are pregnant when they are sent to slaughter.

Because cattle raised for their flesh are slaughtered at about six months of age, the flesh of "spent" cattle is considered low quality. Their bodies, therefore, become ingredients in soups, burgers, or processed foods. It's important to note that both cows exploited for dairy and their calves are destined for slaughter, for human consumption. But unlike the "beef" industry, dairy cattle are cruelly exploited for six years on dairy farms before they're slaughtered. A vegetarian diet that includes dairy products purchased at any U.S. store pays for the ongoing, long-term misery of "dairy" cows and veal calves, and the slaughter of both cows and their calves.

COWS AT SLAUGHTER

As noted, the purchase of dairy products buys slaughter for cows and their calves.

Legislation provides only minimal protection for animals at slaughter. Mammals, including cattle, pigs, and sheep, are, by law, supposed to be "stunned" (rendered unconscious) before they're killed (Humane Slaughter Act of 1958). But slaughtering, like most businesses, is shaped by economic concerns (most significantly, efficiency) and the quest for profits.

In the slaughterhouse, the quicker each animal is killed, the higher the profit margin. Workers must be paid for their time, and while one animal's body is on the dismemberment line, no other body can be processed. Consequently, speed is paramount and stunning is often ineffective. A USDA survey concluded that stunning was either "unacceptable" or a "serious problem" in thirty-six percent of sheep and pig slaughterhouses and sixty-four percent of cattle slaughterhouses. Even more remarkable, chickens, turkeys, ducks—poultry in general—are exempt from the federal Humane Slaughter Act; in the U.S., birds comprise ninety percent of those killed for food.

Several important slaughter details affect cows and calves who have been sent to slaughter by dairy farmers. First, the efficacy of slaughterhouse stunning methods: the captive-bolt pistol (cattle, most calves, and some sheep) and the electric stunner (pigs, most sheep, and some calves); and second, "downers."

The Electric Stunner

When an animal enters the slaughterhouse, a worker clamps an electric stunner (imagine ear phones attached to an insulated handle) onto the victim's head, and then triggers an electric shock. As with all high-speed assembly-line operations, human and mechanical errors are common, and many pigs, calves, and sheep emerge from the stunner fully conscious and still sentient. Further decreasing the effectiveness of electric stunners, it is impossible to determine exactly how much electric current is required to properly stun a large or medium-sized animal. Insufficient current paralyzes the victim, but doesn't prevent sensation. Too much current causes "blown loins" (bruising caused by capillaries that have burst). Blown loins reduce the value of the flesh, so managers often lower the electric current, which means that many mammals go to slaughter fully conscious and sentient, aware of everything that's done to them until they're finally drained of blood.

The Captive-Bolt Pistol

A captive-bolt pistol is placed against a cow or calf's forehead, and then fired, driving a rod through the victim's skull and into the brain. If done properly, the victim will immediately lose consciousness. Poor aim, a hurried shot, or a sudden movement from the cow is likely to result in tremendous pain and terror, but will not stun the victim. Nonetheless, the assembly line keeps moving. Improperly stunned animals are therefore pushed forward, bellowing and struggling as they travel down the assembly line, fully conscious and sentient, on their way to being disassembled.

Downers

Slaughterhouse employees call animals who are too sick or injured to stand or walk "downers."

Transport is hard on farmed animals. When "dairy" cows are transported they are older than cattle raised and transported only for the beef industry. Additionally, their bodies are worn out from repeated production of calves and milk. Cows coming from dairies are therefore more likely to be "downers" than other cattle arriving for slaughter.

Undercover investigators have repeatedly documented slaughterhouse employees kicking and beating "downers," pushing them around with bulldozers, and dragging them from transport trucks with ropes or chain. Unable to rise, let alone flee, these victims are generally fully conscious and in great pain, rolling their eyes to see what might befall them next, and bellowing in fear and pain.

"LAYING" HENS

Cows exploited by the dairy industry, and chickens exploited by the egg industry, are likely the most cruelly exploited of farmed animals. Those who eschew red meat but increase their consumption of eggs or chicken have a right to know what they are supporting.

Shortly after hatching, chicks are "de-beaked" (without anesthesia) in order to reduce injuries caused by stressed birds fighting in overcrowded conditions. Debeaking entails the slicing off of the tips of chicks' sensitive beaks with a hot blade—cutting through bone, cartilage, and soft tissue. Some chicks bleed to death or die of shock shortly thereafter.

At eighteen weeks of age, hens are packed into battery cages that provide just 1.5 square-feet of space shared between four or more birds (slightly bigger than your average microwave oven)—even though the average hen's wingspan is 2.5 feet. Needless to say, the birds cannot stretch their wings and their bodies constantly rub against the wire, causing featherless sore spots. The hens remain in these tiny cages, stacked one on top of the other in giant sheds, laying eggs until they are sent to slaughter. They are usually shipped to slaughter after about a year and a half, though hens can live as long as fifteen years.

Though chickens have a strong urge to dust and peck at insects, nest and sit on their eggs, factory farmed hens cannot satisfy even these basic inclinations. A factory farmed hen's eggs are laid on a cage floor, then roll onto a conveyor belt that carries the eggs away to be boxed.

Hens carry and lay eggs as part of their basic biological functioning—not because they're happy or well cared for. Hens in the wild lay roughly twenty eggs per year, but a factory farmed hen yields 250 eggs (or more) annually. Consequently, factory farmed hens sometimes suffer from "cage layer fatigue," a condition in which they become "egg bound," and die because they're too weak to expel even one more egg.

When a hen's egg production begins to decline as part of their annual cycle, they are put through a "forced molt," in which they're starved and kept in total darkness for as long as eighteen days. Forced molt shocks hen's exhausted bodies into yet another egg cycle, but also causes hens to lose twenty-five percent of their body weight.

Forced-molt claims the lives of five to ten percent of the population, but is economically advantageous to poultry farmers. Hens lost in the process of forced molting are considered to have been of no use, since their egg production had declined below what is profitable.

Factory farmed hens are raised in unhealthy conditions. As a result, they suffer from an assortment of ailments, such as prolapses (the uterus is expelled along with an egg), egg peritonitis, cancers, infectious bronchitis, and severe liver and kidney disease. Because eggshells require a tremendous amount of calcium, hens also suffer frequently from calcium deficiencies, which often result in broken bones, paralysis, and premature death.

Because "laying" hens are bred for maximum egg production, they don't grow quickly or large enough for the flesh industry. Consequently, it's not cost effective to send these birds to slaughter, and many "spent" hens are simply disposed of through a wood chipper. For example, undercover investigators filmed employees at Ward Egg Ranch (California) throwing more than fifteen thousand living hens into a chipper. Despite the outcry from a newly informed and horrified public, the district attorney declined to prosecute, noting that disposing of live hens in a wood chipper is both legal and "common industry practice."

In the poultry industry, the lives of roosters are worth even less than the lives of hens. Male chicks are of no economic value, and are discarded as soon as they hatch. Each year, billions of male chicks are gassed, crushed, or thrown into garbage bins, where they die of dehydration or asphyxiation; their bodies are used as fertilizer or feed for other farmed animals. As with "spent" hens, a common method of eliminating male chicks is to toss them alive into a grinder. Eyewitness accounts describe struggling chicks peeping while they are dismembered by metal blades.

"Spent" egg-laying hens, if they are sent to slaughter, are roughly four times as old as other hens who are sent to slaughter ("broilers"). The flesh of "laying" hens is therefore less desirable, so their bodies are shredded for soups, baby food, stock cubes, school dinners, pot pies, the restaurant trade, animal food, or other low-grade products. Though they likely travel to slaughter at high speeds on major freeways, year round, hens are transported in open cages stacked on open trucks, without food, water, or protection from rain, snow, or sun. Some birds inevitably freeze to death, while others die of heat stress or suffocation. Their brittle, calcium-depleted bones shatter easily during transport, or when they're seized by slaughterhouse workers. But it is cheaper to absorb high transportation mortality rates than pay for enclosed transport trucks, or food and water provisions.

At the slaughterhouse, hens are thrown onto a conveyor belt. Some of the flapping and frightened birds inevitably miss the belt and fall onto the ground, where they're either crushed by machinery or die of starvation or exposure. They are taken from the conveyor belt and their legs are locked into metal shackles. For the sake of efficiency, most slaughterhouses attempt to stun the terrified birds so they won't flap and struggle. As the birds move along the assembly line, hanging upside down, their heads are *supposed* to be dragged through an electrified basin of water. However, some birds raise their heads to avoid the water—a natural reaction—and proceed down the line flapping and struggling.

As with electric stunners used on slaughtered cattle, the amount of current needed to properly stun any given bird is uncertain. In any event, no U.S. laws regulate the slaughter of fowl (even though ninety percent of those killed for food in the U.S. are birds). As with the cattle industry, too much electricity damages flesh, reducing profits, so managers tend to err on the side of lower electric current. As a result, even birds who have touched the electrified water are likely to be immobilized, *but remain fully capable of suffering.*

After the electric water basin, a hen's throat is cut. With slaughter lines running up to eighty-four hundred chickens *per hour*, accuracy in wielding the knife is the exception rather than the rule. After they pass by the blade—whether or not their throat has been cut—hens are submerged in scalding water (to loosen feathers). As a result of these slaughterhouse procedures, millions of hens are boiled alive.

STATISTICS FROM U.S. ANIMAL INDUSTRIES

Cattle

- Every year thirty-five million cattle are destroyed for beef, nine million cows are exploited for milk (and then sent for slaughter), and one million calves are destroyed for veal.
- Cows enslaved by the dairy industry are commonly killed at four to seven years of age, despite a life expectancy of roughly twenty years.
- Without drugs, cows produce just over two tons of milk per year; bovine growth hormone (BGH/BST) has increased milk output so that cows now provide as much as thirty tons of milk annually, enough for *ten* calves.
- One in five factory farmed "dairy" cows secretes pus from their udders, which invariably mixes with her milk.
- In the dairy industry, a cow's horns are scooped, gouged, or cut from her head without anesthesia.
- Cows who are enslaved for milk production endure mechanized milking for ten out of twelve months every year (including seven of the nine months of their pregnancies).
- The veal industry confines one million calves in crates measuring two feet wide by five feet long.
- Every year thousands of factory farmed cattle arrive at slaughter injured or too dispirited to walk; they are kicked, beaten, or forcibly dragged from transport trucks.

Chickens

- Nearly ten billion factory farmed chicks hatch annually.
- Factory farms exploit three hundred million "laying hens" each year.

- Every year, two hundred million male chicks are killed soon after they hatch.
- More than ninety-five percent of "laying" hens are factory farmed in giant warehouses, living their entire lives in less than two square feet of space.
- One million chickens are killed each hour.
- Chickens exploited for their flesh reach market weight just forty-five days after hatching, though they might otherwise live for roughly fifteen years (were their genetic make-up not manipulated to render them biologically unsound beyond youth).

FISH

When people learn about the health problems associated with the consumption of red meat, they sometimes switch to chicken and fish. As a result, the suffering and premature deaths of poultry and fish, and stripping of seas, continue to rise even as the beef industry declines.

As a result of our ongoing and increased fish consumption, a "quarter of the world's commercially important ocean fish populations are depleted or slowly recovering from over-exploitation; another 47 percent are fished to the full extent of their capacity" (Singer and Mason 2006, 111). The Atlantic salmon is commercially extinct, and the adult Atlantic cod population along Cape Cod is 1.1 percent of what it was in the 1960s (Singer and Mason 2006, 111, 114). Other fish devastated by our hooks and jaws are sturgeon, grouper, red snapper, bluefin tuna, swordfish, sharks, Chilean sea bass, and Pacific salmon (Kher 2006, 56–57). Nonetheless, humans continue to eat about one hundred million tons of "seafood" each year.

Bycatch refers to sealife mistakenly pulled from the sea while fishing for "seafood." Annually, *one-quarter* of sealife captured by fishing industries is "bycatch," wasting about twenty-seven million tons of sealife each year (Singer and Mason 2006, 112). Nets and hooks capture billions of creatures that we don't eat—indeed, *cannot*—eat. Commercial fishers tow miles of fishing line laced with baited hooks and nets across many miles of sea. Trawlers destroy everything in their path, leaving a devastated wasteland. Fishers only keep "target" fish (one in four), throwing back the rest—small crabs, shellfish, turtles, dolphins, porpoises, small whales, rays, sharks, and diving seabirds—even if they are dead or dying.

The worst bycatch offender is the shrimp industry, which hauls in only two percent of "edible" sea life, while creating thirty percent of the world's bycatch. Worldwide, the Food and Agriculture Organization (FAO) of the United Nations estimates that eighty-five percent of any given shrimp haul is bycatch (Clucas 1997, n. p.). For every eatable pound, trawlers pull in five inedible pounds (Singer and Mason 2006, 126). Shrimp trawling kills turtles, destroying more endangered turtles than all other human causes combined (Committee 1990, n.p.)..

Fish—like all vertebrates—are sentient, with a central nervous system, including a brain, spinal cord, and nerves. Fishing causes tremendous suffering and billions of premature deaths. Furthermore, consuming fish endangers both species and ecosystems. Fish are sentient, but we tend to ignore or even deny their suffering. We pull eighty to one hundred million tons of "eatable" fish from the oceans, mostly herring, cod, jack, redfish, and mackerel. Whether or not we *admit* that fish suffer, when deep-sea fish are brought to the surface, they experience the pain of decompression; sometimes their organs burst. Routinely, billions of fish are allowed to suffocate on boat decks.

FACTORY FISHING

Aquaculture—the factory farming of fish—is the fastest growing agricultural industry in the world. As a result, thirty to forty percent of salmon (eight hundred million pounds of fish flesh) live in cap-

tivity for most of their lives. Typically, factory fishing entails putting
"50,000 to 90,000 fish in a pen that is only 100 square feet" in order
to raise four hundred thousand to one million fish at a time (Weiss
2002). Confinement itself is problematic because wild salmon cover
hundreds of miles feeding in open waters, migrating to and from
breeding grounds. Additionally, farmed salmon are transferred from
freshwater to saltwater abruptly, leading to a mortality rate of fifty
percent.

ECOSYSTEMS

Not only the creatures that fishers pull from seas are threatened by
our taste for "seafood"; ninety percent of Earth's big sea predators
are now struggling to survive. The fish we consume, if left in the
sea, would feed billions of other creatures who have limited food
options and increasingly limited availability. For example, pollock
(a fish that is now common on the food market) is the main food
source for the endangered Steller sea lion (Singer and Mason 2006,
115). In 2009, hundreds of young penguins washed onto Brazil's
shores, most likely as a result of overfishing, which not only kills
penguins directly, but both exhausts them and puts them at greater
risk by driving them further afield in search of food (FoxNews.com
2008, n. pag.).

When we support fishing, we are responsible for the deaths of
many sea creatures who depend on sealife for survival. For example,
The Marine Mammal Protection Act was amended in 1994 to allow
sea lions to be shot *because* they eat fish that might otherwise profit
the fishing industry. In the same year, the Canadian government and
the province of Nova Scotia debated killing thousands of seals to protect fishing interests ("What About" 1994, 2). The government spent
upwards of three million dollars to kill between sixty and eighty-five
sea lions along the Columbia River for the sake of salmon interests
(Washington 2009, n. p.). When we choose to eat sealife, we pay

for the destruction of ecosystems and individuals, and we further empower the fishing industry.

ADDITIONAL STATISTICS FROM U.S. FISHERIES

- Some ten billion aquatic animals are captured and killed commercially annually.
- Eighty to one hundred million tons of fish are pulled from the seas each year for human consumption.
- Over the latter half of the twentieth century, wild fish catches increased 500 percent.
- Every year, more than 100,000 marine mammals are killed inadvertently by U.S. commercial fisheries (bycatch); endangered sea turtles and whales are among bycatch casualties.
- Annually, worldwide, roughly seven million metric tons of wild-caught fish are discarded as bycatch.

"FREE RANGE," "CRUELTY FREE," AND "ORGANIC" ANIMAL PRODUCTS

"Free range," "cruelty free," and "organic" enterprises exploit animals for flesh, milk, and eggs with little regard for the genuine happiness of their victims. If they were genuinely concerned, they would not exploit farmed animals.

Unlike the "humane" and "cruelty-free" labels, the "organic" label can only be used if it satisfies established guidelines, which are (presumably) monitored by the government. The organic label, however, does little to nothing for the victims, regulating what farmed animals are to be fed (organic foods—no hormones); no other conditions are specified. Therefore, animals who are exploited for "organic" foods need not—and generally *are* not—raised, maintained, transported, or slaughtered any differently than their "nonorganic" counterparts.; they're debeaked, dehorned, detoed, castrated, and/or branded just like their nonorganic counterparts. "Organic" and "cruelty-free" dairy labels do *nothing* for a mother cow who is perpetually impregnated and milked, and loses her calf to the veal industry, or for her calf, who has been sent off at birth to be killed for veal. "Organic" products are designed to optimize human health and reduce environmental degradation, rather than improve the well-being of farmed animals. Nonetheless, it is common for those touting "organic" products to claim that their label includes "rules about the humane treatment of animals" ("What Does" n.d.). One need only look up the Organic Foods Production Act of 1990 to know that this is not the case <www. ams.usda.gov/AMSv1.0/getfile?dDocName=STELPRDC5060370&ac ct=nopgeninf).

Similarly, "free range" and "cruelty free" labels do nothing worth mentioning to prevent the extensive cruelties of factory farming. "Free range" animals, like other factory farmed animals, can be (and almost always are) confined indoors, in conditions similar to those of other factory farmed animals. Hens and eggs sold as "free range" products may or may not have more space than hens in battery cages, and may or may not ever walk outdoors. "Free range" labels do not guarantee any specific amount of space, or even guarantee that all of their animals can reach the small outdoor enclosure that is provided.

"Free range" and "cruelty free" cows and hens are sent to the same slaughterhouses as soon as their milk or egg production drops. "Free range" and "cruelty free" hens are likely to be debeaked, just like other factory farmed chickens, and male chicks are still discarded. What would "cruelty free," "free range," and "organic" egg industries do with millions of roosters? Similarly, "free range" and "cruelty free" cows are impregnated repeatedly, and their calves are taken directly after birth. The male calves of "free range" dairy facilities are sent off to become "veal" just like other factory farmed "dairy" cows. What would "cruelty free," "free range," and "organic" dairy farmers do with hundreds of thousands of male calves?

"Organic," "free range," and "cruelty free" labels offer no comfort worth mentioning to chickens, turkeys, pigs, sheep, or cattle, and should not be considered a solution to those who are genuinely concerned about the plight of farmed animals.

CONCLUSION

We must know something of factory farming to understand why our diet is an ethical and spiritual matter. For cattle, chickens, pigs, turkeys, sheep, ducks, and fish, our choices determine their lives and deaths. Factory farms are exploitative, and conducive neither to health nor happiness.

In North America, those who eat flesh generally consume more than thirty-five animals each year, amounting to 2,600 animals over a seventy-five-year lifetime, including some 2,460 chickens, ninety-six turkeys, thirty-two pigs, and twelve cattle/calves. But this loss of life is only part of the sordid picture. Factory farmed animals are deprived of freedom and their young, and are not permitted to satisfy their most basic instincts.

Perhaps most importantly, if we wish to reduce this suffering and help those who are at the mercy of our consumer dollars, we must reduce or (better yet) omit all animal products from our diet. If we switch to a vegetarian diet, and in the process increase egg or dairy consumption, we merely shift the suffering we cause to "laying" hens and "dairy" cows, who are already among the most cruelly exploited of all living being.

Notes

Preface: The Time Has Come

1. See Whewell (1864, 592*ff.*) and Mill's (1969, 185–87) vehement reply.
2. See Turner (1964) and Lynam (1975) for accounts of the legislative origins of those laws.
3. See Rollin (1989) for a scholarly account of how twentieth century psychology was corrupted to deny that "animals" were sentient.
4. See my *Biology and Christian Ethics* (2000) for further discussion of the effects of various forms of evolutionary theory on our ethical practice.
5. For example, Singer's *Animal Liberation: Towards an End to Man's Inhumanity to Animals* (1977) is often miscalled "the Bible" of the animal rights movement, since Singer has no sympathy with "rights." See Regan (1983).
6. This was especially Chesterton's problem with the "animal rights" movement of his day. See my *G. K. Chesterton: Thinking Backward, Looking Forward* (2006).
7. See *The Moral Status of Animals* (1984) and *Animals and Their Moral Standing* (1997). Andrew Linzey (1987) has also argued from within an orthodox Christian tradition for the moral considerability of the nonhuman.
8. *Wisdom of Solomon* (probably second century B.C.E.) 11.24. The work itself shows some Hellenic influence, but its main theme is Hebraic.

1

Indic Traditions and Animals:
Imitation, Reincarnation, and Compassion

1. For a sampling of verses, see Griffith (1973, 684).
2. For a full description of this tradition and instances of particular *pinjrapoles*, see Lodrick (1981).

3. See www.bishnoi.org, the home page of the Bishnoi.
4. *Ibid.*

2

Vaishnava Hinduism: Ahimsa and Vegetarianism

1. That Vaishnavas constitute the Hindu majority was brought to light in three consequential works: (1) *Hindu Views and Ways and the Hindu–Muslim Interface* by Agehananda Bharati (1981), (2) "The Response of Modern Vaishnavism" by Klaus Klostermaier (1987, 129), and (3) *India's Agony over Religion* by Gerald Larson (1995, 20). The same fact was stated in the *1996 Britannica Book of the Year*.

2. Thus, of the almost 850 million Hindus today, seventy-five percent are Vaishnavas, accounting for almost 640 million people. (For more information on these statistics, see Klostermaier 1987, 129.) Not all practice strictly; nor are all vegetarian. There are Vaishnavas in the state of Orissa, for example, who live off the sea. Their "sea vegetables" often include fish. Those of lower castes might also eat meat out of necessity, and warrior-caste families have a tradition of eating flesh foods, too, especially in the forest as they prepare for battle. But there are few other exceptions in the Vaishnava tradition, with the vast majority adhering to a strict lacto-vegetarian diet.

3. The Vedas as they exist today are said to be but a portion of the original scripture. Regarding monotheism, Vaishnavas aver that the many gods of the Vedas are just aspects of Brahman, the overarching Spirit of the universe. This Spirit, in turn, is merely an impersonal manifestation of Vishnu, the Supreme Godhead. Regarding animal rights, there were, it's true, animal sacrifices in days of old, and these were supported in Vedic texts. But like the biblical prophets, whose esoteric traditions tell us that God "preferred mercy and not sacrifice," Vaishnava sages taught that animal sacrifices were an inferior gift to God, and that He preferred *bhakti*, or devotion. Accordingly, the sacrifice for the current age is the chanting of the holy name, and animal sacrifices are strictly forbidden.

4. The virtue of *sarva-bhuta-hita* is even referred to in the *Bhagavad Gita* 5.25.

5. The Golden Rule, in almost biblical phrasing, can be found in the critical edition of the *Mahabharata* (5.39.57), as part of Vidura's famous sermon:

"Do not do to another that which you would find disagreeable if done to you—this is the summary of all duty." A similar verse appears again much later in the same epic (13.113.8). See the Ganguli translation on the Web: <www.sacred-texts.com/hin/m13/m13b078.htm>. In other editions, see 13.114.8 <www.sacred-texts.com/hin/mbs/mbs13114.htm>.

6. Also see *Brahmanda Purana* 2.63.24 and *Vishnu-smriti* 51.78.
7. For context, see Edwin Bryant's "Strategies of Vedic Subversion: The Emergence of Vegetarianism in Post-Vedic India" (2006, 200).
8. For context, see Christopher Key Chapple, "Ahimsa in the *Mahabharata*" (1996, 109–25).
9. For more on veganism in Vaishnava Hinduism, see Vraja Kishor Das's *The Vegan and the Vedas: A Detailed Examination of Veganism and Krishna Consciousness* (1994).

3

International Society for Krishna Consciousness: Lord Krishna and the Animals

1. The *Bhagavata Purana*, written by Vyasa, is also known as the *Srimad Bhagavatam*.
2. Vaishnavism is a monotheistic faith within Hinduism, but Prabhupada broadened its definition: "Anyone who accepts the supremacy of God, he's a Vaishnava. So Christianity . . . is [also] Vaishnavism" (Prabhupada, 1990, 25:127–28).
3. Chaitanya Vaishnavism, also known as Gaudiya Vaishnavism, is a monotheistic Krishna-centered faith rooted in the teachings of East Bengal's Chaitanya Mahaprabhu (1486–1534).
4. A *dhoti* is a long cotton cloth worn traditionally by men in India.
5. *Prashad* (or *prashadam*) is vegetarian food offered to God and thereafter considered sanctified by Hindus.
6. Prabhupada, *Bhagavad Gita* commentary, verse 5.18, 261. Prabhupada repeated scriptural conclusions that every living being has an individual soul (*atma*) in its body, along with the *paramatma* or Supersoul, a form of God in the heart of every being. *Panditas* honor both.
7. Sartwell's syndicated column appeared in the *Philadelphia Enquirer*. The same article also appeared online at Animal Liberation.com on July 28, 2008: <www.startribune.com/commentary/story/1329238.html>

8. See Goswami and colleagues (1983/2006).

9. Email from Kalakantha Das, Gainesville Hare Krishna temple president, to the author on February 19, 2009. Many of the meals served are entirely vegan. For those that are not, vegans just accept the vegan dishes that are offered and avoid the one dish with dairy.

10. Since its inception in 1974, Hare Krishna Food for Life Global had served an estimated 715 million vegetarian or vegan meals. See <www.ffl.org> (estimate accessed on February 19, 2009).

11. See Rosen's (2004) second chapter, "India's Sacred Cows."

12. See Dasa (1989).

13. *Bhagavad Gita* 18.42 describes the brahminical qualities: "Peacefulness, self-control, austerity, purity, tolerance, honesty, knowledge."

14. Krishna also argued that his father should worship the sacred hill known as Govardhan.

15. See <http://hkrl.com/cowseva.html> and Coyle (1998).

16. In *Bhagavad Gita* 9.26, Lord Krishna states that if a devotee offers him with love and devotion vegan items like "a leaf, a flower, fruit or water" he will accept it and purify it of karmic influences. In other scriptures, such as the *Bhagavata Purana*, Krishna states that he accepts both vegan and lacto-vegetarian foods that are offered with love devotion. But he never indicates that he accepts flesh offerings.

17. Prabhupada's only contact with nonvegetarian food was during an illness as a child. At that time, a doctor tried to force-feed him chicken broth, but he immediately vomited it up.

18. Chaitanya Vaishnavas use leather drumheads in their devotional music and chanting, but traditionally such leather is obtained from cows or bulls that have died natural deaths, not as slaughterhouse casualties.

19. Most Buddhists and Advaitic impersonalists don't practice *bhakti* or devotion to God, believing that ultimately the soul and God are illusory. Yet, at the same time, they practice nonviolence. In an article in *Awareness* magazine <www.awarenessmag.com/marapr4/MA4_IS_THERE_AFTERLIFE.HTML>, Scott S. Smith wrote, "Buddhism and Vedanta (a popular form of Hinduism in the West, but a minority in India) do not teach the existence of even a human soul. The Buddha taught that only a karmic principle reincarnated, while in Vedanta, all individuality is [considered to be] an illusion."

20. See Carman (2003, 118–23).

21. According to *Bhagavad Gita* 3.13: "The devotees of the Lord are released

from all kinds of sins because they eat food which is first offered for sacrifice. Others, who prepare food for personal sense enjoyment, eat only sin."

22. *Bhagavad Gita* 3.9: "Work as a sacrifice for God (Vishnu, Krishna) has to be performed; otherwise, work—karma—binds one to this material world."

23. The threefold miseries are those arising (1) from one's own body or mind, (2) from other living creatures like mosquitoes, tax collectors, or dentists, or (3) from natural forces like snowstorms, hurricanes, or earthquakes.

5

Buddhism and Animal Liberation:
The Family of Sentient Beings

1. For an extensive discussion of this question and other issues surrounding the Buddha's teaching and personal practice concerning vegetarianism, see Phelps (2004, 55–84), Kapleau (1981), and Page (1999).

6

Buddhist Reflections on Animal Advocacy:
Intention and Liberation

1. For an analysis of Buddhist and non-Buddhist practices of animal liberation in Asia see Handlin Smith (1999); for specific reference to Buddhist animal liberation practices in Japan see Williams (1997).

2. For other works on Buddhism and animals see, for example, Kapleau (1981), McDermott (1989), Page (1999), Waldau (2002), and Phelps (2004).

3. Of course, referring to the widely varied schools of thought and religious practices that have been derived from the teachings of Siddhartha Gautama (the Buddha) as "Buddhism" is misleading at best (see Ling 1993). Buddhist traditions have followed very different trajectories of development as they have been carried around the globe and significant doctrinal disagreements separate many of the main schools. Here, however, I'm not attempting to comment on Buddhist practice as a whole, merely on the

benefits of viewing Western practices of animal liberation through the lens of several concepts that emerge from Buddhist doctrine.

4. While these five are the absolute minimum, Buddhist monks must usually abide by more precepts, and there exists an entire system of law (the *Vinaya*) that governs the conduct of monks.

5. Although the term *enlightenment* has come to mean something more basic in the West, this is in essence what enlightenment is: The total cessation of all craving, attachment, and discriminating thought.

6. The workings of karma are very complex and this brief statement should not be taken to mean that Buddhism is a completely deterministic religion. Rather, karma *conditions* our possible futures, while still reserving an element of free will and moral decision-making.

7. Buddhists consider the animal state to be inferior because animals lack the capacity for reflection and meditation that allows one to proceed on the path to enlightenment. However, the doctrines of impermanence and rebirth do allow for the possibility that animals can be reborn as humans, therefore regaining the ability to follow the Buddhist path. For more on the status of animals in Buddhism, see Schmithausen (1997), particularly part VI.

8. See, for example, the Buddha's comments on meat eating in the *Mahaparinirvana Sutra*.

9. While there are many different Buddhist sects and forms of practice, a common distinction is often made between Theravada Buddhism (as practiced in Sri Lanka, Burma, Thailand, Cambodia, and Laos) and Mahayana Buddhism (as practiced in China, Tibet, Korea, Japan, and Vietnam).

10. *Karman* in Sanskrit, the language that was used by the writers of the Upanishads.

11. In Pali, the language of the Buddhist scriptures, the word most often used in this case is *cetana*, understood as the will behind an action.

12. In Pali, *kusala* and *akusala*, respectively.

13. Wrong livelihood is the negative manifestation of a part of the Eightfold Noble Path, a collection of practices that acts as a moral guide for Buddhists. The eight elements of the path are right understanding, right thinking, right speech, right action, right livelihood, right effort, right mindfulness, and right concentration.

14. However, we could reasonably reject some actions as being incompatible with the principle of nonharming. For example, it seems impossible to shout "You can't eat meat with a broken jaw!" in a spirit of compassion.

15. For an interesting and relevant take on intention with regard to environmental damage, see Harvey (2007).

7

Daoism: From Meat Avoidance
to Compassion-Based Vegetarianism

1. As so little research has been done on the place of animals and vegetarianism in Daoism, the historical dimensions of this discussion must be taken as preliminary and tentative. I hope that future research will challenge some of my claims.
2. The ancient Chinese understanding of the connection between blood sacrifice and divine power gives one pause in our contemporary context: human sacrifice (through war) in the name of a supposedly all-powerful cosmocrat.
3. For the ways in which contemporary Zhengyi Daoists accommodate communal demands for animal sacrifice see, for example, Saso (1972, 1978), Schipper (1993 [1982]), and Dean (1993). See also the recent documentary *The Revenge of Han Xin: A Daoist Mystery* directed by Patrice Fava (2005).
4. This was so much the case that members of the cultural elite were often referred to as "meat-eaters" (*roushi zhe*) (Kieschnick 2005, 193; Sterckx 2005, 38). That is, eating meat was (and in many places in the contemporary world still is) a luxury and a privilege. A profitable study could be conducted on the amount of labor and resources required for raising "livestock" (animals for human consumption) in ancient China in comparison to the modern West.
5. It is beyond the confines of the present paper to discuss the various actual and symbolic associations of blood and meat in Chinese culture. For some relevant philosophical discussions of "animals" and "meat" in general see Baker (2001) and Rothfels (2002). See also the important films *Koyaanisqatsi* directed by Godfrey Reggio (1982) and *Baraka* directed by Ron Fricke (1992).
6. In terms of modern ecological concerns, Chinese medicine and Chinese longevity practitioners also have much to answer for with respect to the extinction of rare and endangered species. The Chinese *materia medica* contains references to various "endangered species" (see Bensky, Clavey,

and Stöger 2004, xxx–xxxi, 1063–69), and Asian (patriarchal) tastes continue to crave such substances as rhinoceros horns, tiger bones, and bear gallbladders. The continued modern use of these "substances" is largely a consequence of Asian conceptions of male virility.

7. For translations of the *180 Precepts of Lord Lao* see Hendrischke and Penny (1996) and Kohn (2004, 136–44). For English-language studies see Penny (1996) and Schipper (2001). The latter source discusses the text in terms of Daoism and ecology. Daoist texts are cited according to Komjathy (2002), with numbers for the Ming-dynasty Daoist Canon paralleling Schipper's system.

8. Other prohibitions against specific types of meat consumption appear in the *Lingshu ziwen shangjing* (*Upper Scripture of Purple Texts Inscribed by the Spirits*) (Bokenkamp 1997, 365). For a study of Daoist precepts as a whole see Kohn (2004).

9. Livia Kohn, developing the work of Rolf Stein and Christine Mollier, has offered an alternative interpretation: "These precautions and restraints remained in effect throughout the year and governed the daily life of Celestial Masters practitioners. They were lifted for short periods at the festivals of the Three Primes and other major community occasions" (Kohn 2004, 44).

10. Robert Campany (2005), drawing upon the work of Michael Puett, has provided "internalist" and "externalist" explanations for these alchemical diets. Cf. Saso (1972, 2) on emic and etic distinctions.

11. The same is true with respect to "celibacy" in early Daoist monasticism. In some Daoist "monastic" communities, celibate Daoists, sometimes with their former families, lived side by side with householder Daoists. See Kohn (2003, 39–42).

12. Philosophically speaking, Madhyamika, emphasizing "emptiness," and Yogācāra, emphasizing "consciousness only," views might challenge categorical distinctions between "sentient" and "nonsentient" beings. The Buddhist Tantric tendency towards radical nondualism also might subvert conventional Buddhist arguments for vegetarianism.

13. The fact that Complete Perfection became formally established in the Shandong peninsula would suggest that fish and seafood must have been part of the early community's diet, especially with respect to lay associations and lay patrons.

14. For additional insights on the altruistic activities of the early Complete Perfection adepts see Eskildsen (2004, 155–70).

15. The "five strong-smelling vegetables" (*wuxin*) are leeks, scallions, onions, garlic, and ginger.
16. The research of Vincent Goossaert and Zheng Suchun does not contain information on this important topic.
17. See the relevant contributions to the *Daoism Handbook* (Kohn and Kirkland 2000).
18. My ethnographic fieldwork into Chinese Daoism began in 1997 and has included almost annual return visits. During 2005–2006, I conducted extensive field research using a participant-observer approach at the monasteries of Laoshan and Huashan.
19. For a modern English-language cookbook based on contemporary Complete Perfection monastic diets see Saso (1994).
20. I have written a philosophical "essay" entitled "Theses on the Philosophy of Oecologie," which is currently being prepared for publication. In that essay, I advance a more comprehensive view of "ecology."
21. Compassion for the subsequent layoffs of humans employed as slaughterhouse workers would need to include job training and new employment opportunities. That is, like the promotion of the end of clear-cutting of old-growth forests and the subsequent loss of livelihood, local workers cannot be left in situations of impoverishment.

8

Judaism: Global Warming, Animal Products, and the Vegan Mandate

1. Full text available at: <www.wilsoncenter.org/index.cfm?topic_id=1413&fuseaction=topics.event_summary&event_id=236344>

9

Catholic Exemplars: Recent Popes, Medieval Saints, and Animal Liberation

1. The belief that animals have a soul can be traced through pre-Socratic philosophers as well as Plato and Aristotle. However, the pope was extensively schooled in the teachings of Aquinas, as most popes have been since the nineteenth century.

18

Wicca, Ecofeminism, and Animal Advocacy:
The Earth Path Less Traveled

1. For more on the Clayoquot Sound mass arrests and feminist involvement in the history of civil disobedience, see the documentary *Fury for the Sound: The Women at Clayoquot*, from Bullfrog Films. Made in 1998, this film is available at <www.bullfrogfilms.com/catalog/fury.html>.

2. Feminist Wicca is only one branch of contemporary witchcraft, and there are numerous feminist traditions. See Adler (1979) for an overview of neopaganism and <www.witchvox.com> for a more comprehensive listing of contemporary groups and practices.

3. Not all Witches are Wiccans, but the opposite is true. Many Witches are polytheists, revering multiple deities. The masculine is not seen as subservient to the feminine in traditions that honor both, but as divine son and consort. See Starhawk (1979/1999).

4. Wiccan prayer from the organization Reclaiming, a group focused on, among other things, the tradition of witchcraft. See <www.reclaiming. org> for information on this feminist tradition.

5. Not all ecofeminists include speciesism in their analysis. Contextual rather than universal vegetarianism is advocated by some of those who do. See Gaard (2002).

6. See Coughlin (2002) for a thorough look at the possible origins of the Wiccan Rede and its evolution over time.

7. See "Fireweed Revives the Great Meat Debate" (2003, 16) for my arguments against speciesism and for plant-based dietary choices by those with "the privilege of choice." While I use the term *vegetarian* throughout this essay to distinguish diets that contain animal flesh from those that don't, many ethical vegetarian ecofeminist Wiccans like myself practice and promote veganism as well, pointing out that egg and dairy production exploits the reproductive capacities of female animals.

8. See Perkel (2004).

9. See Wigington (2008) and the Reclaiming community's "FAQ" page about witchcraft at <www.reclaiming.org/about/witchfaq/faq.html#Anchor-16731>.

10. See Weed (2002) and Eisenstein (2002) for a critique of ethical vegetarianism.

11. See various writings by Carol J. Adams, Andree Collard, Dean Curtin,

Maneesha Deckha, Josephine Donovan, Gretta Gaard, Marti Kheel, Val Plumwood, and Marjorie Spiegel on the link between meat eating, privilege, and male violence.

12. See Crockford (1997) for the story of Anthony Marr's involvement in exposing readily available "medicines" in Chinese apothecaries across North America containing tiger bone and other illegal substances from endangered species.

13. The Burning Times refers to the persecution of primarily European women accused of witchcraft between the fourteenth and eighteenth centuries. Animal associates, or "familiars," were sometimes tortured and killed with coaccused human victims. See the National Film Board of Canada documentary *The Burning Times,* directed by Donna Read in 1990. Available at <www.nfb.ca/collection/films/fiche/?id=18315>.

14. See Starhawk (2004, 116) for the author's admonishment that as long as animals raised for food are treated with "respect" and endure a minimum of suffering, *and gratitude is given to their spirits for their lives,* then she is "happy to eat them."

15. See Adams (1994). Chapter 5 explores ecofeminism and the eating of animals and how the logic of domination theoretically resisted by ecofeminism is inadvertently reinforced when biotic environmentalist discourse is willing to sacrifice individual animals as edible bodies. Also, see Donovan (1996).

Appendix
The Egg and Dairy Industries

1. The basic ideas in the appendix are taken from a previous work by Lisa Kemmerer, published with Oxford University Press (*Rightful Relations: Religion and Animals,* 2011). Information included in this appendix was taken from a handful of websites, including:
   VIVA! USA <www.vivausa.org/visualmedia/index.html>
   PETA <www.petatv.com>
   HSUS <http://video.hsus.org/>
   PCRM <www.pcrm.org/resources/>
   Farm Sanctuary <www.farmsanctuary.org/mediacenter/videos.html>
   Vegan Outreach <www.veganoutreach.org/whyvegan/animals.html>
   For specific information on "dairy" cattle and "laying" hens see:

HSUS Factory Farming Campaign <www.hsus.org/farm/resources/ research/welfare/welfare_overview.html#76>

Farm Sanctuary's FactoryFarming.com <www.farmsanctuary.org/ issues/factoryfarming/>

VIVA!USA Guides <www.vivausa.org/activistresources/guides/mur-dershewrote1.htm#>.

2. Here are some suggestions:

For U.S. footage, visit Mercy for Animals <www.mercyforanimals. org/> and Compassion Over Killing <www.cok.net<.www.cetfa. com> and <www.defendhorses.org>.

For Australian footage, visit Animals Australia <www.animalsaustra-lia.org/>.

For European footage, visit Vier Pfoten (Four Paws) <www.vier-pfo-ten.org/website/output.php>

For footage from France, visit <www.l214.com>, Eyes on Animals <http://eyesonanimals.com/> and Varkens in Nood <www.varken-sinnood.nl/>.

For excellent footage from The Netherlands (and also for an overall view) visit the website of Compassion in World Farming <www. ciwf.org.uk/>.

I also highly recommend these two short online videos: <www.youtube.com/watch?v=vCX7f_s1CA4> <www.petatv.com/ tvpopup/Prefs.asp?video=mym2002>.

For more information about factory farming, also visit:

VIVA! USA <www.vivausa.org/visualmedia/index.html> (or VIVA! UK)

PCRM <www.pcrm.org/resources/>

Farm Sanctuary <www.farmsanctuary.org/mediacenter/videos.html>

PETA

HSUS <http://video.hsus.org/>

Vegan Outreach <www.veganoutreach.org/whyvegan/animals.html>

Bibliography

Foreword

Bannerjee, Neela. 2008. "A Fluid Religious Life Is Seen in U.S. with Switches Common." In *New York Times*, February 28.

Blackstone, William. 1765a. *Commentaries on the Laws of England*. Oxford: Clarendon Press.

———. 1765b. *Commentaries on the Laws of England vol. 2*. Oxford: Clarendon Press.

Scully, Matthew. 2002. *Dominion: The Power of Man, the Suffering of Animals, and the Call to Mercy*. New York: St. Martin's Press.

Preface

Clark, Stephen R. L. 2006. *G. K. Chesterton: Thinking Backward, Looking Forward*. West Conshohocken, Penn.: Templeton Foundation Press.

———. 2000. *Biology and Christian Ethics*. Cambridge: Cambridge University Press.

———. 1997. *Animals and their Moral Standing*. London: Routledge.

———. 1984. *The Moral Status of Animals*. 2nd ed. Oxford: Oxford University Press.

Conway, Anne. 1996. *Principles of the Most Ancient and Modern Philosophy*, eds. A. P. Coudert and T. Course. Cambridge: Cambridge University Press. (Originally published in 1690.)

Linzey, Andrew. 1987. *Christianity and the Rights of Animals*. London: Society for Promoting Christian Knowledge.

Lynam, Shevawn. 1975. *Humanity Dick: A Life of Richard Martin*. London: Hamilton.

Mill, John Stuart. 1969. "Whewell on Moral Philosophy." In *Essays in Ethics, Religion and Society*, ed. J. M. Robson, pp. 165–202. Toronto: University of Toronto. (Originally published in 1867).

Primatt, Humphrey. 1992. *The Duty of Mercy and the Sin of Cruelty to Brute Animals*, ed. Richard D. Ryder. Fontwell, U.K.: Centaur Press. (Originally published in 1776.)

Regan, Tom. 1983. *The Case for Animal Rights*. Berkeley: University of California Press.

Rollin, Bernard. 1989. *The Unheeded Cry: Animal Consciousness, Animal Pain and Science*. New York: Oxford University Press.

Singer, Peter. 1977. *Animal Liberation: Towards an End to Man's Inhumanity to Animals* London: Paladin.

Turner, E. S. 1964. *All Heaven in a Rage*. London: Michael Joseph: London.

Whewell, William. 1864. *Elements of Morality*. 4th ed. Cambridge, U.K.: Deighton, Bell: Cambridge.

Wilson, E. O. 1978. *On Human Nature*. Cambridge, Mass.: Harvard University Press.

Introduction

Cadman, S. Parkes. n.d. "Quotes about the Relationship between Animals and Humans." Kansas State University website <www.k-state.edu/womenscenter/W.A.R/Animal%20Quotes.pdf> (accessed Jan. 21, 2010).

Schweitzer, Albert. n.d. "Trans-Species Institute: Creating Knowledge and Community with Animals." Trans-Species Institute website <www.trans-species.org> (accessed Jan. 21, 2010).

1

Indic Traditions and Animals:
Imitation, Reincarnation, and Compassion

Chapple, Christopher Key. 2006. "Inherent Value without Nostalgia: Animals and the Jaina Tradition." In *A Communion of Subjects: Animals in Religion, Science, and Ethics*, eds. Paul Waldau and Kimberley Patton, pp. 241–49. New York: Columbia University Press.

———. 1997. "Animals and Environment in Buddhist Birth Stories." In *Buddhism and Ecology: The Interconnection of Dharma and Deeds*, eds. Mary Evelyn Tucker and Duncan Ryuken Williams, pp. 131–48. Cambridge, Mass.: Harvard University Center for the Study of World Religions.

Cowell, E. B., ed. 1895–1907. *The Jataka or Stories of the Buddha's Former Births.* 6 vols. London: Pali Text Society.

Eliade, Mircea. 1953. *Shamanism: Archaic Techniques of Ecstasy.* Princeton, N.J.: Princeton University Press.

Gheranda. 1979. *The Gheranda Samhita.* Trans. Rai Bahadur Srisa Chandra Vasu. Delhi: Sri Satguru Publications. First published in 1914/1915.

Griffith, Ralph T. H. 1973. *The Hymns of the Rgveda.* Revised reprint. Delhi: Motilal Banarsidass.

Hardy, Adam, trans. 1990. "Karmic Retribution: The Story of Yasodhara from the *Brhatkathakosa.*" In *The Clever Adulteress and Other Stories: A Treasury of Jain Literature,* ed. Phyllis Granoff, pp. 118–39. Oakville, Ontario: Mosaic Press.

Hume, Robert Ernest, trans. 1921. *The Thirteen Principal Upanishads.* Oxford: Oxford University Press.

Jacobi, Hermann, trans. 1884. *Jaina Sutras Translated from the Sanskrit. Part I. The Acaranga Sutra and the Kalpa Sutra.* Oxford: Clarendon Press.

Jain, Pankaj. 2008. *Sustaining Dharma, Sustaining Ecology: Perspectives from Swadhyayis, Bishnois, and Bhils in India.* Ph.D. diss., University of Iowa.

Jaini, Padmanabh S. 2000. *Collected Papers on Jaina Studies.* Delhi: Motilal Banarsidass.

Kenoyer, Jonathan. 1998. *Ancient Cities of the Indus Valley Civilization.* Karachi, Pakistan: Oxford University Press.

Lodrick, Deryck O. 1981. *Sacred Cows, Sacred Places: Origins and Survivals of Animal Homes in India.* Berkeley: University of California Press.

Rosen, Steven J. 2004. *Holy Cow: The Hare Krishna Contribution to Vegetarianism and Animal Rights.* New York: Lantern Books.

Svatmarama. 1997. *The Hatha Yoga Pradipika.* Trans. Pancham Sinh. New Delhi: Munshiram Manoharlal.

Tatia, Nathmal, trans. 1994. *That Which Is: Tattvartha Sutra.* San Francisco: Harper Collins.

Warren, William Clarke. 1896. *Buddhism in Translations.* Cambridge, Mass.: Harvard University Press.

Williams, Duncan Ryuken. 1997. "Animal Liberation, Death, and the State: Rite to Release Animals in Medieval Japan." In *The Interconnection of Dharma and Deeds,* eds. Mary Evelyn Tucker and Duncan Ryuken Williams, pp. 149–64. Cambridge, Mass.: Harvard University Center for the Study of World Religions.

2

Vaishnava Hinduism: *Ahimsa* and Vegetarianism

Bharati, Agehananda. 1981. *Hindu Views and Ways and the Hindu–Muslim Interface*. New Delhi: Munshiram Manoharlal.

Bryant, Edwin. 2006. "Strategies of Vedic Subversion: The Emergence of Vegetarianism in Post-Vedic India." In *A Communion of Subjects: Animals in Religion, Science, and Ethics*, eds. Paul Waldau and Kimberley Patton, pp. 194–206. New York: Columbia University Press.

Chapple, Christopher Key. 1996. "Ahimsa in the *Mahabharata*." In *Journal of Vaishnava Studies* 4, no. 3 (Summer):109–25.

Chakravarthi, A. 1953. "Thirukural in English with Commentary." In *Madras*: n.p., Verse 320, p. 154.

Das, Vraja Kishor. 1994. *The Vegan and the Vedas: A Detailed Examination of Veganism and Krishna Consciousness*. Towaco, N.J.: Krishnafest North America.

Klostermaier, Klaus. 1987. "The Response of Modern Vaishnavism." In *Modern Indian Responses to Religious Pluralism*, ed. Harold G. Coward, pp. 83–109. Albany: State University of New York Press.

Larson, Gerald. 1995. *India's Agony over Religion*. Albany: State University of New York Press.

Nelson, Lance. 2006. "Cows, Elephants, Dogs, and other Lesser Embodiments of Atman: Reflections on Hindu Attitudes toward Nonhuman Animals." In *A Communion of Subjects: Animals in Religion, Science, and Ethics*, eds. Paul Waldau and Kimberley Patton, pp. 179–93. New York: Columbia University Press.

Subramuniyaswami, Satguru Shivaya. 1993. *Dancing with Siva: Hinduism's Contemporary Catechism*. Concord, Calif.: Himalayan Academy.

3

International Society for Krishna Consciousness: Lord Krishna and the Animals

Berry, Rynn. 1999. *Famous Vegetarians and their Favorite Recipes*. New York: Pythagorean.

Carman, Judy. 2003. *Peace to All Beings: Veggie Soup for the Chicken's Soul*. New York: Lantern Books.

Coyle, Stuart. 1998. *Protecting Cows: A Handbook of the Principles and Practices of Vegetarian Cow Husbandry.* Sussex, U.K.: Hatagra Publishing.

Dasa, Drutakarma. 1985. "A New Spirit in San Diego." In *Back to Godhead*, Vol. 20, No. 2–3, February/March 1985:28–34.

Dharma, Krishna. 1999. *Mahabharata.* Badger, Calif.: Torchlight.

———. 1989. "Mother Mild." In *Back to Godhead*, Vol. 24, No. 6, June 1989:20–22.

Dasa, Satsvarupa. 2003. *Srila Prabhupada Nectar.* Port Royal, Penn.: Gita Nagari Press.

Goswami, Jayadeva. 2003. *Gita-Govinda.* Los Angeles: Bhaktivedanta Book Trust.

Goswami, M., Dasa, B., Dasa, D. and Dasa, K. 1983/2006. *Higher Taste.* Los Angeles: Bhaktivedanta Book Trust.

Prabhupada, A. C. Bhaktivedanta Swami. 1994. *Science of Self-Realization. Thou Shalt not Kill.* Los Angeles: Bhaktivedanta Book Trust.

———. 1993. *Collected Lectures on Srimad Bhagavatam*, Vol. 5/11. Los Angeles: Bhaktivedanta Book Trust.

———. 1990. *Conversations with Srila Prabhupada*, Vol. 20/37. Los Angeles: Bhaktivedanta Book Trust.

———. 1987. *Srimad Bhagavatam.* Los Angeles: Bhaktivedanta Book Trust.

———. 1974. *Sri Caitanya-caritamrta.* Los Angeles: Bhaktivedanta Book Trust.

Rosen, Steven J. 2004. *Holy Cow: The Hare Krishna Contribution to Vegetarianism and Animal Rights.* New York: Lantern Books.

Smith, Scott S. 2004. "Is There an Afterlife for Animals?" Awareness Magazine website. www.awarenessmag.com/marapr4/MA4_IS_THERE_AFTERLIFE.HTML (accessed Dec. 31, 2009).

Stanford Report. Stanford University website. <http://news-service.stanford.edu/news/2005/june15/jobs-061505.html> (accessed Dec. 31, 2009).

Subramanian, V. K. 1990. *Maxims of Chanakya.* New Delhi: Abhinav.

4

The Jain Center of Southern California:
Theory and Practice across Continents

Babb, Lawrence A. 1996. *Absent Lord: Ascetic Kings in a Jain Ritual Culture.* Berkeley: University of California Press.

Chapple, Christopher Key. 2006. "Inherent Value without Nostalgia:

Animals and the Jaina Tradition." In *A Communion of Subjects*, eds. Paul Waldau and Kimberley Patton. New York: Columbia University Press.

———. 1993. *Nonviolence to Animals, Earth, and Self in Asian Traditions*. Albany: State University of New York Press.

Chatterjee, Asim Kumar. 1978. *A Comprehensive History of Jainism*. 2 vols. Calcutta: Firma KLM Private Limited.

Glera, M. R. 2002. *Science in Jainism*. Ladnun, Indian: Jain Visha Bharati Institute.

Jacobi, Hermann, trans. 1884a. "The Gaina Sutras." In *Sacred Books of the East*, ed. F. Max Muller, pp. 79–87. Oxford: Clarendon Press.

———. 1884b. *Jaina Sutras Translated from the Prakrit*. Oxford: Clarendon Press.

Jaini, Padmanabh S. 1979. *The Jaina Path of Purification*. Delhi: Motilal Banarsidass.

Koller, John M. 2006. "Jain Ecological Perspectives." In *Jainism and Ecology: Nonviolence in the Web of Life*, ed. Christopher Key Chapple, pp. 30–2. Delhi: Motilal Banarsidass.

Lodrick, Deryck O. 1981. *Sacred Cows, Sacred Places: Origins and Survivals of Animal Homes in India*. Berkeley: University of California Press.

Mehta, Mohan Lal. 1969. *Jaina Culture*. Varanasi, India: P. V. Research Institute at Hindu University.

Narvi, Sri Jinendra. 1993. *Saman Suttam*. Varanasi, India: Sarva Seva Sangh Prakashun.

Nevaskar, Balwant Nevaskar. 1971. *Capitalists without Capitalism*. Westport, Conn.: Greenwood Publishing Corporation.

Noss, John B. 1956. *Man's Religions*. New York: Macaulay Company.

Rampuria, S. C. 1947. *Cult of Ahimsa*. Calcutta: Sri Jain Swetamber Terapanthi Mahasabha.

Rousselet, Louis, and Charles Randolph Buckle. 1876. *India and Its Native Princes: Travels in Central India and in the Presidencies of Bombay and Bengal*. London: Chapman and Hall.

Shah, Pravin K. 2001. *Jainism: Religion of Compassion and Ecology*. Raleigh, N.C.: JAINA Education Committee.

———. 1994. *Essence of World Religions*. Cary, N.C.: Jain Study Center of North Carolina.

Tatia, Nathmal, trans. 1994. *That Which Is: Tattvartha Sutra*. San Francisco: Harper Collins.

Tobias, Michael. 1991. *Life Force: The World of Jainism*. Berkeley: Asian Humanities Press.

Von Glasenapp, Helmuth. 1942. *The Doctrine of Karman*. Varanasi, India: P. V. Research Institute.

5

Buddhism and Animal Liberation:
A Family of Sentient Beings

Dhammapada: The Path of Perfection, The. 1973. Trans. from the Pali with an introduction by Juan Mascaro. London: Penguin.

Hanh, Thich Nhat. 1997. *Stepping into Freedom: An Introduction to Buddhist Monastic Training*. Berkeley: Parallax Press.

Harvey, Peter. 1990. *An Introduction to Buddhism: Teachings, History, Practice*. Cambridge: Cambridge University Press.

Kapleau, Philip. 1981. *To Cherish all Life: A Buddhist Case for Becoming Vegetarian*. Rochester, N.Y.: The Zen Center.

Lankavatara Sutra: A Mahayana Text, The. 1999. Trans. D. T. Suzuki. New Delhi: Munshiram Manoharlal Publishers.

Narada, Mahathera. 1988. *The Buddha and His Teachings*. 2nd ed. Kandy, Sri Lanka: Buddhist Publication Society.

Page, Tony. 1999. *Buddhism and Animals: A Buddhist Vision of Humanity's Rightful Relationship with the Animal Kingdom*. London: UKAVIS (United Kingdom Anti-Vivisection Information Society) Publications.

Phelps, Norm. 2004. *The Great Compassion: Buddhism and Animal Rights*. New York: Lantern Books.

Rabten, Geshe. 1984. *Essential Nectar: Meditations on the Buddhist Path*. Boston: Wisdom Publications, Boston.

6

Buddhist Reflections on Animal Advocacy:
Intention and Liberation

Handlin Smith, Joanna F. 1999. "Liberating Animals in Ming-Qing China: Buddhist Inspiration and Elite Imagination." In *The Journal of Asian Studies* 58, no. 1:51–84.

Harvey, Peter. 2007. "Avoiding Unintended Harm to the Environment and the Buddhist Ethic of Intention." Journal of Buddhist Ethics website. <www.buddhistethics.org/14/harvey-article.html> (accessed Jan. 16, 2010).

Kapleau, Philip. 1981. *To Cherish All Life: A Buddhist View of Animal Slaughter and Meat Eating.* Rochester, N.Y.: The Zen Center.

Ling, Trevor, ed. 1993. *Buddhist Trends in Southeast Asia.* Singapore: Institute of Southeast Asian Studies.

McDermott, James P. 1989. "Animals and Humans in Early Buddhism." In *Indo-Iranian Journal* 32, no. 4:269–80.

Page, Tony. 1999. *Buddhism and Animals: A Buddhist Vision of Humanity's Rightful Relationship with the Animal Kingdom.* London: UKAVIS (United Kingdom Anti-Vivisection Information Society) Publications.

Phelps, Norm. 2004. *The Great Compassion: Buddhism and Animal Rights.* New York: Lantern Books.

Schmithausen, Lambert. 1997. "The Early Buddhist Tradition and Ecological Ethics." *Journal of Buddhist Ethics* 4. <www.buddhistethics.org/4/schm1.html> (accessed 1/16/10).

Waldau, Paul. 2002. *The Specter of Speciesism: Buddhist and Christian Views of Animals.* New York: Oxford University Press.

Williams, Duncan Ryukan. 1997. "Animal Liberation, Death, and the State: Rites to Release Animals in Medieval Japan." In *Buddhism and Ecology: The Interconnection of Dharma and Deeds,* eds. Mary Evelyn Tucker and Duncan Ryukan Williams, pp. 149–62. Cambridge, Mass.: Harvard University Center for the Study of World Religions.

7

Daoism: From Meat Avoidance to Compassion-Based Vegetarianism

Baker, Steve. 2001. *Picturing the Beast: Animals, Identity, and Representation.* Champaign: University of Illinois Press.

Bensky, Dan, Steven Clavey, and Erich Stöger. 2004. *Materia Medica.* 3rd ed. Seattle, Wash.: Eastland Press.

Bokenkamp, Stephen. 1997. *Early Daoist Scriptures.* Berkeley: University of California Press.

Campany, Robert. 2005. "Eating Better than Gods and Ancestors." In *Of Tripod and Palate,* ed. Roel Sterckx, pp. 96–122. New York: Palgrave Macmillan.

_____. 2002. *To Live as Long as Heaven: A Translation and Study of Ge Hong's Traditions of Divine Transcendents*. Berkeley: University of California Press.

_____. 2001. "Ingesting the Marvelous: The Practitioner's Relationship to Nature According to Ge Hong." In *Daoism and Ecology*, eds. Norman Girardot *et al.*, pp. 125–46. Cambridge, Mass.: Harvard University Press.

Dean, Kenneth. 1993. *Taoist Ritual and Popular Cults of Southeast China*. Princeton, N.J.: Princeton University Press.

Douglas, Mary. 2002 (1966). *Purity and Danger: An Analysis of Concepts of Pollution and Taboo*. London and New York: Routledge.

Eskildsen, Stephen. 2004. *The Teachings and Practices of the Early Quanzhen Taoist Masters*. Albany: State University of New York Press.

_____. 1998. *Asceticism in Early Taoist Religion*. Albany: State University of New York Press.

Fava, Patrice *et al.*, dirs. 2005. *The Revenge of Han Xin: A Daoist Mystery*. Paris and Honolulu: CNRS Media.

Fricke, Ron, dir. 1992. *Baraka*. Orland Park, Ill.: MPI Home Video.

Hendrischke, Barbara, and Benjamin Penny. 1996. "*The 180 Precepts Spoken by Lord Lao*: A Translation and Textual Study." In *Taoist Resources* 6.2:17–29.

Kieschnick, John. 2005. "Buddhist Vegetarianism in China." In *Of Tripod and Palate*, ed. Roel Sterckx, pp. 186–212. New York: Palgrave Macmillan.

Kleeman, Terry. 2005. "Feasting without the Victuals: The Evolution of the Daoist Communal Kitchen." In *Of Tripod and Palate*, ed. Roel Sterckx, pp. 140–62. New York: Palgrave Macmillan.

_____. 1994. "Licentious Cults and Bloody Victuals: Sacrifice, Reciprocity, and Violence in Traditional China." In *Asia Major* 3.7:185–211.

Kohn, Livia. 2004. *Cosmos and Community: The Ethical Dimension of Daoism*. Cambridge, Mass.: Three Pines Press.

_____. 2003. *Monastic Life in Medieval Daoism: A Cross-Cultural Perspective*. Honolulu: University of Hawaii Press.

Kohn, Livia, and Russell Kirkland. 2000. "Daoism in the Tang (618–907)." In *Daoism Handbook*, ed. Livia Kohn, pp. 339–83. Leiden: Brill.

Komjathy, Louis. 2008. *Handbooks for Daoist Practice*. Hong Kong: Yuen Yuen Institute.

_____. 2007. *Cultivating Perfection: Mysticism and Self-Transformation in Early Quanzhen Daoism*. Leiden: Brill.

_____. 2002. *Title Index to Daoist Collections*. Cambridge, Mass.: Three Pines Press.

Lagerwey, John. 1987. *Taoist Ritual in Chinese Society and History*. New York: Macmillan.

Lévi, Jean. 1983. "L'abstinence des Céréales chez les Taoïstes." *Études Chinoises* 1:3–47.

Lewis, Mark Edward. 1990. *Sanctioned Violence in Early China*. Albany: State University of New York Press.

Marsone, Pierre. 2001. "Accounts of the Foundation of the Quanzhen Movement: A Hagiographic Treatment of History." In *Journal of Chinese Religions* 29:95–110.

Penny, Benjamin. 1996. "Buddhism and Daoism in *The 180 Precepts Spoken by Lord Lao*." In *Taoist Resources* 6.2:1–16.

Puett, Michael. 2002. *To Become a God: Cosmology, Sacrifice, and Self-Divinization in Early China*. Cambridge, Mass.: Harvard University Press.

Reggio, Godfrey, dir. 1982. *Koyaanisqatsi: Life out of Balance*. Santa Fe, N.M.: Institute for Regional Education.

Robinet, Isabelle. 1993. *Taoist Meditation: The Mao-Shan Tradition of Great Purity*. Translated by Julian Pas and Norman Girardot. Albany: State University of New York Press.

———. 1989. "Visualization and Ecstatic Flight in Shangqing Taoism." In *Taoist Meditation and Longevity Techniques*, ed. Livia Kohn, pp. 159–91. Ann Arbor: Center for Chinese Studies, University of Michigan.

Rothfels, Nigel, ed. 2002. *Representing Animals*. Bloomington: Indiana University Press.

Saso, Michael. 1994. *A Taoist Cookbook*. North Clarendon, Vt.: Tuttle Publishing.

———. 1978. *The Teachings of Taoist Master Chuang*. New Haven, Conn.: Yale University Press.

———. 1972. *Taoism and the Rite of Cosmic Renewal*. Pullman: Washington State University Press.

Schipper, Kristofer. 2001. "Daoist Ecology: The Inner Transformation: A Study of the Precepts of the Early Daoist Ecclesia." In *Daoism and Ecology*, eds. Norman Girardot *et al.*, pp. 79–94. Cambridge, Mass.: Harvard University Press.

———. 1993 (1982). *The Taoist Body*. Translated by Karen C. Duval. Berkeley: University of California Press.

Sterckx, Roel. 2002. *The Animal and the Daemon in Early China*. New York: State University of New York Press.

_____, ed. 2005. *Of Tripod and Palate: Food, Politics, and Religion in Traditional China*. New York: Palgrave Macmillan.

Veith, Ilza. 1949. *The Yellow Emperor's Classic of Internal Medicine*. Berkeley: University of California Press.

Xu Hairong, ed. 1999. *Zhongguo Yinshi Shi* (History of Chinese Diet). 6 vols. Beijing: Huaxia.

Yifa. 2002. *The Origins of Buddhist Monastic Codes in China: An Annotated Translation and Study of the Chanyuan Qinggui*. Honolulu: University of Hawaii Press.

8

Judaism: Global Warming, Animal Products, and the Vegan Mandate

Animal Rights Group. n.d. "Facts about World Farm Animal Day." FARM website <www.wfad.org/about.htm> (accessed June 25, 2009).

Chill, Abraham. 1974. *The Commandments and Their Rationale*. Jerusalem: Urim Publications.

Durning, Alan B. 1986. "Cost of Beef for Health and Habitat." In *Los Angeles Times*, September 21, A3.

Easterbrook, Gregg 2006. *Case Closed: The Debate Over Global Warming Is Over*. Washington: Brookings Institution.

Energy and Resources Institute 2008. "Lifestyles, Energy Security, and Climate." The Energy and Resources Institute website. <www.teriin.org/index.php?option=com_events&task=details&sid=14> (accessed June 24, 2009).

Food and Agriculture Organization (FAO) 2006. "Livestock a Major Threat to Environment." Food and Agriculture Organization of the United Nations website <www.fao.org/newsroom/en/news/2006/1000448> (accessed June 24, 2009).

Gore, Al, Jr., 2006. *An Inconvenient Truth*. Emmaus, Penn.: Rodale Press.

Goveg.com. n.d. "Wasted Resources." PETA website <www.goveg.com/environment-wastedResources-food.asp> (accessed June 25, 2009).

Hansen, James. 2008. "Tipping Point: Perspective of a Climatologist." Columbia University in the City of New York website <www.columbia.edu/~jeh1/2008/StateOfWild_20080428.pdf> (accessed July 2006).

Hirsch, Rabbi Samson Raphael. 1962. *Horeb*. New York, N.Y.: Soncino Press.

Hoffmann, Hillel J. 2000. "The Permian Extinction." National Geographic website <ngm.nationalgeographic.com/ngm/0009/feature4/fulltext.html> (accessed June 24, 2009).

Intergovernmental Panel on Climate Change (IPCC) 2007. "Fourth Assessment Report." Intergovernmental Panel on Climate Change website <www.ipcc.ch/> (accessed June 24, 2009).

Johnson, Brad. 2008. "Global Boiling: In California It's 'Fire Season All Year Round.'" The Wonk Room website <wonkroom.thinkprogress.org/2008/11/17/schwarzenegger-always-wildfires> (accessed June 24, 2009).

Knickerbocker, Brad. 2007. "Humans' Beef with Livestock: A Warmer Planet." Christian Science Monitor website <www.csmonitor.com/2007/0220/p03s01–ussc.html> (accessed June 24, 2009).

McKie, Robin, and Caroline Davies. 2008. "Is Our Taste for Sunday Roast Killing the Planet?" In *The Guardian*, September 7, 2008.

Moore Lappé, Frances. 1991. *Diet for a Small Planet*. New York: Ballentine Books.

Norris, John. 2003. "Hans Blix: Caught between Iraq and a Hard Place." MTV website <www.mtv.com/bands/i/iraq/news_feature_031203/index5.jhtml> (accessed June 25, 2009).

Robbins, John. 1987. *Diet for a New America*. by John Robbins, Walpole, N.H.: Stillpoint Pub.

Singer, Robert. 2009. "Meat, Milk and Motors: The New China Syndrome Part 1." War on You website <waronyou.com/forums/index.php?topic=8137.0> (accessed June 25, 2009).

Schwartz, Richard. H. 2001. *Judaism and Vegetarianism*. New York: Lantern Books.

Tell Youth Tell Truth. 2007. "Animal Agriculture Equates to Wasted Resources and Environmental Degradation." All-Creatures.org website <www.all-creatures.org/tytt/env-animalag.html> (accessed June 25, 2009).

Timmer, John. 2007. "Ex-Military Leaders Call Climate Change a National Security Issue." Ars Technica website <http://arstechnica.com/news.ars/post/20070528–ex-military-leaders-call-climate-change-a national-security-issue.html> (accessed June 24, 2009).

Walsh, Bryan. 2007. "Climate Change: Case Closed." Time website <www.time.com/time/health/article/0,8599,1584992,00.html> (accessed June 25, 2009).

9

Catholic Exemplars: Recent Popes, Medieval Saints, and Animal Liberation

Agius, Dom, A. n.d. "Cruelty to Animals." Catholic Pamphlets website <www.catholicpamphlets.net/pamphlets/CRUELTY%20TO%20ANI-MALS.pdf> (accessed Sep. 1, 2010).

AnimalChaplains.com. n.d. "Spiritual Inspirations from Many Faiths." Animal Chaplains website <www.animalchaplains.com/MultifaithScripturalReadings.html> (accessed Sep. 1, 2010).

Aquinas, Thomas. 1994. *Commentary on Aristotle's De Anima.* Trans. Kenelm Foster, O.P. and Silvester Humphries, O.P.. New Haven, Conn.: Yale University Press.

———. 1964. *Summa Theologica.* Trans. Blackfriars. New York: McGraw-Hill.

———. 1953. *The Disputed Questions on Truth.* Trans. James McGlynn. Chicago: Regnery Publishing Inc..

Celano, Thomas. 1200–1260/1270. "Excerpts from the First Life of St. Francis." Five Franciscan Martyrs Region Secular Franciscan Order website <www.franciscan-sfo.org/ap/vita1n2.htm> (accessed July 3, 2009).

Francis Assisi. n.d. "Spiritual Inspirations from many Faiths." Animal Chaplains website <www.animalchaplains.com/MultifaithScripturalReadings.html> (accessed June 24, 2009) and Evanston Public Library website <www.epl.org/library/strategic-plan-00.html> (accessed June 24, 2009).

Hyland, J. R. n.d. "The Pope and the Homeless Cats: John Paul II had a Dream." PETA website <www.jesusveg.com/popecats.html> (accessed June 24, 2009).

Pacifici, Mimmo. 1990. "The Pope Has Said: Animals Too Have Souls, Just Like Men." Rocky Rococo's Animal Rights News and Action website <www.dreamshore.net/rococo/pope.html> (accessed Sep. 1, 2010).

People for the Ethical Treatment of Animals. n.d. "Benedict XVI continues Tradition of Papal Concern for Animals." PETA website <www.goveg.com/f-popebenedictxvi.asp> (accessed Sep. 1, 2010).

Pope Pius XII. n.d. "Selections of Brief Quotations." All-Creatures.org website <www.all-creatures.org/ca/archive-quotes.html> (accessed July 2, 2009).

Ugolino, B. 2007. *Little Flowers of St. Francis of Assisi.* Trans. W. Heywood. New York: Cosimo Classics.

10

Christian Mysticism: Unity and Love for All

Armstrong, Regis J., and Ignatius C. Brady. 1982. *Francis and Clare: The Complete Works*. London: SPCK.

Carmichael, Alexander. 1992. *Charms of the Gaels: Hymns and Incantations with Illustrative Notes on Words, Rites and Customs, Dying and Obsolete*. Edinburgh: Floris Books.

Davies, Oliver, and Thomas O'Loughlin. 1999. *Celtic Spirituality*. New York: Paulist Press.

Fox, Matthew. 1991. *Creation Spirituality: Liberating Gifts for the Peoples of the Earth*. San Francisco: HarperCollins.

————. 1983. *Original Blessing*. New York: Penguin.

Inge, William R. 1947. *Mysticism in religion*. London: Hutchison.

————. 1899. *Christian Mysticism: Considered in Eight Lectures Delivered before the University of Oxford*. New York: Charles Scribner's Sons.

James, William. 1902/1982. *The Varieties of Religious Experience*. New York: Penguin.

King, Ursula. 2003. *Christian Mystics: Their Lives and Legacies throughout the Ages*. London: Routledge.

Plotinus. 1991. *The Enneads*. Trans. S. MacKenna. New York: Penguin.

Sellner, Edward C. 1993. *Wisdom of the Celtic Saints*. Notre Dame, Ill.: Ave Maria Press.

Soelle, Dorothee. 2001. *The Silent Cry: Mysticism and Resistance*. Trans. B. and M. Rumscheidt. Minneapolis: Fortress Press.

Troeltsch, Ernst. 1912/1992. *The Social Teaching of the Christian Churches*. Trans. O. Wyon. Louisville, Ky.: Westminster/John Knox Press.

Waddell, Helen, and Robert Gibbings. 1934/1995. *Beasts and Saints*. London: Darton, Longman and Todd.

11

A Society of Friends (Quaker-Christian) View: Prophets and the Hidden Paradise

Brinton, Howard H. 1972. *Quaker Journals*. Wallingford, Penn.: Pendle Hill.

————. 1965. *Friends for 300 Years*. Wallingford, Penn.: Pendle Hill.

Britain Yearly Meeting. n.d. "Online Exhibition: Quakers and the Path to Abolition." Quakers in Britain website <www.quaker.org.uk/Templates/Internal.asp?NodeID=93433> (accessed Nov. 9, 2008).

Cowper, William. n.d. *The Task and other Poems*. n.p.: Dodo Press.

Ellwood, Gracia Fay. 2008. "The Peaceable Table." Vegetarian Friends website <www.vegetarianfriends.net> (accessed Oct. 9, 2008).

Fox, George. 2008. "The Letters of George Fox." The Way to Righteousness website <www.hallvworthington.com/Letters/gfsection6.html> (accessed July 5, 2008).

_____. 2007. "Epistles." University of Oregon website <www.uoregon.edu/~rbear/foxep.htm> (accessed June 11, 2007).

_____. 1997. *The Journal of George Fox*. Ed. John L. Nickalls. Philadelphia: Religious Society of Friends.

Gilbert, Joan. 2005. "Joshua Evans: Consistent Quaker." Vegetarian Friends website <www.vegetarianfriends.net/issue6.html> (accessed Jan. 1, 2005) (Originally from the *The Friendly Vegetarian*, No. 15, Spring 1986).

Hatkoff, Isabella, Craig Hatkoff, and Dr. Paula Kahumbu. 2006. *Owen & Mzee*. New York: Scholastic.

Henderich, Garret, Derick up den Graeff, Francis Daniell Pastorius, and Abraham up den Graef. 1688. "A Minute Against Slavery." Faith and Interpractice of Intermountain Yearly Meeting website <http://home.earthlink.net/~imym-faith-and-practice/id37.html> (accessed Aug. 15, 2008).

Hussenbux, Marian. 2007. E-mail personal communication, Feb. 20, 2007.

Masson, Jeffrey Mossaieff. 1999. *The Emperor's Embrace*. New York: Pocket Books.

Shideler, Mary McDermott. 1962. *The Theology of Romantic Love*. New York: Harper.

Spiegel, Marjorie. 1996. *The Dreaded Comparison: Human and Animal Slavery*. New York: Mirror.

Suchocki, Marjorie Hewitt. 1999. *The Fall to Violence*. New York: Continuum.

Traherne, Thomas. 1960. *Centuries*. New York: Harper.

Williams, Charles. 2005. *The Figure of Beatrice*. Berkeley: Apocrophile.

Woolman, John. 1971. *The Journal and Major Essays of John Woolman*, ed. Phillips P. Moulton. New York: Oxford.

Wordsworth, William. 1952. "Ode" and "Tintern Abbey." In *Immortal Poems of the English Language*, ed. Oscar Williams, pp. 260–66 and pp. 255–59. New York: Pocket Books.

12

Christianity and Scapegoating:
Understanding and Responding to Oppression

Becker, Ernest. 1973. *The Denial of Death*. New York: Free Press.

Fiddes, Nick. 1991. *Meat: A Natural Symbol*. New York: Routledge.

Girard, René. 1973. *Violence and the Sacred*. Baltimore: Johns Hopkins Press.

Pyszczynski, Thomas A., Sheldon Solomon, and Jeff Greenberg. 2003. *In the Wake of 9/11: The Psychology of Terror*. Washington, D.C.: American Psychological Association.

13

Islam: Muhammad, Sacred Writings, and Animal Liberation

Attar, Farid Al-Din. 1990. *Muslim Saints and Mystics: Episodes from the Tadhkirat al-Auliya'*. Trans. A. J. Arberry. New York: Arkana.

Bakhtiar, Laleh. 1987. *Sufi: Expressions of the Mystic Quest*. New York: Thames and Hudson.

Berry, Rynn. 1998. *Food for the Gods: Vegetarianism and the World's Religions*. New York: Pythagorean.

Cragg, Kenneth, and R. Marston Speight. 1988. *The House of Islam*. Belmont, Calif.: Wadsworth.

Denny, Frederick M. 1987. *Islam and the Muslim Community*. San Francisco: HarperSanFrancisco.

Dutton, Yasin. 2003. "The Environmental Crisis of our Time: A Muslim Response." In *Islam and Ecology: A Bestowed Trust*, ed. Richard C. Foltz et al., pp. 323–40. Cambridge, Mass.: Harvard University Press.

Foltz, Richard C. 2005. *Animals in Islamic Tradition and Muslim Cultures*. Oxford: Oneworld.

_____. 2004. "Is Vegetarianism Un-Islamic?" in *Food for Thought: The Debate on Vegetarianism*, ed. Steven Sapontzis, pp. 209–22. Amherst: Prometheus.

_____. 2003. "Islamic Environmentalism: A Matter of Interpretation." In *Islam and Ecology: A Bestowed Trust*, ed. Richard C. Foltz et al., pp. 249–80. Cambridge, Mass.: Harvard University Press.

Friedlander, Shems. 1977. *Submission: Sayings of the Prophet Muhammad*. New York: Harper Colophon.

Grisell, Ronald. 1983. *Sufism.* Berkeley: Ross.

"Halal—Into the Future." *Halal Food Authority.* <http://www.halalfoodauthority.co.uk/seminars-halalfoodexhibit.html> (accessed Oct. 19, 2010).

"Halal V/s Haraam Food in a Non-Muslim Country." *ShiaChat.com: Forums.* <http://www.shiachat.com/forum/index.php?/topic/234916013-halal-vs-haraam-food-in-a-non-muslim-country/#top> (accessed Oct. 19, 2010).

Hamid, Rehana. 1998. "Conversation/Islam: Dr. Rehana Hamid." In *Food for the Gods: Vegetarianism and the World's Religions,* ed. Rynn Berry, pp. 256–69. New York: Pythagorean.

Haq, S. Nomanul. 2003. "Islam and Ecology: Toward Retrieval and Reconstruction." In *Islam and Ecology: A Bestowed Trust,* ed. Richard C. Foltz *et al.*, pp. 121–54. Cambridge, Mass.: Harvard University Press.

"Hazrat Ibrahim Bin Adham (RA)." *Thecurrentaffairs.Com: Pakistan News and Current Events.* <http://thecurrentaffairs.com/hazrat-ibrahim-bin-adham-ra.html> (accessed Oct. 19, 2010).

Hind, Jamaat-e-Islami. *Human Face of Religion.* "10. The Religion of Compassion." Kerala. n.d. <http://www.jihkerala.org/htm/english/RELIGION/10.html> (accessed October 19, 2010).

Holy Qur'an Pages. n.d. "Agriculture." In *Sahih Bukhari Book – 39. Vol. 3, No. 513.* <http://www.quranmalayalam.com/hadees/bukhari/039.sbt.html> (accessed December 16, 2010).

"Animals in Islam II." n. d. *Islam: The Modern Religion.* <http://www.themodernreligion.com/misc/an/an2.htm> (accessed October 19, 2010).

Khawaja, Masood. November 24, 2005. "Halal—Into the Future." Halal Food Authority website. <http://www.halalfoodauthority.co.uk/seminars-halalfoodexhibit.html> (accessed October 19, 2010).

Llewellyn, Othman Abd-ar-Rahman. 2003. "The Basis for a Discipline of Islamic Environmental Law." *Islam and Ecology: A Bestowed Trust,* ed. Richard C. Foltz *et al.*, pp. 185–248. Cambridge, Mass.: Harvard University Press.

Masri, Al-Hafiz Basheer Ahmad. 2007. *Animal Welfare in Islam.* Leicestershire: Islamic Foundation.

Mishkat al-Masabih (Book 6, Chapter 7). *Islam, the Modern Religion.* "Animals in Islam II." <http://www.themodernreligion.com/misc/an/an2.htm> (accessed Oct. 19, 2010).

Muhaiyaddeen, M. R. Bawa. 1985. *Come to the Secret Garden: Sufi Tales of Wisdom.* Philadelphia: Fellowship Press.

Muhaiyaddeen, M. R. Bawa. 1985. "The Hunter Learns Compassion from the

Fawn." *Come to the Secret Garden: Sufi Tales of Wisdom.* Philedalphia: Fellowship Press. <http://books.google.com/books?id=_JKbdJtLbZMC&pg=PA28&lpg=PA28&dq=Muhaiyaddeen+if+we+remember+that+every+creation+was+young+once,+we+will+never+kill+another+life&source=bl&ots=wRk-_CbM5Y&sig=6K7DMPtNJzcOjViXBxHJJ5Bdfsc&hl=en&ei=X1m-TOXBFYKisQOxkbTIDA&sa=X&oi=book_result&ct=result&resnum=1&ved=0CBMQ6AEwAA#v=onepage&q&f=false> (accessed Oct. 19, 2010).

Muttaqi, Shahid 'Ali. n. d. "The Sacrifice of 'Eid al-Adha': An Islamic Perspective Against Animal Sacrifice." *Islamic Concern.* <http://www.islam-veg.com/sacrifice01.asp> (accessed June 29, 2004).

Muwatta Malik. Guided Ways: Hadith. <http://www.guidedways.com/book_display-book-54-translator-4-start-30-number-54.12.31.htm> (accessed Oct. 19, 2010).

Nasr, Seyyed Hossein. 2003. "Islam, the Contemporary Islamic world, and the Environmental Crisis." In *Islam and Ecology: A Bestowed Trust*, ed. Richard C. Foltz *et al.*, pp. 85–106. Cambridge, Mass.: Harvard University Press.

Ozdemir, Ibrahim. 2003. "Toward an Understanding of Environmental Ethics from a Qur'anic Perspective." In *Islam and Ecology: A Bestowed Trust*, ed. Richard C. Foltz *et al.*, pp. 3–38. Cambridge, Mass.: Harvard University Press.

Qur'an. 1956. Trans. N. J. Dawood. Harmondsworth: Penguin.

Rumi, Jelaluddin. 2007. *Divan-i Kabir*, in "Rumi's Path of Love and 'Being Freed' with the Sama," by Mehmet Seker. In *Rumi and His Sufi Path of Love*. 1–8, eds. Fatih Çitlak and Hüseyin Bingül. Somerset, N.J.: The Light Inc.

Sahih Bukhari. Guided Ways: Hadith. <http://www.guidedways.com/searchHadith.php> (accessed October 19, 2010).

Sahih Bukhari 67. Guided Ways: Hadith. <http://www.guidedways.com/book_display-book-67-translator-1-start-60-number-442.htm> (accessed October 19, 2010).

Sahih Bukhari referenced on *Jamaat e Islami Hind, Kerala.* "10. The Religion of Compassion." <http://www.jihkerala.org/htm/english/RELIGION/10.html> (accessed Oct. 19, 2010).

Said, Abdul Aziz, and Nathan C. Funk. 2003. "Peace in Islam: An Ecology of the Spirit." In *Islam and Ecology: A Bestowed Trust*, ed. Richard C. Foltz *et al.*, pp. 155–84. Cambridge, Mass.: Harvard University Press.

Schuon, Frithjof. 1979. *Sufism: Veil and Quintessence.* Bloomington, Ind.: World Wisdom Books.

"Selected Comments on Islamic Teachings." *ReligiousTolerance.Org.* <http://www.religioustolerance.org/tomek14.htm> (accessed October 19, 2010).

Siddiq, Mohammad Yusuf. 2003. "An Ecological Journey in Muslim Bengal." In *Islam and Ecology: A Bestowed Trust*, ed. Richard C. Foltz *et al.*, pp. 451–62. Cambridge, Mass.: Harvard University Press.

Stoddart, William. 1985. *Sufism: The Mystical Doctrines and Methods of Islam.* New York: Paragon Publishing.

Ullah, Najib.1963. *Islamic Literature: An Introductory History with Selections.* New York: Washington Square.

14

Al-Hafiz B. A. Masri: Muslim, Scholar, Activist—Rebel with a Just Cause

Amin, Muhammad. 1965. *Wisdom of Prophet Mohammad.* Pakistan: Lion Press.

Haque, Nadeem. 2007. "Book Review: Animals in the Islamic Tradition and Muslim Cultures," by Richard C. Foltz. In *Journal of Agricultural and Environmental Ethics.* Vol. 20, Issue 6.

Masri, Al-Hafiz B. A. 1991. "An Islamic Viewpoint on Animal Protection." In *ANIMALS International.* Vol. XI, Issue 36.

———. 1989. *Animals in Islam.* Petersfield: The Athene Trust.

———. 1988. *The Bane of Mirzaiyat.* South Africa: Young Men's Muslim Association.

———. 1986. "Animal Experimentation: The Muslim Viewpoint." In *Animal Sacrifices: Religious Perspectives on the Use of Animals in Science*, ed. Tom Regan, pp. 171–98. Philadelphia: Temple University Press.

Qur'an. 2008. Trans. M. A. S. Abdel Haleem. U.K.: Oxford University Press.

15

Indigenous Peoples: Kinship and Killing

Associated Press. 1999. "Colville Tribal Elder Shows Herself to be a 'Natural' Resource." In *Skagit Valley Herald*, December 28, C5.

Bierlein, J. F. 1994. *Parallel Myths.* New York: Ballantine.

Brown, Dee. 1979. *Folktales of the Native American: Retold for Our Times.* New York: Henry Holt.

Cajete, Gregory. 2001. "Indigenous Education and Ecology: Perspectives of an American Indian Educator." In *Indigenous Traditions and Ecology: The Interbeing of Cosmology and Community*, ed. John A. Grim, pp. 619–38. Cambridge, Mass.: Harvard University Press.

Dunagan, Christopher. 1998. "Whale Watch: Tribal Views on Whaling." Kitsap Sun website <http://web.kitsapsun.com/packages/whalehunt/story30.html> (accessed Oct. 19, 2010).

Erdoes, Richard, and Alfonso Ortiz, ed. 1984. *American Indian Myths and Legends*. New York: Pantheon.

Feinup-Riordan, Ann. 2001. "A Guest on the Table: Ecology from the Yup'ik Eskimo Point of View." In *Indigenous Traditions and Ecology: The Interbeing of Cosmology and Community*, ed. John A. Grim, pp. 541–58. Cambridge, Mass.: Harvard University Press.

Gill, Sam D. 1982. *Native American Religions: An Introduction*. Belmont, Calif.: Wadsworth.

Harrod, Howard L. 1987. *Renewing the World: Plains Indian Religion and Morality*. Tucson: University of Arizona.

Henare, Manuka. 2001. "*Tapu, Mana, Mauri, Hau, Wairua*: A Maori Philosophy of Vitalism and Cosmos." In *Indigenous Traditions and Ecology: The Interbeing of Cosmology and Community*, ed. John A. Grim, pp. 197–221. Cambridge, Mass.: Harvard University Press.

Ides, Isabelle, *et al.* 2000. "Whale Hunt Issue." In *Peninsula Daily News*, June 16.

Kelley, Peter. 2000. "Reaching Out in Friendship." In *Skagit Valley Herald*, January 28, A1.

Kinsley, David. 1995. *Ecology and Religion: Ecological Spirituality in Cross-Cultural Perspective*. Englewood Cliffs, N.J.: Prentice-Hall.

Montejo, Victor D. 2001. "The Road to Heaven: Jakaltek Maya Beliefs, Religion, and the Ecology." In *Indigenous Traditions and Ecology: The Interbeing of Cosmology and Community*, ed. John A. Grim, pp. 175–96. Cambridge, Mass.: Harvard University Press.

Nelson, Richard K. 1983. *Make Prayers to Raven: A Koyukon View of the Northern Forest*. Chicago: University of Chicago Press.

Noske, Barbara. 1997. "Speciesism, Anthropocentrism, and Non-Western Cultures." In *Anthrozoos* 10, no. 4:183–90.

Opoku Kofi. 2006. "Animals in African Mythology." In *A Communion of Subjects: Animals in Religion, Science, and Ethics*, eds. Paul Waldau and Kimberley Patton, pp. 351–59. New York: Columbia University Press.

Prabhu, Pradip. 2001. "In the Eye of the Storm: Tribal Peoples of India." In *Indigenous Traditions and Ecology: The Interbeing of Cosmology and Community*, ed. John A. Grim, pp. 47–70. Cambridge, Mass.: Harvard University Press.

Rosenberg, Donna. 1994. *World Mythology: An Anthology of the Great Myths and Epics*. Lincolnwood, Ill.: NTC Publishing Group.

Serpell, James. 1992. "Animal Protection and Environmentalism: The Background." In *Animal Welfare and the Environment*, ed. Richard D. Ryder, pp. 27–39. Melksham, U.K.: Duckworth.

Silva, Javier Galicia. 2001. "Religion, Ritual, and Agriculture among the Present-day Nahua of Mesoamerica." In *Indigenous Traditions and Ecology: The Interbeing of Cosmology and Community*, ed. John A. Grim, pp. 303–24. Cambridge, Mass.: Harvard University Press.

Spence, Lewis. 1985. *North American Indians: Myths and Legends*. London: Studio.

Suzuki, David, and Peter Knudtson. 1993. *Wisdom of the Elders: Sacred Native Stories of Nature*. New York: Bantam.

Tauli-Corpuz, Victoria. 2001. "Interface between Traditional Religion and Ecology among the Igorots." In *Indigenous Traditions and Ecology: The Interbeing of Cosmology and Community*, ed. John A. Grim, pp. 281–302. Cambridge, Mass.: Harvard University Press.

Valladolid, Julio, and Frederique Apffel-Marglin. 2001. "Andean Cosmovision and the Nurturing of Biodiversity." In *Indigenous Traditions and Ecology: The Interbeing of Cosmology and Community*, ed. John A. Grim, pp. 639–70. Cambridge, Mass.: Harvard University Press.

VanStone, James W. 1974. *Athapaskan Adaptations: Hunters and Fishermen of the Subarctic Forests*. Chicago: Aldine.

Watson, Paul. 1999. "1999 Captain's Log:1998–99: Gray Whale Protection Campaign, Part II: Bury my Heart at Neah Bay." In *Sea Shepherd Log: Sea Shepherd Conservation Society* 52.

17

Wiccan Spirituality and Animal Advocacy:
Perfect Love and Perfect Trust

Ahimsa. 2008. Wikipedia website <http://en.wikipedia.org/w/index.php?title=Ahimsa&oldid=185174738> (accessed Jan. 29, 2008).

Duchene, Lisa. 2006. "Are Pigs Smarter than Dogs?" ResarchPennState website <www.rps.psu.edu/probing/pigs.html> (accessed Jan. 20, 2008).

Hutton, Ronald. 1999. *The Triumph of the Moon: A History of Modern Pagan Witchcraft*. New York: Oxford University Press.

Rede. n.d. The American Heritage Dictionary of the English language. 4th ed. Website <http://dictionary.reference.com/browse/rede> (accessed Jan. 28, 2008).

Robinson, B. A. 2001. "Religious Identification in the U.S.: How American Adults View Themselves." Ontario Consultants on Religious Tolerance website <www.religioustolerance.org/chr_prac2.htm> (accessed Jan. 20, 2008).

18

Wicca, Ecofeminism, and Animal Advocacy: The Earth Path Less Traveled

Abbot, Sally. 1990. "The Origins of God in the Blood of the Lamb." In *Reweaving the World: The Emergence of Ecofeminism*, eds. Irene Diamond and Gloria Feman Orenstein, pp. 35–40. San Francisco: Sierra Club Books.

Adams, Carol. 2004. *The Pornography of Meat*. New York: Continuum.

———. 1998. *The Sexual Politics of Meat*. New York: Continuum.

———. 1994. *Neither Man nor Beast*. New York: Continuum.

Adler, Margot. 1979. *Drawing Down the Moon*. Boston: Beacon Press.

Bowman, Marion. 2000. "Nature, the Natural and Pagan Identity." Philipps-Universität Marburg website <www.uni-marburg.de/religionswissenschaft/journal/diskus/bowman_2.html> (accessed Jan. 15, 2010).

Coughlin, John. 2002. "The Wiccan Rede: A Historical Journey." Waningmoon website <www.waningmoon.com/ethics/rede.shtml> (accessed Jan. 15, 2010).

Crockford, Ross. 1997. "Bad Medicine." The New Internationalist website <www.newint.org/issue288/bad.htm> (accessed Jan. 15, 2010).

Donovan, Josephine. 2000. "Attention to Suffering: Sympathy as a Basis for Ethical Treatment of Animals." In *Beyond Animal Rights: A Feminist Caring Ethic for the Treatment of Animals*, eds. Josephine Donovan and Carol J. Adams, p. 16. New York: Continuum.

Eisenstein, Charles. 2002. "The Ethics of Eating Meat: A Radical View." Weston A. Price Foundation website <www.westonaprice.org/healthissues/ethicsmeat.html> (accessed Feb. 13, 2009).

Fireweed. 2002. "Fireweed Revives the Great Meat Debate." In *The Island Word* 1, no. 20 (June):19.

Gaard, Greta. 2002. "Vegetarian Ecofeminism: A Review Essay." In *Frontiers: A Journal of Women Studies*, ed. Susan Armitage, vol. 23, no. 3:117–46. Lincoln: University of Nebraska Press.

jones, pattrice. 2004. "Mothers with Monkeywrenches: Feminist Imperatives and the ALF." In *Terrorists or Freedom Fighters? Reflections on the Liberation of Animals*, ed. Steve Best and Anthony J. Nocella II, p. 142. New York: Lantern Books.

Kheel, Marti. 2004. "Toppling Patriarchy with a Fork: The Feminist Debate over Meat." In *Food for Thought: The Debate over Eating Meat*, ed. Steve F. Sapontzis, pp. 327–43. Amherst, N.Y.: Prometheus.

Perkel, Colin. 2004. "Anti-Meat Ads Referencing Pickton Case 'Grotesque.'" Missing People website <www.missingpeople.net/anti_meat_ads.htm> (accessed Jan. 15, 2010).

Starhawk. 2004. *The Earth Path: Grounding your Spirit in the Rhythms of Nature*. New York: HarperCollins.

———. 1989. "Feminist, Earth-Based Spirituality and Ecofeminism." In *Healing the Wounds: The Promise of Ecofeminism*, ed. Judith Plant, p. 174. Philadelphia: New Society Publishers.

———. 1979/1999. *The Spiral Dance: Rebirth of the Ancient Religion of the Goddess*. San Francisco: HarperSanFrancisco.

Weed, Susun. 2002. "Nutrition—The Wise Woman Way. Weed Wanderings 2." Herbal

Medicine and Spirit Healing the Wise Woman Way website <www.susunweed.com/herbal_ezine/weed_letter_Mar-02.htm> (accessed Mar., 2002).

Wigington, Patti. 2008. "Animal Sacrifice: Protected Under First Amendment or Not?" About.com website <http://paganwiccan.about.com/b/2008/01/15/animal-sacrifice-protected-under-first-amendment-or-not.html> (accessed Jan. 15, 2010).

Appendix
Factory Farming and Fishing

Clucas, Ivor. n.d. "A Study of the Options for Utilization of Bycatch and Discards from Marine Capture Fisheries." Food and Agriculture Organization of the United Nations <www.fao.org/docrep/w6602e/w6602e00.htm> (accessed Oct. 19, 2010).

Committee on Sea Turtle Conservation, National Research Council. 1990. *Decline of the Sea Turtles: Causes and Prevention.* Washington D.C.: National Academic Press.

FoxNews.com. 2008. "HundredsofDeadPenguinsWashUponBrazilBeaches." Fox News website <www.foxnews.com/story/0,2933,386578,00.html> (accessed Mar., 2009).

Kher, Unmesh. November 13, 2006. "Oceans of Nothing: Study Says Overfishing Will Soon Destroy the Seafood Supply." In *Time* Magazine, pp. 56–7.

Singer, Peter, and Jim Mason. 2006. *Eating: What We Eat and Why it Matters.* London: Arrow.

Washington Department of Fish and Wildlife. n.d. "Questions and Answers: Sea Lion Predation on Columbia River Salmon and Steelhead." Washington Department of Fish and Wildlife website <http://wdfw.wa.gov/wlm/sealions/questions.htm> (accessed Mar., 2009).

Weiss, Kenneth R. 2002 "Fish Farms Become Feedlots of the Sea." *Los Angeles Times,* December 9.

"What About Fish?" 1994. In *Animal People: News for People Who Care About Animals.* Vol.

3.7, Issue, 2. Clinton: Animal People, Inc..

"What Does the 'Organic' Label Really Mean?" n.d. NC State University: North Caroline

Cooperative Extension: Extension's Successful Family website <http://www.ces.ncsu.edu/successfulfamily/Nutrition%20&%20Wellness/organlab.htm > (accessed Dec., 2010).

About the Contributors

JUDITH BARAD is a professor of philosophy and women's studies at Indiana State University, and is active in her local parish. After graduating magna cum laude from Loyola University of Chicago in 1980, she attended Northwestern University. She received her Ph.D. in philosophy from Northwestern in 1984. In 1985, she accepted a position in philosophy at Indiana State, where she served as the chair of the department for nine years. She is the author of three books and numerous articles on ethics and the philosophy of religion, including such topics as feminist ethics, the role of emotion in moral judgments, the treatment of animals, the philosophy of St. Thomas Aquinas, and a book titled *The Ethics of Star Trek*. She has given dozens of national and international presentations, has been an ethics consultant for Boeing, and is a member of the Secular Franciscan Order.

CHRISTOPHER KEY CHAPPLE is Doshi Professor of Indic and Comparative Theology at Loyola Marymount University. Dr. Chapple received his undergraduate degree in comparative literature and religious studies from the State University of New York at Stony Brook and his doctorate in the history of religions through the theology department at Fordham University. He served as assistant director of the Institute for Advanced Studies of World Religions and taught Sanskrit, Hinduism, Jainism, and Buddhism for five years at the State University of New York at Stony Brook before joining the faculty at LMU. Dr. Chapple's research interests focus on renouncer religious traditions of India: Yoga, Jainism, and Buddhism. He has published several books, including *Karma and Creativity* (1986); a cotranslation of the

Yoga Sutras of Patanjali (1991); *Nonviolence to Animals, Earth, and Self in Asian Traditions* (1993); *Hinduism and Ecology* (coedited, 2000); *Jainism and Ecology: Nonviolence in the Web of Life* (edited, 2002), and *Reconciling Yogas: Haribhadras Array of Views on Yoga* (2003).

STEPHEN R. L. CLARK, PH.D., has been a professor of philosophy at the University of Liverpool, U.K., since 1983, having previously lectured at Oxford and Glasgow universities. His writings include *The Moral Status of Animals* (1977), *The Nature of the Beast* (1982), *How to Think about the Earth* (1993), *Animals and Their Moral Standing* (1997), and *Biology and Christian Ethics* (2000). (For a complete list see http://pcwww.liv.ac.uk/~srlclark/srlc.htm.) He has served on the Farm Animal Welfare Council and on the Animal Procedures Committee (which advise relevant government departments on issues related to the treatment of animals). He is at present researching the ethics and psychology of the third century Platonist, Plotinus.

KRISHNA KRIPA DASA, originally from Alabama, joined the International Society for Krishna Consciousness (ISKCON) in Texas, in 1978. He served briefly as vice president of Dallas's Radha-Kalachandji Temple, and for many years was head priest of the Houston Hare Krishna Temple. From 1985 to 2005 he directed a vegetarian cooking class at Rice University and helped produce an online vegetarian cookbook. Krishna Kripa resides in Houston with his wife and two children, and frequently visits Vrindavan, India, where Lord Krishna spent his youth.

GRACIA FAY BOUWMAN ELLWOOD was born in 1938 in the Puget Sound area of Washington State, and spent her formative years on a traditional family farm amid a divine beauty that often called to her. Farm life also awakened a sense of compassionate kinship with baby animals, which evaporated under cultural pressures that named these creatures "commodities" as they grew to adulthood. It was not until she encountered principled vegetarians in the 1970s and 1980s that she again opened her heart to farmed animals and began to study and think about this form of exploitation in a disciplined way. In the early 1980s she joined the Society of Friends and is presently active in the Animal Kinship Committee in her Quaker meeting, particularly as editor of the monthly online journal *The Peaceable Table*. Ellwood received her M.A. in religion and literature from the University of Chicago, and her Ph.D. in philosophy of religion at Claremont Graduate University. She taught religious studies at California State University, Long Beach, and is the author of *The Uttermost Deep: The Challenge of Near-Death Experiences*, as well as other books and essays, and the booklet *Are Animals Our Neighbors?*

FIREWEED is a Wiccan, ecofeminist, animal rights activist who lives with her partner and four cats in the woods of Denman Island, British Columbia. She is an honors graduate from the Emily Carr College of Art and Design (Vancouver, British Columbia, 1982) and has exhibited her work both across Canada and internationally. She currently works in graphic design and digital photography. In 1991, Fireweed founded Women and the Earth, a conference and workshop series dedicated to women's personal empowerment through activism. She has participated on the front lines of numerous logging blockades, in solidarity with First Nations and antibiotech activists, and in anti-G8 protests. She spearheaded a successful regional bylaw opposing exotic animals in entertainment, founded Citizen Support for Marine Mammal Protection, and Companion Animal Allies Network. Fireweed coordinates a community vegan potluck series highlighting environmental and social justice issues and organizes work bees called "garden parties" to support organic growers. She has successfully galvanized local government opposition "in principle" to genetically modified crops and is helping found a community food security co-op for local potato production. Fireweed has addressed a variety of British Columbian women's events, college classes, environmental gatherings, and community groups on ecofeminism, art and activism, animal rights, and women's Earth-based spirituality. Her writings have appeared in the *Island Word, Comox Valley Record, Comox Valley Echo*, the *Denman Island Flagstone, Witch Words*, and *Pagans for Peace* newsletter (www.fireweed.ca).

LINDA G. FISHER, aka Nightfeather, is a professional artist and animal activist who has dedicated much of her life to educating society about the plight of captive parrots. As an eleven year old, she was thrust into animal activism when she witnessed the suffering of a tiny parakeet who lay dying in a cage in a department store. Early in life, Linda discovered that she had an uncanny ability to communicate with animals and to feel their emotions; she was eventually inspired to tell their stories through art. Linda's sensitivity and remarkable connection to animals inspires her work, which has gained international recognition. Linda lives in the San Francisco Bay area and shares her home with a family of rescued animals, including parrots. She is part Ojibway and Cherokee and is a tribal member of the Ojibway Nation.

ANDREW FITZ-GIBBON is associate professor in philosophy, and chair of the Center for Ethics, Peace and Social Justice (CEPS) at SUNY, Cortland. He is bishop-abbot of the Lindisfarne Community, a neomonastic religious order in the broadly Anglican/Celtic tradition. He holds a Ph.D. from the University of Newcastle-upon-Tyne, U.K.

NADEEM HAQUE is a professional engineer, with a degree in economics from the University of Toronto and in civil engineering from the University of London, King's College. His extensive and deep academic interests, however, concern philosophical questions relating to human beings and nature. He is the coauthor of a handful of books, including *From Facts to Values: Certainty, Order, Balance and Their Universal Implications*, and a series titled *From Microbits to Everything*, in which he and his co-authors attempt to solve the "Big Questions," including the issue of consciousness, eschatology, proofs for God's existence, and the nature of God. He has also researched and written on the Qur'an, including an unpublished treatise on Islam and the Environment entitled *Ecolibrium*. His latest novella is in an extremely rare genre, Islamic Science Fiction, called: *Escape From Sirius: The Doomsday Protocol*.

STEPHEN R. KAUFMAN, M.D. is an ophthalmologist and an assistant professor at Case Western Reserve University School of Medicine. He has been active in animal protection for over three decades and is chair of the Christian Vegetarian Association, co-chair of the Medical Research Modernization Committee, and president of the Cleveland-area group Vegetarian Advocates. He was editor of the seven-volume monograph series *Perspectives on Medical Research*, and has written two books, *Guided by the Faith of Christ: Seeking to Stop Violence and Scapegoating* (2008) and, with Nathan Braun, *Good News for All Creation: Vegetarianism as Christian Stewardship* (2002). He has written numerous other articles including (with Neal Barnard, M.D.) "Animal Research is Wasteful and Misleading" (*Scientific American*, February 1997).

LISA KEMMERER (B.A. in international studies, Reed College; M.T.S. in comparative religions, Harvard Divinity School; Ph.D. in philosophy, University of Glasgow, Scotland) is a philosopher-activist, artist, and lover of wild places, who has hiked, biked, kayaked, backpacked, and traveled widely. She is the author of *In Search of Consistency: Ethics and Animals* (Brill 2006) and *Religion and Animals: Rightful Relations* (Oxford 2011), and (in addition to co-editing this volume) the editor of *Sister Species: Women, Animals, and Social Justice* (University of Illinois Press, 2011) and *Primate People: Personal Stories of Advocacy and Adventure* (University of Utah Press, 2011). She is currently editing three other anthologies (*Women as Animal Advocates and Activists: International Insights from the Front Lines*; *Links of Life: Earth and Animal Liberation*; and an untitled anthology on activism on behalf of bears). She has published a dozen chapters in books and encyclopedias, and has nearly thirty articles in print. Kemmerer is currently associate professor of philosophy and religions at Montana State University, Billings.

LOUIS KOMJATHY (Ph.D., Religious Studies, Boston University) is assistant professor of theology and religious studies at the University of San Diego and research associate in the Institute of Religion, Science and Social Studies of Shandong University (PRC). He also serves as co-director of the Center for Daoist Studies and as co-chair of the Daoist Studies Group of the American Academy of Religion. He has previously published *Title Index to Daoist Collections* (Three Pines Press, 2002), *Cultivating Perfection: Mysticism and Self-Transformation in Early Quanzhen Daoism* (Brill, 2007), and *Handbooks for Daoist Practice* (Yuen Yuen Institute, 2008).

CHARLOTTE LAWS holds a doctorate in religion and social ethics from the University of Southern California, in addition to two master's degrees and two bachelor's degrees. She is the founder and president of two animal organizations: League for Earth and Animal Protection, and the Los Angeles Directors of Animal Welfare. She was recently elected to serve a third term on the Greater Valley Glen Council in Southern California and was appointed by Mayor Antonio Villaraigosa (2006) to serve as a Los Angeles city commissioner. She is the author of two books and contributed a chapter to the 2006 anthology, *Igniting a Revolution*. Laws' articles have appeared in numerous publications, including *Newsweek*, the *Los Angeles Times*, and *E the Environmental Magazine*. She has also been a guest on dozens of TV shows, such as *Larry King Live*, *Fox News*, and *The Late Show*. Laws is the recipient of the 2006 Los Angeles Animal Humanitarian Award.

PETER ALAN MEDLEY (SARVABHAUMA DAS) graduated from the University of California at Berkeley in English literature. He joined the Hare Krishna movement in 1981, becoming an ordained priest in 1985. He writes a blog for the *Houston Chronicle*'s religious blog page, HoustonBelief.com: "Spirit Soul: A Hare Krishna Priest Looks at Today's World." He is the author of *Servant of Love: The Saintly Life of Kirtida Devi* and editor of *TKG Memories*, volumes 1–3. He has also written a chapter on death and dying in the Hindu religious tradition for the anthology, *Ultimate Journey: Death and Dying in the World's Major Religions* (edited by Steven Rosen, Greenwood Publishing, 2008).

ANTHONY J. NOCELLA II, a Quaker and long-time animal advocate, is finishing his Ph.D. in Social Science at Syracuse University, while teaching at Le Moyne College, SUNY Cortland, and Hillbrook Youth Detention Center. He is an associate with a number of scholarly institutes, including the Program for the Advancement of Research on Conflict and Collaboration (PARCC). He has provided conflict transformation workshops and classes to NGOs, the ROTC, the U.S. military, law enforcement, and public safety groups and also in prisons, youth detentions, middle schools, and high schools with the Alternative to Violence Program, Save the Kids, and the American Friends Service Committee. He has been involved in numerous political campaigns, organizations, and international demonstrations fostering direct democracy and is a co-founder of more than twenty active NGOs, four peer-reviewed book series, and four scholarly journals. He has contributed to more than two-dozen publications and is editing his fifteenth anthology. His publications include: *A Peacemaker's Guide for Building Peace with a Revolutionary Group* (PARC, 2004), co-edited (with Dr. Steve Best) *Terrorists or Freedom Fighters? Reflections on the Liberation of Animals* (Lantern Books, 2004), *Igniting a Revolution: Voices in Defense of the Earth* (AK Press, 2006), and *Contemporary Anarchist Studies* (Routledge, 2009). Nocella's website is www.anthonynocella.org.

NORM PHELPS, a Buddhist practitioner and Unitarian-Universalist, studied with a Tibetan lama for twelve years. An animal rights activist for nearly twenty-five years, he is the former spiritual outreach director for the Fund for Animals, and a founding member of the Society of Ethical and Religious Vegetarians (SERV). He is the author of *The Great Compassion: Buddhism and Animal Rights*; *The Dominion of Love: Animal Rights according to the Bible*; and *The Longest Struggle: Animal Advocacy from Pythagoras to PETA*, all published by Lantern Books. He lives in Funkstown, Maryland, with his wife, Patti Rogers, and their family of rescued cats (n.phelps@myactv.net).

STEVEN ROSEN (Satyaraja Dasa) is an initiated disciple of His Divine Grace A. C. Bhaktivedanta Swami Prabhupada. He is also founding editor of the *Journal of Vaishnava Studies* and associate editor for *Back to Godhead*. He has published twenty-one books in numerous languages, including the recent *Essential Hinduism* (Rowman & Littlefield, 2008) and *The Yoga of Kirtan: Conversations on the Sacred Art of Chanting* (FOLK Books, 2008).

RICHARD H. SCHWARTZ, PH.D., is professor emeritus of mathematics at the College of Staten Island, New York. He created a unique course, Mathematics and the Environment, which he taught for over twenty-five years. He is the author of *Mathematics and Global Survival*, *Judaism and Global Survival*, and *Judaism and Vegetarianism*, as well as over 140 articles, which can be accessed at www.jewishveg. com/schwartz, where there are also 25 podcasts of his talks and interviews. He is president of both Jewish Vegetarians of North America (JVNA) and the Society of Ethical and Religious Vegetarians (SERV), and director of Veg Climate Alliance. He frequently speaks and contributes articles on vegetarianism, environmental issues, and related issues, often focusing on Jewish teachings. In 2005 he was inducted into the Vegetarian Hall of Fame of the North American Vegetarian Society (NAVS). He is married, has three children and ten grandchildren, and lives in Staten Island, New York.

DIANNE SYLVAN, author of *The Circle Within: Creating a Wiccan Spiritual Tradition* and *The Body Sacred*, has been a practicing Wiccan since the age of sixteen, an ethical vegetarian since the age of twenty-six, and an aspiring spiritual vegan since the age of twenty-eight. She is founder of the fledgling EarthDance tradition of Wicca, and writes about her beliefs, experiences, and foibles on her website *Dancing Down the Moon* (www.dancingdownthemoon.com). Sylvan lives, writes, and teaches in Austin, Texas.

MATTHEW J. WALTON is a Ph.D. student in the political science department at the University of Washington, Seattle. His primary research is in political theory, examining connections between Buddhism and democracy in Southeast Asia. He also writes about radical animal rights and environmental activism, and most recently coauthored a chapter with Jessica Widay in *Igniting a Revolution: Voices in Defense of the Earth* (2006).

STEVEN M. WISE is president of the Coral Springs, Florida-based Center for the Expansion of Fundamental Rights, Inc. (CEFR), a long-term "Nonhuman Rights Project" that works to attain such basic common law rights as bodily integrity and bodily liberty for at least some nonhuman animals. He is the author of *Rattling the Cage: Toward Legal Rights for Animals* (2000), *Drawing the Line: Science and the Case for Animal Rights* (2002), *Though the Heavens May Fall—The Landmark Trial That Led to the End of Human Slavery*, (2005), and *An American Trilogy: Death, Slavery, and Dominion along the Banks of the Cape Fear River* (2009). He has taught Animal Rights Jurisprudence at Harvard, Vermont, Lewis and Clark, John Marshall, University of Miami, and St. Thomas law schools, and practiced animal protection law throughout the United States for twenty-nine years.

QUANTUM MECHANICS
OF ONE- AND TWO-ELECTRON
ATOMS